Robert W. Ottman

North Texas State University

ADVANCED HARMONY
Theory and Practice
THIRD EDITION

Prentice-Hall, Inc., Englewood Cliffs, New Jersey 07632

Library of Congress Cataloging in Publication Data

OTTMAN, ROBERT W.
   Advanced harmony.

   Bibliography: pp. 337, 358
   Includes index.
   1 Harmony.   I. Title.
   MT50.0923 1984   781.3   83-21233
   ISBN 0-13-011370-0

Printed in the United States of America

10   9   8   7   6

Editorial production/supervision: Dan Mausner
Page layout: William Schwartz
Manufacturing buyer: Raymond Keating

ISBN   0-13-011370-0

Prentice-Hall International (UK) Limited, *London*
Prentice-Hall of Australia Pty. Limited, *Sydney*
Prentice-Hall Canada Inc., *Toronto*
Prentice-Hall Hispanoamericana, S.A., *Mexico*
Prentice-Hall of India Private Limited, *New Delhi*
Prentice-Hall of Japan, Inc., *Tokyo*
Simon & Schuster Asia Pte. Ltd., *Signapore*
Editora Prentice-Hall do Brasil, Ltda., *Rio de Janeiro*

Contents

PREFACE   vii

1   MODULATION   1

Theory and Analysis   1
Secondary Dominant Chords, 1   The V/V-V at the Cadence, 3
Modulation   5
Relationship of Keys, 5   Modulation by Pivot Chord, 6   Choice of Pivot Chord, 8
Modulation by Sequence, 9   Direct Change of Key, 11   Secondary Tonal
Levels, 13
Application   20
Written Materials, 20   Ear Training, 26   Keyboard Harmony, 27

**2   FURTHER DOMINANT RELATIONSHIPS: THE LEADING TONE
CHORDS**   31

Theory and Analysis   31
Secondary Leading Tone Triads, 31   Diminished Seventh Chords, 34   Characteristics
of the Diminished Seventh Chord, 35   Terminology Variant, 36   The Leading Tone
Seventh Chord, 37   Secondary Leading Tone Seventh Chords, 39   Regular Resolution
of Secondary Leading Tone Seventh Chords, 40   Resolution of vii°⁷/V to Tonic Six-
Four, 42   Other Resolutions, 43   Spelling Variants, 45   The Nondominant Use of
Diminished Seventh Chords, 46   The Melodic Augmented Second, 46   Modulation
with Diminished Seventh Chords, 52
Application   64
Written Materials, 64   Ear Training, 72   Keyboard Harmony, 74

3   BINARY AND TERNARY FORMS   77

Binary Form   77
Ternary Form   79
The Three-Part Period, 83
Rounded Binary or Incipient Ternary   84

**4   LESS COMMON CHORD PROGRESSIONS—EXTENDED PART-
WRITING PROCEDURES**   97

Theory and Analysis   97
Review of Commonly Used Progressions, 97   Review of Commonly Used Exceptions,
98   Harmonic Progressions that Include a Chromatic Melodic Line, 99   Other Less
Common Progressions, 101   Extended Part-Writing Procedures, 107
Application   113
Written Materials, 113   Ear Training, 115   Keyboard Harmony, 115

**5   APPLICATION OF PART-WRITING PROCEDURES TO
INSTRUMENTAL WRITING   116**

Theory and Analysis   116
   Similarities Between Vocal and Instrumental Writing, 117   Differentiating Instrumental
   from Vocal Writing, 120   A Note on Compositional Style, 127
Application   129
   Written Materials, 129   Keyboard Harmony, 151

6   DIATONIC SEVENTH CHORDS   152

Theory and Analysis   152
   The Major Seventh Chord, 152   The Single Diatonic Seventh Chord, 153   Diatonic
   Seventh Chords in Sequence, 155
Application   166
   Written Materials, 166   Ear Training, 172   Keyboard Harmony, 173

**7   BORROWED CHORDS, THE NEAPOLITAN SIXTH CHORD,
AUGMENTED TRIADS   177**

Theory and Analysis   177
   Borrowed Chords, 177   Tonicizing the Borrowed Chord, 180   Temporary Change of
   Mode, 181   Modulation by Change of Mode, 183   The Neapolitan Sixth Chord,
   191   The Secondary Dominant of the Neapolitan Chord, 193   The Neapolitan Chord
   in a Sequence, 195   The Neapolitan as a Pivot Chord, 196   The Augmented Triad,
   197   The Augmented Triad in a Key, 197   Other Augmented Sonorities, 200
Application   207
   Written Materials, 207   Ear Training, 213   Keyboard Harmony, 215

8   AUGMENTED SIXTH CHORDS   217

Theory and Analysis   217
   Characteristics of the Interval of the Augmented Sixth, 217   Derivation of the
   Augmented Sixth, 218   Types of Augmented Sixth Chords, 219   Conventional Use of
   Augmented Sixth Chords in a Minor Key, 220   Conventional Use of Augmented Sixth
   Chords in a Major Key, 222   Augmented Sixth Chords with Bass Notes Other than the
   Sixth Scale Step, 224   Augmented Sixth Chords Built on Scale Steps Other than ii, ♯ii,
   or ♯iv, 226   Augmented Sixth Chords in which the Interval of the Augmented Sixth
   does not Resolve to the Octave, 227   Augmented Minor Seventh Chords, 228   The
   German Sixth Chord as a Pivot in Modulation, 234
Application   242
   Written Materials, 242   Ear Training, 250   Keyboard Harmony, 252

9   CHORDS OF THE NINTH, ELEVENTH, AND THIRTEENTH   255

Theory and Analysis   255
     Chords of the Ninth, 255   Eleventh and Thirteenth Chords, 262
Application   269
     Written Materials, 269   Keyboard Harmony, 270

10   UNCLASSIFIED CHORD STRUCTURES AND COMPLEX HARMONIC PROGRESSIONS   273

Individual Less Common Altered Chords   273
Complex Harmonic Progressions   275
Chord Functions Produced by Sequence and Enharmonicism   276
Chords Produced by Sequence and by Change of Mode   276
The Interlocking Sequence   279
Secondary Tonal Level Combined with First Inversions in Series and with Change of Mode   281

11   THE CLOSE OF THE NINETEENTH CENTURY—THE BEGINNING OF NEW DIRECTIONS   290

Review of Traditional Harmony   290
Triads in Chromatic Third Relationship   291
Root Movement by Tritone   296
Evasion of Tonic   297
     Evasion of Tonic by Deceptive Cadence, 299   Evasion of Tonic by Chromatic Inflection, 300
Unconventional Root Movement   303
Indeterminate Tonic Implication   305

12   DEBUSSY AND IMPRESSIONISM   316

Impressionism   316
Tonality and Cadence Structure   316
The Whole Tone Scale   317
The Pentatonic Scale   319
The Medieval Modes   319
Chords and Harmonic Progressions   321
Conventional Chords   321
Quartal and Quintal Harmony; Added Tone Chords   323
Tritones and Augmented Fifths   325
Conclusions   327
Method for Analysis   327

13   AFTER DEBUSSY: AN INTRODUCTION TO TWENTIETH-CENTURY MUSIC   336

14   TWENTIETH-CENTURY MUSIC: MELODY, RHYTHM, AND HARMONY   339

Melody   339
Meter and Rhythm   343
Harmony   350
Analysis   357
Suggested Writing Activities   364

15   SERIAL COMPOSITION: LATER TWENTIETH-CENTURY PRACTICES   366

Atonality   368
Twelve-Tone Systems   371
Row Variants   379
    Three-note Cells, 379   Combinatoriality, 382   Conservative Use of the Row, 384
Other Uses of Serialism   385
Music Since 1950   388
New Sound Sources   393
Summary   396

APPENDIX 1   THE ESSENTIALS OF PART-WRITING   397

The Single Chord   397
    Triad Position, 397   Usual Doubling, 397
Chord Connection   398
    Triad Roots, 398   Triads in Inversion, 399   Position Changes, 399   Nonharmonic Tones, 399   Seventh Chords, 399   Altered Chords, 399   General Rule, 400

APPENDIX 2   INSTRUMENTATION: RANGES, CLEFS, TRANSPOSITION   401

    String Instruments, 401   Woodwind Instruments, 402   Brass Instruments, 404

INDEX   405

Preface

Advanced Harmony, Theory and Practice, together with its preceding volume, *Elementary Harmony, Theory and Practice*, third edition (Prentice-Hall, Inc., 1982)* are designed to meet the needs of college courses in basic music theory. These include not only studies in analysis and written harmony, but also a complete course of instruction in ear training and keyboard harmony. Studies in sight singing are correlated throughout with the author's *Music for Sight Singing*, second edition (Prentice-Hall, Inc., 1967) and *More Music for Sight Singing* (Prentice-Hall, Inc., 1981). The subject matter of each chapter and its application to each of these areas are so presented that they can be taught successfully either in the correlated class (all areas in one class), or in several classes, each devoted to one or more of these areas.

The present, third edition of *Advanced Harmony* maintains the format and general pedagogical procedures that have characterized the usefulness of previous editions of the text. Users of earlier editions will find a number of new features in the present edition:

1. Inclusion of music scores for analysis in all chapters.

2. Placement of all chords of dominant function in the opening two chapters of the text.

3. Adoption of "functional symbols" for chords of dominant function, such as V/V, vii°/ii, vii°⁷/V, ii°⁷/III, etc. Symbols for augmented sixth chords have been simplified, using only the initials of their geographical terms, such as Gr6 for the German sixth chord.

4. The presentation of each new sonority includes the use of that sonority in the modulatory process.

5. Special instruction in combining various analytical techniques to produce logical and satisfactory analyses of particularly difficult passages often found in music literature.

6. A study of late nineteenth-century music in its function as a link to twentieth-century practices.

7. Studies in early twentieth-century music (especially Debussy) followed by chapters devoted to twentieth-century compositional systems, such as the twelve-tone concept, and to the analysis of other contemporary music derived from both earlier compositional practices and from ideas novel to the twentieth century.

The pedagogical and musical effectiveness of these texts is a result of many years of experimentation and use in the theory classes of North Texas State University. Many thanks are due to the thousands of undergraduate students, to the many graduate students and teaching fellows, and to the members of the theory faculty whose reactions and constructive criticisms have helped shape the format and contents of these texts.

R. W. O.

*References in this text to *Elementary Harmony* apply to the third edition.

CHAPTER ONE

Modulation

The closing chapter of *Elementary Harmony, Theory and Practice* presented secondary dominant chords, elementary modulation, and their relationship to each other. The material of this chapter includes much of that presentation for review integrated with more advanced considerations of these topics.

Theory and Analysis

Secondary Dominant Chords

When a single V-I progression occurs other than on the tonic of the key, a very short impression of a new key is established. In fact, it could be called a modulation consisting of two chords. But more conveniently, the progression is called a secondary dominant progression (or applied dominant), as in Figure 1.1. The analysis V^6_5/vi to vi acknowledges that a V-I feeling is present (V-I in F♯ minor) but that this impression is so fleeting that analysis in the original key is more satisfactory. The F♯ minor triad in this case is said to be *tonicized,* and the process is called *tonicization*.

Fig. 1.1.

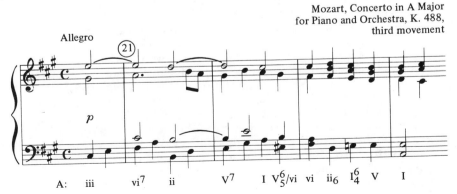

Mozart, Concerto in A Major
for Piano and Orchestra, K. 488,
third movement

A: iii   vi^7 ii   V^7 I   V$^6_5$/vi   vi   ii$_6$ I$^6_4$ V   I

Figure 1.2 shows the commonly used secondary dominant triad for each of the diatonic triads in a key. Each can also be found as a secondary dominant seventh chord by adding a minor seventh above its root. Observe that in a major key, only a seventh chord is used as a secondary dominant to IV (V^7/IV); V/IV-IV is simply the diatonic progression, I-IV. Also, the seventh of this chord, as well as that of V^7/VI in a minor key, requires an accidental not in the key: V^7/IV in C major is C E G B♭, and V^7/VI in C minor is E♭ G B♭ D♭.

Fig. 1.2

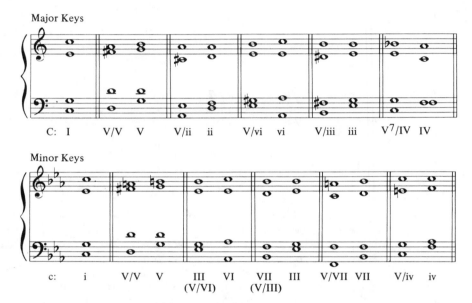

Major Keys

C: I   V/V V   V/ii ii   V/vi vi   V/iii iii V^7/IV IV

Minor Keys

c: i   V/V V   III   VI   VII   III   V/VII VII   V/iv iv
                      (V/VI)   (V/III)

The III and VII triads in minor are diatonic triads and rarely function as secondary dominant triads. However, their seventh chords usually are designated V^7/VI and V^7/III. Additional secondary dominant chords, those in dominant relationship to altered chords, will be described in later chapters as the altered chords are presented.

Additional uses of secondary dominant chords (examples of which are found in *Elementary Harmony,* Chapter 18) are:

1. *Deceptive resolution.*   Just as V-vi constitutes a deceptive resolution of V, a secondary dominant can resolve similarly, up by step, such as V/vi-IV (root movement III-IV). (See Figure 18.9 in *Elementary Harmony.*)

2. *Interruption of a common progression.*   Any common progression (*Elementary Harmony,* Table 12.I, page 259, and, in this volume, Figure 4.1) can be interrupted with the secondary dominant of the second chord of the progression; for example, instead of IV-ii, interrupt with IV-V/ii-ii (see *Elementary Harmony,* Figure 18.10). Also, the secondary dominant may be preceded and followed by its chord of resolution, V-V/V-V, sometimes called an *embellishing* secondary dominant (*Elementary Harmony,* Figure 18.11).

3. *Harmonic sequence* (review *Elementary Harmony,* Chapter 16).   In any harmonic sequence which contains a root movement down a fifth and up a fourth, any chord preceding a major or minor triad may be a secondary dominant. (See Figure 18.13 in *Elementary Harmony.*) Here are some possibilities:

diatonic progression	I	IV	vii°	iii	vi	ii	V	I
secondary dominants	I	IV	V/iii	iii	V/ii	ii	V	I
	I	IV	vii°	V/vi	vi	V/V	V	I
	I	IV	V/iii	V/vi	V/ii	V/V	V	I

Occasionally, the V/iii may be preceded by its secondary dominant, for example,

C:	I	V/VII	V/iii	iii......etc.
	C E G	F♯ A♯ C♯	B D♯ F♯	E G B......

For an example of V/vii (vii = minor triad built on the leading tone), see the harmonic sequence of Figure 10.3

The V/V-V at the Cadence

While we have said that a V-I progression at a cadence point can be the mark of the location of a modulation, such a progression whose final chord is V of the original key and is preceded by its secondary dominant (V/V-V) often does not impart enough impression of finality to be considered anything but a half cadence in the original key.

In Figure 1.3, a simple tonicization of F A C in the key of B flat takes place at the cadence, (measure 8), but no feeling of rest resides here. To most listeners, this progression must proceed to the original tonic, which is exactly what happens in the score. The progression as illustrated here is best analyzed as a tonicization of V(V/V-V), though other terminologies sometimes encountered include *progressive cadence, transient cadence,* or *transient modulation.*

Fig. 1.3

Adagio cantabile

Haydn, Sonata in E♭ Major for Piano

B♭:

V⁷/V   V   I

In Figure 1.4, the tonicization of the cadential B♭ triad in measure 9 is begun four measures earlier. With the sounding of the B♭ major triad in each of measures six through nine, many ears will be convinced of an accomplished modulation to B♭ major.

Fig. 1.4

*D = Deutsch, Otto Erich, who catalogued and numbered Schubert's works in 1951.

Modulation

A modulation exists when the music provides a given listener the aural impression that a new tonal center or key has definitely been achieved. In contrast to the cadence on the dominant in a major key, reaching a cadence on any other scale step, or on the dominant of the minor key, poses fewer problems in analysis, since the aural effect more likely than not will be that of stability in the newly achieved key. The cadence on G, last measure of Figure 1.5, is sufficiently strong as to require no immediate return to the key of B minor. This stability indicates that a modulation has taken place.

Fig. 1.5

Schumann, *Myrten*, Op. 25,
"Hochländers Abschied"

Relationship of Keys

In a modulation, a key may progress to any other key. The keys to which it may progress are divided into two groups:

1. *Closely related keys.*   There are five keys closely related to any given key. These can be identified in several ways, three of which are as follows:

a) The closely related key has a signature the same as, or one accidental more or less than, the original key. The closely related keys to D major (two sharps) consist of all the keys with a signature of one sharp, two sharps, or three sharps—G major, E minor, B minor, A major, and F♯ minor.

b) A closely related key is one whose tonic triad is found as a diatonic major or minor triad in the original key. In D major, the diatonic triads are ii, E minor; iii, F♯ minor; IV, G major; V, A major; and vi, B minor.

In a minor key, calculation of the diatonic triads is made on the basis of the natural (pure) minor scale. In D minor the closely related keys are III, F major; iv, G minor; v, A minor; VI, B♭ major; and VII, C major.

c) The tonic, dominant, and subdominant keys and their related keys produce the six closely related keys.

D major:		D			B	
	G		A	E		F♯
	(major keys)			(minor keys)		
D minor:		D			F	
	G		A	B♭		C
	(minor keys)			(major keys)		

Modulation may be made from keys with seven accidentals to keys with eight accidentals, though no key signatures exist for the latter and such modulations are quite uncommon. For example, see Bach, *Well-tempered Clavier,* Volume 2, Prelude No. 3, measures 1–6 for a modulation from C♯ major to G♯ major (eight sharps).

2. *Remote keys.*   A key other than a closely related key is known as a remote or foreign key.

In musical practice, modulations to closely related keys are more common than remote modulations. Modulation to closely related keys will be the principal concern of this chapter.

Assignment 1.1.   Write out, or name, the five closely related keys to each of the 15 major keys and 15 minor keys.

Modulation by Pivot Chord

Although there are several means of modulation, that by *pivot chord* (or *common chord*) is the most frequent. A pivot chord is one that can function in both the old key and the new key simultaneously. It often appears just before the first chord of dominant function (V, vii°, or I$_4^6$) in the new key. Observe in Figure 1.6 that the pivot i = iv occurs just before the V of the new key, and that the pivot can function as i in G minor and as iv in D minor. Note also that in modulating to the dominant in minor, the cadence sounds final enough as not to require an immediate return to G minor, compared to the usual lack of such stability when reaching a cadence on the dominant from a major key.

Fig.   1.6

Mozart, Sonata in C Major for Piano, K. 545,
first movement

Allegro

g: i   V⁷   i =
                                          d: iv

V   i   V⁷   i

Looking back at Figure 1.5, the pivot iv = vi precedes a IV-I progression (rather than V-I), followed by a confirming V⁷-I cadence in G major.

The pivot may also be found two or even three chords preceding the new dominant, most often before a strong I-IV-v or ii-V-I cadence in the new key, as shown in Figure 1.7.

Fig.   1.7

Bach, *Herr Christ, der ein'ge Gotts Sohn* (No. 303)*

F: I   IV   I   V   vi =   o   V   i
                                 d: i   ii6   i
                                      5

*The number in parentheses refers to the number of the chorale in the collected editions of J. S. Bach's chorales, such as *The 371 Chorales of Johann Sebastian Bach*, edited, with English texts, by Frank D. Mainous and Robert W. Ottman (New York: Holt, Rinehart and Winston, Inc., 1966).

Choice of Pivot Chord

Any diatonic triad common to two keys can be used as a pivot between those two keys. (Studies of chromatically altered chords as pivots will be considered in later chapters). Obviously, a large number of possibilities are available, as listed in Table 1.1. But in music literature, pivots in which one of the two chords is tonic appear to be the most frequently used, most likely because of their simplicity:

a) C: I IV V I=
      e:VI iv V i

b) C: I IV V I ii=
      d: i iv V i

The dominant chord is rarely considered a pivot because of its strength and its pull to the tonic of its key. The principal exception is in the modulation from a major key to its subdominant, where I of the original key may become V, usually followed by V^7 to help strengthen the stability of the new key (see Figure 1.8).

Fig. 1.8

Schubert, Symphony in B Minor, *Unfinished*, D. 759, second movement

TABLE 1.1

AVAILABLE PIVOT CHORDS IN MODULATING FROM A GIVEN KEY TO A CLOSELY RELATED KEY (ILLUSTRATED IN C MAJOR AND C MINOR)

Modulation from a Major Key to its . . .		*Modulation from a Minor Key to its . . .*	
Supertonic key (C major - D minor)	ii = i iii = ii* IV = III vi = v*	Mediant key (C minor to E♭ major)	i = vi III = I iv = ii VI = IV
Mediant key (C major - E minor)	I = VI iii = i vi = iv	Subdominant key (C minor - F minor)	i = v* iv = i v = ii* VI = III VII = IV*
Subdominant key (C major - F major)	I = V ii = vi IV = I vi = iii		
		Dominant key** (C minor - G minor)	i = iv III = VI v = i
Dominant key (C major - G major)	I = IV iii = vi vi = ii		
		Submediant key (C minor - A♭ major)	i = iii iv = vi VI = I
Submediant key (C major - A minor)	ii = iv IV = VI vi = i		
		Subtonic key (C minor - B♭ major)	i = ii III = IV

*In minor keys, ii and IV contain the raised sixth scale step which ordinarily ascend; v contains the lowered seventh scale step which ordinarily descends.

**From a minor key, the closely related key on the dominant is also minor, for example, C minor to G minor, one accidental difference, but *not* C minor to G major, four accidentals difference.

For lack of space, illustration of all the pivot chords is not feasible. Five pivot chord modulations have been shown so far in this chapter; they serve as a guide to the remaining possibilities in Table 1.1.

Figure 1.4 E♭ major to B♭ major, I = IV
Figure 1.5 B minor to G major, iv = vi
Figure 1.6 G minor to D minor, i = iv
Figure 1.7 F major to D minor, vi = i
Figure 1.8 D major to G major, I = V

Modulation by Sequence

1. *Harmonic sequence.* Secondary dominant chords in sequence provide an easy way to modulate, simply by continuing the sequence until the dominant of the desired key is reached. In Figure 1.9, modulation from D minor to F major, a series of secondary dominants beginning with the chord E G♯ B D continues until a C seventh chord appears as V^7 in the new key. Analysis is easily accomplished by considering the first chord of the sequence as a member of the new key.

Fig. 1.9

Mozart, Symphony No. 41, K. 551,
second movement

*German sixth chord (see Chapter 8)

2. *Formal sequence.*   A formal pattern, usually a motive or a short phrase, repeated at different pitch levels will accomplish a change of key by stopping the
sequence at the desired key. Like any sequence, only a small number of repetitions is desirable. In Figure 1.10, Chopin reaches G major from B major through
three successive two-measure motives, each with the same chord progression.
Note that the achieved key is *not* closely related to the opening key. Such *remote*
or *foreign* keys will be observed frequently in the study of chromatic harmony.

Fig. 1.10

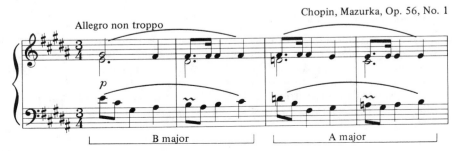

Chopin, Mazurka, Op. 56, No. 1

G major

Direct Change of Key

A new key may be reached simply by going to it directly. Since there is no process involved, the term modulation is not entirely appropriate, but is commonly used.

    1. *By Phrase.*　Material following a cadence may simply begin in another key. Figure 1.11 shows a remote relationship, A♭ major to F♯ minor. For a simpler relationship, D major to B minor, see Bach chorale number 120, measures 1-4.

Fig. 1.11

Schubert, *Moments musicals*, D. 780

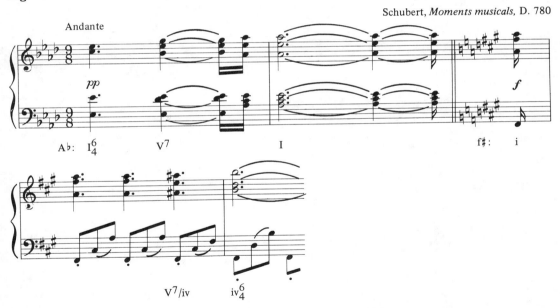

    2. *By Melodic Chromatic Alteration.*　This occurs when, during the course of the phrase, there can be found one melodic line (any voice part) that proceeds by chromatically altered half step (two notes of different pitch with the same letter name). In Figure 1.12, the chromatically altered bass line, F–F♯, indicates the location of the direct chromatic modulation. In this example, designating any chord as the pivot will result in an awkward harmonic analysis.

Fig. 1.12

Bach, *Jesu, der du meine Seele* (No. 297)

Bb: I   I₆   V   g: V₆   i   iv₆   V

3. *By Pivot Tone.* Two different keys may be connected by a tone common to both keys. This procedure is particularly useful in connecting keys in a remote relationship. In Figure 1.13, the tone E is common to both keys, while in Figure 1.14, the pivot tone is spelled enharmonically, D flat = C sharp.

Fig. 1.13

E major to
G major
Pivot tone—E (root of I in E major = 5th of ii, A C E, in G major)

Allegro commodo
non agitato

L'istesso tempo ma moderato

Smetana, *The Moldau*

E: I   G: ii   V   I

Fig. 1.14

Bb minor to
F# minor
Pivot tone spelled enharmonically, Db - C# (Db, third of tonic
triad in Bb minor = C#, fifth of tonic triad in F# minor)

Wagner, *Tristan und Isolde*,
Act I, Scene V

Langsamer

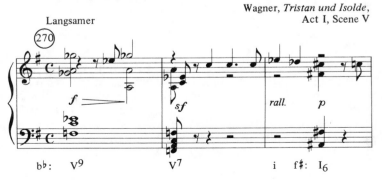

bb: V⁹   V⁷   i   f#: I₆

$$N_6 \; (\flat II_6)^* \qquad\qquad i_4^6 \qquad\qquad V \qquad\qquad i$$

*N_6 or $\flat I_6$ symbolizes a Neapolitan sixth chord (see Chapter 7)

Secondary Tonal Levels

There are times when a chord within a phrase is tonicized not only by its secondary dominant, but by an additional one or more chords preceding the secondary dominant. Such a series of chords might be called a modulation, but the fact that the series is followed by a cadence in the original key prevents the tonicized chord from achieving any status other than that of a temporary tonic. In measure two of the next figure, an analysis of V/V–V/vi–vi could be appropriate. But the aural effect of the two chords preceding vi so strongly reinforces its tonic quality that an alternate symbolization is in order:

$$\frac{IV_5^6 - V_5^6 - i}{vi}$$

(The presence of sevenths in this example does affect the system of analysis). The symbols above the line indicate the relationship to the single symbol representing the tonicized chord number placed below the line, or, in this case, a secondary tonal progression, IV-V-i on the level of vi of the original key.

Fig. 1.15

Bach, *Wach auf, mein Herz, und singe* (No. 93)

$$V/vi \quad IV_5^6 \; V_5^6 \quad I \quad IV_5^6 \; V_5^6 \quad i \quad I_6 \quad ii_5^6 \quad V \qquad I$$

$$\overline{\hphantom{IV_5^6 \; V_5^6 \quad I \quad}vi}$$

(oboe)

The next example, Figure 1.16, includes a secondary tonal level on F, the length of which might seem to justify a modulation to that key were it not for the Phrygian cadence[1] in D minor with which the phrase ends.

[1] iv_6–V in a minor key. Review *Elementary Harmony*, chapter 16.

Fig. 1.16

Brahms, Sextet, Op. 18,
second movement

Three analyses are possible, the third of which we have chosen for the analysis above.

1. no change of key: d:i V i IV VII III i ii° III iv₆ V
2. modulation: d:i V i=
                          F:vi V/V V I ii vii° I=
                                                    d:III iv ₆ V
3. secondary tonal level   : i V i V/V V I ii vii° I iv₆ V
                                      ⎯⎯⎯⎯⎯⎯⎯⎯⎯⎯⎯⎯⎯⎯⎯⎯⎯
                                      III

Analysis 1 implies the use of several less common progressions which do not seem that unusual to the ear. In 2, the use of two keys of equal importance is implied, while in 3, the digression into F major (III) is recognized, but the implication of D minor as the principal key of the phrase is maintained.[2]

Assignment 1.2. Harmonic Analysis.   Analyze the harmony and the modulations in these excerpts. In some cases, a progression may be either a modulation or a secondary dominant progression. Consider this alternative carefully and be prepared to justify your choice.

[2]If measures 1–3 were considered vi–V/vi–vi, no secondary tonal level on F would be necessary. But since these are the opening measures of a D minor movement, the establishment of a tonic on D minor is strongly implied.

Beethoven, Sonata for Piano, Op. 10, No. 3,
first movement

Rimksy-Korsakov, *Scheherazade*, Op. 35,
third movement

Beethoven, Sonata for Violin and Piano, Op. 47,
"Kreutzer," first movement

The modulation in the following excerpt is from A flat minor to its submediant. Spell the submediant, and explain how to achieve its enharmonic spelling.

Beethoven, Sonata for Piano, Op. 13,
second movement

(4)   Adagio cantabile

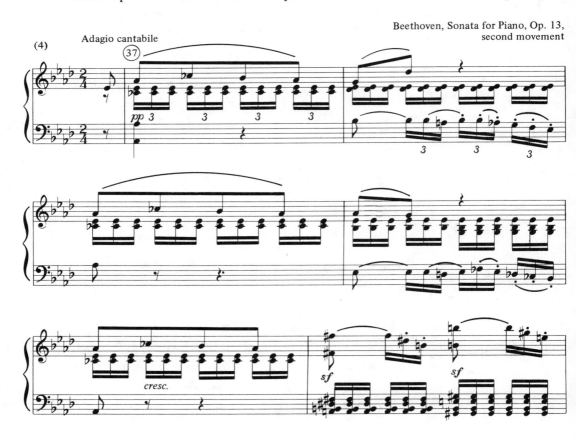

Bach, Mass in B Minor,
"Et in unum dominum"

(5) (28)

Rossini, *Anodine I I I I*,
from "Sins of My Old Age"

(6)   Allegro moderato
(61)

me.   Cru - del! ___   Non   lo ___ spe -

Mozart, Trio for Violin, Cello, and Piano, K. 542,
first movement (piano score only)

(8)   Bach, *Es ist genug!* (No. 216)

It   is   e - nough!   So   take   my   spir - it,   Lord.

Bach, *Eins ist Not! Ach Herr, dies eine* (No. 280)

(9)

(10)   *più lento*   Brahms, Intermezzo, Op. 118, No. 2

Application

Written Materials

Part-Writing Modulations   No new part-writing procedures are necessary when writing a modulation.

A concise statement of the essentials of part-writing will be found in Appendix 1. For a more thorough review of the basic principles and reasons for formal part-writing procedures, review Chapter 4 of *Elementary Harmony*, and for amplification of the material of each specific rule, consult the index under "Part-writing" in that text.

Part-writing assignments in four voices, such as Assignment 1.3 below and similar assignments in the remaining chapters of this text, may be worked out in two ways other than that indicated:

1. *For choral or instrumental performance.* Review *Elementary Harmony* pages 201–202. Appendix 2, "Instrumentation," in the present text provides pertinent and specific information helpful in writing for instruments.

2. *In open score.* Write each voice on a separate staff, using the treble, alto, tenor, and bass clefs. Review *Elementary Harmony* page 151.

Assignment 1.3. Part-writing.   Add alto and tenor voices. Make harmonic analysis, including location and type of modulation.

5   6   7 6 4♮   ♭6   6
2   6 —   5

Assignment 1.4. Write the following chord progressions in four voices. Devise a satisfactory rhythmic pattern within each measure. Other keys may be used.

a) G minor. $\frac{3}{4}$i $\Big|$ VI ii$^{\circ}_{6}$ V $\Big|$ i$_6$ iv $=$
i $\Big|$ VI ii$^{\circ}_{6}$ V $\Big|$ i $\Big\|$

b) E♭ major. $\frac{4}{4}$ V$_6$ $\Big|$ I V^7 vi V$_4$ $\Big|$ i$_6$ iv i V $\Big|$ I$_6$ IV I$_6$ V $\Big|$ I $\Big\|$
5   2   4
ii

c) F♯ major. $\frac{6}{8}$ I $\Big|$ ii$_4$ V$_6$ I I$_6$ $\Big|$ IV I$_6$ V I iii$\Big|$
2   5   4
vi $=$
iv   V$_4$ i$_6$ ii$^{\varnothing}_6$ V $\Big|$i $\Big\|$
2   5

Melody Harmonization   To harmonize a phrase containing a modulation, follow this procedure:

1. Analyze the cadence. Is the cadence in a new key? Choose harmony for the cadence and write chord numbers below the staff.
2. Locate the pivot chord. Look for the first V-I progression in the new key, then look immediately ahead of this progression for the location of the pivot. Indicate the pivot below the staff.
3. Choose harmony for the remainder of the phrase.
4. Write the three lower voices, including non-harmonic tones where appropriate.

For an example, Figure 1.17 is an excerpt from Assignment 1.5, melody 6. It begins with the final note of phrase 3, followed by all of phrase 4. Observe that phrase 3 ends in A major, while phrase 4 ends in B minor. Following these steps produces the first harmonization shown in Figure 1.17.

1. Identify the soprano notes of the last measure as 2–1 in B minor, implying a V–I cadence in B minor.

2. Look for the pivot chord. Since the cadence is the first V–I progression in B minor, the two preceding notes (D's) can be analyzed as i in B minor.

3. Harmonize from the beginning of the phrase. The simplest harmonization is V-I-ii. At ii (B D F♯) the soprano note D also implies i (B D F♯) of B minor. Following the first and simplest harmonization are just a few of many other possibilities. In most modulatory situations it is possible to find several different harmonizations; therefore, do not necessarily expect your first solution to be the most desirable one.

Fig. 1.17

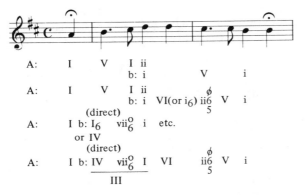

Assignment 1.5. Melody harmonization   Harmonize the melodies below, as assigned.

(6)

After completing your harmonization, it will be both interesting and instruct-ive to compare your solution with that of Bach, as found in the 371 chorales. Where Bach has provided more than one harmonization,[3] study each one. (1) 102, (2) 236, (3) 95, (4) 120, (5) 340, (6) 153.

Assignment 1.6. Writing modulations.   Select an opening key, major or minor. From Table 1.1., choose a key relationship and one of the pairs of pivot chords indicated for that modulation; for example, E minor, modulation to the submediant, iv = vi. Write an example in four voices or for four instruments. Be sure that the original key is firmly established by at least one cadential progres-sion, as in the examples in Assignment 1.4 and that the chords leading up to and away from the pivot chord are good acceptable progressions. Strive for a good soprano melody line.

Ear Training

Exercise 1.1. Harmonic dictation.   In taking harmonic dictation which in-cludes modulation, it is usually not possible to hear the modulation until the pivot chord is passed. This is because the pivot chord functions in the old key; it sounds as a chord in the old key, and when the new key becomes apparent the pivot is no longer sounding. Follow these suggestions for listening to modula-tion, particularly when taking down chord numbers only (without staff nota-tion). These suggestions are repeated from *Elementary Harmony*, Chapter 18, where a full discussion of the listening process may be found.

a) Sing aloud or to yourself (as instructed) the tonic of the new key. Sing the tonic of the old key.

b) Compare the tonic of the new key with the tonic of the old key. The interval between the two tonic notes will indicate the location of the new key.

c) In subsequent hearings listen for a chord immediately preceding the first cadential progression in the new key—a chord which seems to function in both keys. This will be the pivot chord.

---

[3]Bach made as many as nine different harmonizations of some chorales. In the Mainous-Ottman edition, cross references to all the harmonizations are given with each chorale.

Exercise 1.2. Writing a melody with modulation from dictation. The principles involved in harmonic and melodic analysis of modulation apply here also. Listen for the cadential progression in the new key and establish mentally the new tonic pitch. The interval relationship between the old and new tonic notes will indicate the name of the new key. Check this information against the name of the new key as found in writing the pitches by interval relationships. Review *Elementary Harmony,* "Modulation in the Melodic Line," page 425.

Keyboard Harmony

Exercise 1.3. Playing modulations to closely related keys at the keyboard.
The ten progressions supplied for this exercise represent modulations to each closely related key from C major and C minor. In each, except as noted, the tonic triad of the old key is the pivot chord. In numbers 2, 3, 4, and 8, the tonic triad of the old key or the following triad may be considered the pivot chord.

a) Play each progression in all keys. Any progression may be played beginning with the first chord in a different soprano position—positions of following chords will be determined by basic part-writing procedures.

b) Modulate to a closely related key and return to the original key. For example, modulate from C major to the submediant and return to C major. Follow these steps.

(1) modulate to the submediant (A minor) as in progression number 3.

(2) determine relationship of new key (A minor) to original key (C major)—C major is the mediant of A minor.

(3) from A minor, modulate to the mediant as in progression number 9.

To play a modulation from a major key to:	Play progression no.	Followed by progression no.
dominant and return	1	2
subdominant and return	2	1
submediant and return	3	9
supertonic and return	4	10
mediant and return	5	8

To play a modulation from a minor key to:	Play progression no.	Followed by progression no.
dominant and return	6	7
subdominant and return	7	6
submediant and return	8	5
mediant and return	9	3
subtonic and return	10	4

(6) to the dominant

i   iv   V   i   i =
                        iv   V   i

(7) to the subdominant

i   iv   V   i   i =
                        v   VI   iv   V   i

(8) to the submediant

i   iv   V   i   i =   iv =
                        iii   vi   ii$_6$ V   I

(9) to the mediant

i   iv   V   i   i =
                        vi   IV   V   I

(10) to the subtonic

i   iv   V   i   i =
                        ii   vii$_6^o$ I

29

Exercise 1.4. Playing modulations to closely related keys.   Modulation from one key to another can be accomplished with pivots other than those practiced in Exercise 1.3. Table 1.1 lists a variety of pivots for each modulatory goal from a given key. For example, a modulation from C major to D minor (modulation to the supertonic) is shown in Exercise 1.3 (4), pivot IV = III, while the example below shows the same modulation with the pivot vi = v. Using Table 1.1, practice the various ways of achieving the same modulatory goal. Be sure to follow the pivot chord with commonly used progressions as listed in Figure 4.1 (review also *Elementary Harmony,* pages 258–259).

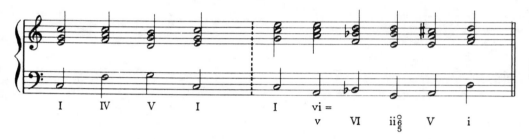

Exercise 1.5.   Play exercises from Assignment 1.3 at the keyboard.

Exercise 1.6. Melody harmonization.   At the keyboard harmonize melodies as assigned from the author's *Music for Sight Singing,* third edition (Prentice-Hall, Inc., 1986), Chapter 11, section 2 and Chapter 12, and *More Music for Sight Singing* (Prentice-Hall, Inc., 1981), melodies 693-742.

CHAPTER TWO

Further Dominant Relationships:
The Leading Tone Chords

Theory and Analysis

The importance of the dominant relationship has been stressed from the beginning of our study of harmony and has included consideration of the dominant triad, the dominant seventh chord, the leading tone triad, and the secondary dominant triads and their seventh chords. Our continuing study of dominant relationships will include use of diminished triads in a secondary function, and the diminished seventh chords in both primary and secondary dominant functions.

Secondary Leading Tone Triads

Just as the tonic of a key can be preceded by the leading tone triad, vii°, in a progression of dominant function, so can other major and minor triads in the key be tonicized by their secondary leading tone triads. These are diminished triads which progress in a manner identical to the vii°-I progression but at other scale step locations in the key. Figure 2.1 shows, in root position, the secondary

Fig. 2.1

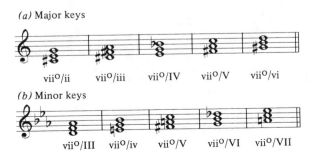

(a) Major keys

    vii°/ii   vii°/iii   vii°/IV   vii°/V   vii°/vi

(b) Minor keys

    vii°/III   vii°/iv   vii°/V   vii°/VI   vii°/VII

leading tone triad to each diatonic major or minor traid in major and minor keys. It is understood, of course, that like all diminished triads, these are ordinarily used only in first inversion. Figure 2.2 shows the vii°-I and the vii°/V-V-I progressions in C major, illustrating the similarity between the use of the diminished triad as a vii° triad and as a secondary leading tone triad.

Fig. 2.2

C: vii$^o_6$ I   vii$^o_6$/V   V   I

Assignment 2.1.   Spell each of the secondary leading tone triads in any major or minor key. For example, to spell vii°/iv in E minor, (1) the root of iv is A, (2) the leading tone to A is G♯, and (3) a diminished triad spelled on G♯ is G♯ B D.

Observe that all the secondary leading tone triads except vii°/III in minor include an accidental not in the key signature. This one exception is spelled the same as ii° in the key; the two are differentiated by their resolutions: ii°-V and vii°/III-III.

Our examples of the uses of secondary leading tone triads begin with the common quasi-modulation at the cadence, shown in figure 2.3. Here, instead of the secondary dominant progression I-V/V-V, we find the secondary leading tone progression I-vii°/V-V (which, if modulation to D were considered, would be analyzed as I = IV-vii°-I).

Fig. 2.3

Bach, *Der Tag, der ist so Freudenreich* (No. 158)

G: V$_6$ I   vii$^o_6$/V   V   V$^6_5$ I

    or: V$_6$ IV   vii$^o_6$ I   V$^6_5$ I
                                                        V

Using the lower analysis, the composer's choice of vii°/V becomes clear: when the melody ascends after a IV triad, a diminished triad is commonly used. (Review *Elementary Harmony*, pages 263–64.)

The secondary leading tone traid is frequently used in a I-vii°$_6$-I$_6$ (or reverse) progression, but on a pitch level other than tonic. In Figure 2.4, there are two such occurrences, one on the level of vi—

$$\underset{\text{vi}}{\underline{\text{i-vii}^{\circ}\text{-i}_6}}$$

—followed immediately by the same progression on the level of ii.

Fig. 2.4

Moderato   (19)   Schumann, *Album for the Young*, Op. 68, No. 43

A: vi vii°/vi vi$_6$ ii vii°/ii ii$_6$

$\underset{\text{vi}}{\underline{\text{I vii}^{\circ}_6 \quad \text{i}_6}}$ $\underset{\text{ii}}{\underline{\text{i vii}^{\circ}_6 \quad \text{I}_6}}$

The diatonic ii° triad, used as a secondary leading tone triad, vii°/III, is shown in Figure 2.5. The seemingly incorrect resolution of the soprano note B♭ (third note), the lowered seventh scale degree in C minor, is easily explained when the G B♭ D triad is correctly related to the tonicized E♭ triad (III), resulting in this analysis:

$$\underset{\text{III}}{\underline{\text{iii–vii}^{\circ}_6\text{–I}}}$$

Fig. 2.5

Bach, *So wahr ich lebe, spricht dein Gott* (No. 110)

c: i   iii vii$^{\circ}_6$ I   V^7 VI   V   I

$\underset{\text{III}}{\underline{\qquad}}$

In Figure 2.6, the vii°/V resolves to i_4^6. Observe the clever use of nonharmonic tones to allow the D♯ in the melody ultimately to descend.

Fig. 2.6

Andante   Bach, *English Suite II*, "Sarabande"

vii°₆/V i_4^6 V^7 i

Diminished Seventh Chords

Adding a seventh above the root of a diminished triad will produce a diminished seventh chord. There are two varieties, depending on the size of the seventh.

1. The diminished-diminished seventh chord is so named because it consists of a diminished triad and the interval of a diminished seventh above its root. Its name is commonly shortened simply to *diminished seventh chord*. Its Roman numeral symbol includes the superscript ^{o7}, as in Figure 2.7*a*.

2. The diminished-minor seventh chord is so named because it consists of a diminished triad and the interval of a minor seventh above its root. It is usually called a *half diminished seventh chord*. Its Roman numeral symbol includes the superscript ^{ø7}, as in Figure 2.7*b*.

Fig. 2.7

(a)   *(b)*

c minor: vii^{o7} ii^{ø7}

Assignment 2.2. Spell the diminished seventh chords above these pitch names. (The spelling can also be accomplished by adding a minor third above the diminished triad. Example, B D F + m3 (A♭) = B D F A♭).

E, C♯, A G♯, F♯, C×, E♯, D♯ G, B♭

Assignment 2.3. Spell the half diminished seventh chords above these pitch names. (The spelling can also be accomplished by adding a major third above the diminished triad. Example, D F A♭ + M3 (C) = D F A♭ C.)

B, E, F♯, A G♯, F×, C, G, B♭, D♯

Characteristics of the Diminished Seventh Chord

The diminished seventh chord (referring to the diminished-diminished variety) displays features unlike other chords studied thus far. Composers have taken advantage of its many unique features, as will be shown later in this and other chapters.

    1. The chord is made up exclusively of minor thirds, including the interval from the seventh of the chord up to its root, which, though written as an augmented second, is enharmonic with the minor third.

Fig. 2.8

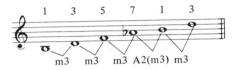

In addition, every interval located by skipping a member of the chord is a tritone: a diminished fifth or its enharmonic equivalent, an augmented fourth. For these reasons, the diminished seventh chord lacks any semblance of stability; it is a "restless" chord which must seek its resolution.

Fig. 2.9

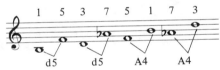

    2. Though on paper the chord can be inverted, its sound remains the same, regardless of the arrangement of the tones. The equal division of the octave prevents any inversion from having a characteristic sound of its own, as in inversions of other chords. In fact, each inversion can be spelled enharmonically, so that the lowest sounding note can be considered a root, or all lowest notes could be thirds, and so on.

Fig. 2.10

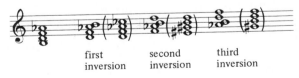

first   second   third
inversion inversion inversion

    3. There are only three diminished seventh chord sounds, as shown in Figure 2.11 *a*, *b*, and *c*. At *d*, the chord, though spelled differently from *a*, is simply the inversion of *a*. Any other possible spelling of any diminished seventh chord will also prove to be a respelling of one of the three sounds represented by *a*, *b*, and *c*. Different spellings of the same sound are necessary in the score to indicate

Fig. 2.11

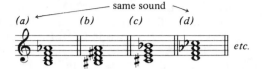

differing functions of the sound. For example, both chords in Figure 2.12 sound the same, but are spelled differently to express different uses of that sound: vii°⁷ progresses to I while vii°⁷/vi progresses to vi.

Fig. 2.12

C: vii°⁷ I   vii°⁷/vi vi₆

4. The seventh of either the diminished seventh chord or the half diminished seventh chord may resolve in either of two ways. It may resolve as in other seventh chords, that is, with a change of harmony at the point of resolution (Figure 2.13*a,* showing this resolution in both V⁷ and vii°⁷), or it may resolve while other members of the chord remain stationary. In the latter case, at the point of resolution a major minor seventh chord results (Figure 2.13*b*).

Fig. 2.13

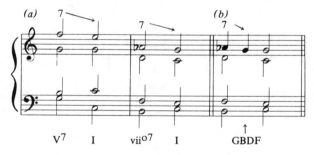

V⁷   I   vii°⁷   I   GBDF

In many cases, the seventh resolving "prematurely," as at *b* above, will be better analyzed as a simple nonharmonic tone over a chord of the dominant seventh type (see Figure 2.18).

Terminology Variant

Both the diminished triad and the diminished seventh chord may be considered as dominant chords, each with its root missing. In this view, the vii° triad is V⁷ with a missing root, symbolized V⁰₇ (review *Elementary Harmony,* pages 262–63), while the diminished seventh chord is a V⁹ with its root missing, symbolized V⁰₉♭. This concept will often be helpful in certain analyses.

Fig. 2.14

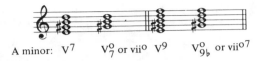

A minor: V^7 V^O_7 or vii^O V^9 $V^O_{9\flat}$ or vii^{O7}

The Leading Tone Seventh Chord

There are three useful seventh chords built on the leading tone of a key (Fig. 2.15). The vii^{O7} in minor is a diatonic seventh chord (in C minor, B D F A$\flat$, considering B natural a diatonic tone). To produce the same chord in a major key, it is necessary to lower the sixth scale step, B D F A$\flat$, the resultant chord often known as one "borrowed" from the minor. The vii^{O7} in either major or minor is very commonly used, while the remaining chord, the $vii^{\varnothing7}$ is less frequently encountered. The $vii^{\varnothing7}$ in minor (not shown) is extremely rare. Its seventh, which should resolve down, is also the raised sixth scale step of the key, which should ascend.

Fig. 2.15

C major: $vii^{\varnothing7}$ vii^{O7} C minor: vii^{O7}

Assignment 2.4.   *a)* Spell the vii^{O7} in each major and minor key.
b) Spell the $vii^{\varnothing7}$ in each major key.
Use of any diminished seventh chord in any inversion is acceptable, and indeed, common. Figures 2.16 and 2.17 show the vii^{O7} in first inversion and in second inversion respectively.

Fig. 2.16

Bach, *Ist Gott mein Schild und Helfersmann,*
(No. 122)

vii^{O7}_6 $i6$
5

Fig. 2.17

Mozart, Sonata for Piano, K. 279,
second movement

Figure 2.18 shows a very simple example of the premature resolution of the seventh. The note B♭ is obviously an upper neighbor of the V$_5^6$ chord.

Fig. 2.18

Bach, *Jesu, meine Freude* (No. 356)

Slightly more complex is the repeated upper neighbor, E♭, in the left hand of the music of Figure 2.19, which seems to create a vii°[7], a VI$_6$, and another vii°[7]. Because of the early resolution of the upper neighbors, the progression is simply i-V-i-V-i. The "VI$_6$," the first chord of measure 2, is an excellent example of the "harmonic" nonharmonic tone first described in *Elementary Harmony*, page 231.

Fig. 2.19

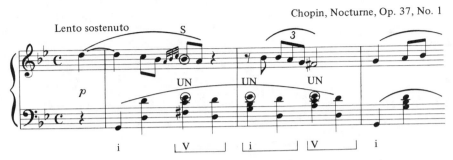

The less common vii$^{\varnothing 7}$ is found in the next example at the point of a dramatic climax in the theme of this scherzo movement.

Fig. 2.20

Secondary Leading Tone Seventh Chords

Adding a seventh to each secondary leading tone triad of Figure 2.21 produces a secondary leading tone seventh chord. A fully diminished seventh chord is possible in each case, while in some cases the half diminished seventh chord is impossible. As before, the fully diminished seventh chords are very common in music scores, the half diminished chords much less so. In the list of these chords (Figure 2.21), note that the $^{\varnothing 7}$ chord on the second scale step in minor, usually a ii$^{\varnothing 7}$, is a secondary leading tone chord when progressing to III (vii$^{\varnothing 7}$/III– III).

Fig. 2.21

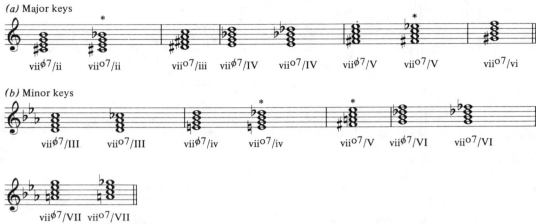

(a) Major keys

vii$^{\varnothing 7}$/ii vii^{o7}/ii   vii^{o7}/iii vii$^{\varnothing 7}$/IV vii^{o7}/IV   vii$^{\varnothing 7}$/V vii^{o7}/V   vii^{o7}/vi

(b) Minor keys

vii$^{\varnothing 7}$/III   vii^{o7}/III   vii$^{\varnothing 7}$/iv   vii^{o7}/iv   vii^{o7}/V vii$^{\varnothing 7}$/VI   vii^{o7}/VI

vii$^{\varnothing 7}$/VII vii^{o7}/VII

*These chords, together with the vii^{o7} in major and minor, are by far the most commonly used of all the diminished seventh chords.

Assignment 2.5.   Spell the secondary leading tone seventh chords in all major and minor keys.

Regular Resolution of Secondary Leading Tone Seventh Chords

Each chord of Figure 2.21 resolves as does any diminished seventh chord: the root (a leading tone function) rises a half step, while the seventh resolves down stepwise. Figures 2.22 and 2.23 show various secondary leading tone seventh chords. In each of these, the seventh resolves simultaneously with the chord as a whole. Each of these examples illustrates these chords as used in harmonic sequences.

Fig. 2.22

Schumann, Concerto in A Minor
for Piano and Orchestra, Op. 54, first movement
Allegro affetuoso

G: I   vii^{o7}/V V   vii^{o7}/IV IV   vii^{o7} I

Fig. 2.23

Mozart, String Quartet, K. 458, second movement

B♭: vii⌀7   I   vii°7/vi   vi   vii⌀7/IV   IV   I⁶₄   vii°7/vi   vii°7/V   I⁶₄   V7   I

When found in inversion, there is no change of spelling in these diminished seventh chords, even though to the ear the lowest sounding note could be the root of the chord. The actual root and seventh resolve exactly as in the root position of the chord, as shown in Figure 2.24.

Fig. 2.24

Brahms, Intermezzo, Op. 76, No. 7

(a) Moderato simplice

a: i₆   vii°7₄/V   V₆
                   ₃

(b)

C: vii°7₄/ii   V⁶₄/V   vii°7₄   I⁶₄
            ₂   ₂

vii°7/ii   V/V   vii°7   I

41

The principle of the "premature" resolution of the seventh, described earlier in this chapter in connection with the vii°⁷ chord, applies equally to secondary leading tone seventh chords. Figure 2.25 shows a chord spelling G♯ B D F with the F resolving prematurely to E, creating a V⁷/V before the resolution of the sonority as a whole. Because the G♯ B D F sonority is held for two full beats, the aural impression may well be that of a diminished seventh sound followed by a dominant seventh sound. Such situations as these cannot always be evaluated objectively, and in this case, either analysis is acceptable.

Fig. 2.25

*The part for clarinet in A has been transposed to concert pitch.

Resolution of vii°⁷/V to Tonic Six-Four

It has been established that the tonic six-four functions as a dominant chord, containing two nonharmonic tones. Therefore, the vii°⁷/V chord can just as easily resolve to I⁶₄ or i⁶₄ as to V.

In minor, this is easily accomplished, as the seventh of the diminished seventh chord is simply held over to become the sixth above the bass note of i⁶₄, as in Figure 2.26a. In major, a notational problem arises: the seventh of the diminished seventh chord must ascend in this same situation, as shown in Figure 2.26b, where the seventh, E♭, of vii°⁷/V ascends to the E♮ of I⁶₄. Most composers let this stand, as can be seen at the cadence of Figure 2.23, D♭–D♮. Some composers, on the other hand, prefer to respell the diminished seventh chord, changing the seventh to its enharmonic equivalent showing a ♯ sign, as in Figure 2.26c, and Figure 2.27. Although the chord appears to be spelled as a vii°⁷/iii, it functions as a vii°⁷/V.

Fig. 2.26

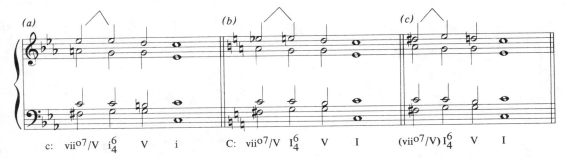

Fig. 2.27

Haydn, Quartet in G Major, Op. 77, No. 1,
first movement

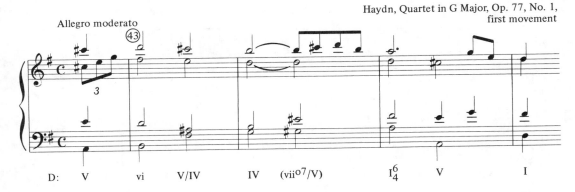

Other Resolutions

We have learned that in dominant and secondary dominant harmonies, the leading tone often descends by half step to a pitch using the same letter name. Since the root of a diminished seventh chord functions as a leading tone, it too can resolve in this manner, as shown in Figure 2.28, B♮–B♭ in the progression vii°^{7}/V- ii$^6_5$.

Fig. 2.28

Wagner, *Lohengrin*, **Act III**

Fig. 2.29

Bizet, *Les Pêcheurs des Perles*,
Act II, No. 8, "Duo"

Diminished seventh chords are often used freely in succession and without concern for resolution of sevenths or of altered tones. In such a succession, any feeling for a specific key is often lost until the final diminished seventh chord, which usually resolves normally. In this situation, Roman numeral symbols are without value, except to identify the spelling of the chord. In Figure 2.29, four successive diminished seventh chords effectively eliminate a sense of key until the last of the four, C♯ E G B♭, assumes the role of a vii°⁷/V chord in resolving to i_4^6.

Spelling Variants

Composers occasionally spell diminished seventh chords other than as described in this chapter. Often this is done to simplify notation, as shown in the simple progression in Figure 2.30, I-vii°⁷/VI-V/ii-IV-V-I. Though it is possible that Beethoven intended the notation E♭ G B♭ to reflect a new key feeling, more likely the E♭ triad represents an easier spelling of D♯ F✕ A♯ (V/ii). Spelled as E♭ G B♭, it is preceded by its secondary leading tone chord, D F A♭ C♭, respelled as shown in the score from E♯ G♯ B D, itself an easier respelling of the vii°⁷/VI in F♯ major, C✕ E♯ G♯ B. Such manipulation of accidentals is justified from a performance point of view, but an analysis of the music should reflect the actual function of the chord structure.

Fig. 2.30

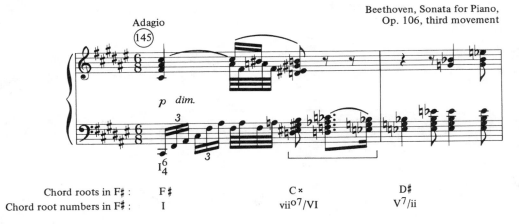

Beethoven, Sonata for Piano, Op. 106, third movement

Chord roots in F♯:	F♯	C✕	D♯
Chord root numbers in F♯:	I	vii°⁷/VI	V⁷/ii

	B	C♯	F♯
	IV	V	I

The Nondominant Use of Diminished Seventh Chords

There are two other diminished seventh chords commonly used in music that do not function as secondary leading tone chords. They are the $\sharp ii^{o7}$ and $\sharp vi^{o7}$ in major keys. In each of these, the root of the chord resolves up a half step to the third of the following chord: $\sharp ii^{o7}\text{-}I_6$ and $\sharp vi^{o7}\text{-}V_6$ (or V_5^6).

Fig. 2.31

Figure 2.32 includes both chords, the $\sharp vi^{o7}$ being in inversion. When used in inversion, the roots of these chords still resolve up one half step to the third of the following chord.

Fig. 2.32

Beethoven, Quartet, Op. 18, No. 3, second movement

Assignment 2.6. Spell in each major key the $\sharp ii^{o7}$ and $\sharp vi^{o7}$ chords.

The Melodic Augmented Second

When using diminished seventh chords, the melodic interval of the augmented second sometimes appears. When the chord is arpeggiated, the interval from the seventh up to the root is an augmented second. The same is true when the chord is repeated in different positions (Figure 2.29, measures 93, 94, and 96).

Composers occasionally use this interval other than in a diminished seventh chord. In a minor key, a scale passage displayed prominently in the musical texture may include all or part of the harmonic form of the scale, ascending or descending.

Fig. 2.33

Beethoven, Quartet, Op. 59, No. 3,
second movement

The interval is also used as an appoggiatura figure where the second note of the augmented second is the dissonant tone (Figure 2.34, measure 1, E-F✕).

Fig. 2.34

Mozart, Serenade, No. 7, K. 250,
"Haffner" sixth movement

Assignment 2.7. Harmonic analysis.   Each excerpt contains one or more of the various uses of diminished sonorities described in this chapter. Make a Roman numeral analysis below the staff, and describe the use of the diminished sonorities.

Mozart, Sonata in F Major for Piano, K. 280,
second movement

(2) Bach, *Gottes Sohn ist kommen* (No. 18)

(3) Offenbach, *La Créole*, No. 18b

(4) Allegro
Haydn, Quartet, Op. 71, No. 1

Beethoven, Symphony No. 5, Op. 67,
fourth movement

Brahms, *Dein Herzen mild*, Op. 62, No. 4

Thou gen - tle heart, how pure thou art, in child - hood's qui - et

dream - ing. In but a day will love's hot ray through thee / through thee be fierce - ly

through thee be fierce - ly gleam - ing.

gleam - ing, through thee, through thee, through thee be fierce - ly gleam - ing.
fierce - ly gleam - ing, through thee, _____ through

thee be fierce - ly,

Sehr lebhaft

Schumann, *Novelletten*, Op. 21, No. 6

(7) ㉖

Immer schneller und schneller

(8) Andantino   Chopin, Nocturne, Op. 48, No. 2

(9) Note the composer's procedure in the first two diminished seventh chords: the seventh resolves while the remaining members of the chord are held over as multiple suspensions, or these tones may be considered collectively as an "appoggiatura chord" (review *Elementary Harmony,* page 231) over the chord of resolution.

Adagio sostenuto

Rachmaninoff, Concerto for Piano
and Orchestra, No. 2, Op. 18

V⁹/V   ii∅7

Modulation with Diminished Seventh Chords

Quick and effective modulation to any major or minor key can be accomplished through any diminished seventh chord. This is possible because of the chord's ambiguity: 1) the chord sounds the same in all inversions, and 2) each position of a given chord can usually be respelled enharmonically. Consequently, any single diminished seventh chord in the original key will function in some way in any other major or minor key. This is demonstrated in Table 2.1, where the vii°⁷ in C major or C minor can act as a pivot to any other key. For purposes of this table, only the most commonly used diminished seventh chords are used: in major, vii°⁷, vii°⁷/ii, and vii°⁷/V; in minor, vii°⁷, vii°⁷/iv and vii°⁷/V. These represent the three possible sounds (Figure 2.11) of a diminished seventh chord in major and minor keys. Spellings of any other diminished seventh functions will be enharmonic with one of these (for example, in C major, vii°⁷/vi, G♯ B D F is enharmonic with vii°⁷, B D F A♭).

When the spelling of the diminished seventh chord is the same in both keys, the pivot relationship is usually obvious, as in Figure 2.35, where D♯ F♯ A C is the spelling for vii°⁷/ii in D major and vii°⁷/V in A major. If one wishes to consider the cadence at measure 95 simply a half cadence, we find a short progression on the level of V beginning at measure 5:

$$\text{I} \quad \underline{\text{vii°⁷} \quad \text{I}_4^6 \quad \text{V} \quad \text{V}}$$
$$\text{V}$$

Regardless of which analysis is correct, (or both), analysis as modulation clearly shows the modulatory process in using diminished seventh chords.

TABLE 2-1

THE DIMINISHED SEVENTH CHORD AS A PIVOT CHORD

Modulation to all major and minor keys from C major
or C minor using the vii°7, B D F A♭, as the pivot chord

vii°7 in C spelled as	Major Key	Minor Key
B D F A♭ =	vii°7/V in F major	vii°7/V in F minor
=	vii°7/ii in B♭ major	vii°7/iv in G minor
D F A♭ C♭ =	vii°7 in E♭ major	vii°7 in E♭ minor
=	vii°7/V in A♭ major	vii°7/V in A♭ minor
=	vii°7/ii in D♭ major	vii°7/iv in B♭ minor
C✕ E♯ G♯ B =		vii°7 in D♯ minor
=		vii°7/V in G♯ minor
=	vii°7/ii in C♯ major	vii°7/iv in A♯ minor
F A♭ C♭ E♭♭ =	vii°7 in G♭ major	
=	vii°7/V in C♭ major	
E♯ G♯ B D =	vii°7 in F♯ major	vii°7 in F♯ minor
=	vii°7/V in B major	vii°7/V in B minor
=	vii°7/ii in E major	vii°7/iv in C♯ minor
G♯ B D F =	vii°7 in A major	vii°7 in A minor
=	vii°7/ii in G major	vii°7/iv in E minor
=	vii°7/V in D major	vii°7/V in D minor

Fig. 2.35

D major, vii°7/ii, D♯ F♯ A C =
A major, vii°7/V, D♯ F♮ A C (same spelling in both keys)

Haydn, Symphony No. 101 *(Clock)*,
third movement

Fig. 2.36

B♭ major, vii°⁷/ii, B D F A♭ =
F♯ minor, vii°⁷,   E♯ G♯ B D (both spellings shown)

Schubert, Sonata in B♭ Major for Piano,
D. 960, first movement

Often the spelling of the diminished seventh pivot differs for each of the two keys it represents. Figure 2.36 is an excerpt showing an uncommon display, in measure 46, of the pivot as spelled in both keys. Note also that the seventh of the respelled diminished seventh chord resolves prematurely, creating a V^7 before progressing to its tonic. Figure 2.37 shows this modulatory process reduced to its basic chords.

Fig. 2.37

More likely, when the pivot involves two spellings, only that of the new key is shown in the score, as in Figure 2.38 where the spelling A C E♭ G♭ is that of its function as vii°⁷/V in the new key of E♭ minor.

Fig. 2.38

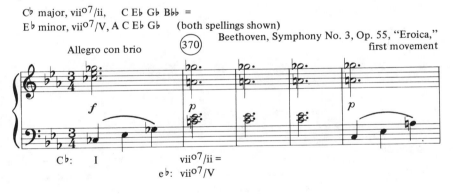

Use of diminished seventh chords with functions other than those listed in Table 2.1 are also common, as in Figure 2.39 where vii^{o7}/V = $\sharp$ii^{o7}, the latter one of the two nondominant diminished seventh chords described earlier in this chapter. (The chord labeled N$_6$ is presented in Chapter 7.)

Fig. 2.39

A major, vii^{o7}, G$\sharp$ B D F =
F major, $\sharp$ii^{o7}, G$\sharp$ B D F

Brahms, *Dein blaues Auge*, Op. 59, No. 8

*Note the two uses of G$\sharp$ B D F: at the first * it is the nondominant $\sharp$ii^{o7}; at the second * it is the alternate spelling of the vii^{o7}/V

†D F A: passing six-four between two positions of the $\sharp$ii^{o7}

Alternate spellings of the pivotal diminished seventh chord are occasionally seen. Usually the reason is obvious: to provide a simpler spelling for the benefit of the performer, as in Figure 2.40, where D$\sharp$ F$\sharp$ A C replaces G$\times$ B$\sharp$ D$\sharp$ F$\sharp$.

Fig. 2.40

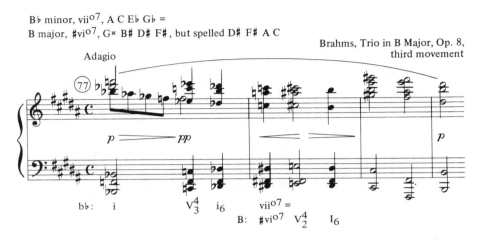

B♭ minor, vii°7, A C E♭ G♭ =
B major, #vi°7, G× B♯ D♯ F♯, but spelled D♯ F♯ A C

Brahms, Trio in B Major, Op. 8,
third movement

It will be recalled from discussion earlier in this chapter that the seventh of a diminished seventh chord often resolves before the resolution of the chord as a whole (premature resolution), resulting in a dominant seventh chord (e.g., B D F A♭-B D F G). This principle is sometimes extended to other members of the diminished seventh chord to produce various dominant seventh chords useful in modulatory situations. Using the same B D F A♭ chord as an example,

lowering the root B to B♭ produces	B♭ D F A♭
or B to A♯	A♯ C× E♯ G♯
lowering the third D to D♭ produces	D♭ F A♭ C♭
or D to C♯	C♯ E♯ G♯ B
lowering the fifth F to F♭ produces	F♭ A♭ C♭ E♭♭
or F to E	E G♯ B D

Each of these may be used as a dominant seventh or any secondary dominant seventh in the new key.

In Figure 2.41 the root of the vii°7 is lowered, E♯ G♯ B D to E G♯ B D, the

Fig. 2.41

Beethoven, Sonata for Piano,
Op. 28, first movement

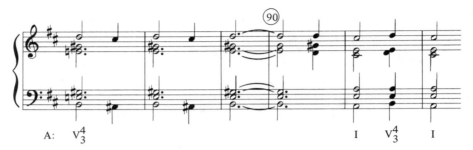

latter becoming the dominant seventh of the new key. This illustration shows only the harmonic skeleton of the composition. For the full pianistic figuration, and for the definite establishment of each of the two keys involved, F♯ minor and A major, refer to measures 71–109 of the sonata quoted.

In the excerpt from *Siegfried,* Figure 2.42, the composer uses this device repeatedly in short motives in close succession, using both half diminished and fully diminished seventh chords. In the first of these motives, the A of B D F A moves down a half step to G♯, creating G♯ B D F, the D of which moves down a half step to C♯, creating a dominant seventh chord requiring an enharmonic spelling of C♯ E♯ G♯ B.

Note that no attempt is made to resolve the achieved dominant seventh in each case, except to proceed to another similar motive. At this point in the score this process continues for a total of nineteen measures during which the listener feels time after time that the music is arriving at a new key, only to start over at another functional level.

Fig. 2.42

*denotes the beginning of a similar figure, each either two or three chords in length.

Assignment 2.8. Harmonic analysis of modulations involving diminished seventh chords.   Include key relationships, the dual function of the diminished seventh chord, or any other manipulation of the chord.

Beethoven, Sonata for Piano, Op. 27, No. 2, first movement

(1)   Adagio sostenuto

Schubert, Sonata in D Major for Piano, D. 850, first movement

(2)   Allegro vivace

Haydn, Quartet, Op. 74, No. 1,
second movement

(3)

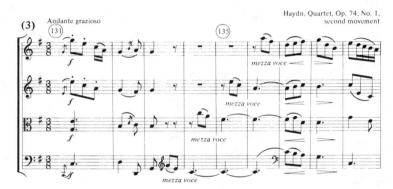

(4)

Schubert, Quintet in C Major,
D. 956, first movement

Allegretto ma non troppo

(6) In this passage, at each * is a diminished seventh chord, each spelled identically, but each serving a different harmonic function. Determine the function of each diminished seventh chord and respell it (if applicable) according to its function. (While Beethoven usually spells diminished seventh chords functionally, we can assume a single spelling is used here because of the proximity of their appearances.)

Beethoven, Symphony No. 7,
Op. 92, second movement

Application

Written Materials

Part-Writing the Secondary Leading Tone Chords   Part-writing procedures for secondary leading tone triads and seventh chords are similar to procedures already established for diatonic diminished triads and for seventh chords. Following is a brief review of these, as well as suggestions for certain less conventional situations.

1. Secondary leading tone triads are almost invariably in first inversion.
2. In both triads and seventh chords, the root of the chord (the secondary leading tone) will ascend. Exception: the root may descend a half step to a pitch with the same letter name, for example, in E major, A♯ to A♮ in the progression A♯ C♯ E to B D♯ F♯ A (vii°/V-V$^4_2$). A similar example is shown in Figure 2.28.
3. The seventh of the chord progresses down by step.
4. When diminished seventh chords are used in succession, altered notes may move in any direction.
5. Any cross relation between a note in a diminished seventh chord and a note in the preceding or following chord is acceptable. The strong sound characteristic of the diminished seventh chord distracts the ear from the usual unpleasant effect of the cross relation.
6. Intervals not otherwise commonly used may occur when progressing to or from a diminished triad or seventh chord. Here a few examples:

Diminished fourth (d4)	Figure 2.23, A up to D♭, measures 26-27
Diminished seventh (d7)	Assignment 2.7 (1), A up to G♭, measure 59
Diminished third (d3)	Assignment 2.7 (3), G down to E♯, measure 3
Augmented fifth (A5)	Assignment 2.7 (6), D♭ up to A♮, measure 3

7. In the half diminished seventh chord, when its seventh is in the soprano, care must be taken to avoid parallel fifths, like those in Figure 2.43a. Use of Rule 5[1] (double the third of the second chord) is effective, as in Figure 2.43b and Figure 2.23, the first two chords. Two other possibilities are shown in Figure 2.43c and d.

---

[1]See Appendix 1, page 397.

Fig. 2.43

Assignment 2.9. Part-writing secondary leading tone triads. Fill in alto and tenor voices. Write in harmonic analysis.

Assignment 2.10. Part-writing secondary leading tone seventh chords.
Fill in alto and tenor voices. Make harmonic analysis.

Assignment 2.11. Part-writing extended exercises including secondary leading tone chords.

(5)

Assignment 2.12. Part-writing chord progressions listed in Exercise 2.1, page 72. Choose key and meter. Add nonharmonic tones where feasible.

Assignment 2.13. Melody harmonization. The following phrases are from Bach chorales. In each, Bach has used a diminished seventh chord as studied in this chapter. Harmonize melodies as assigned, adding alto, tenor, and bass voices. Upon completion, compare your harmonization with that of Bach.

Sources: 1, chorale 47, last phrase; 2, chorale 67, last phrase; 3, chorale 94, last phrase; 4, chorale 128, fourth phrase; 5, chorale 237, last phrase; 6, chorale 303, fourth phrase; 7, chorale 340, fourth phrase.

Assignment 2.14. Part-writing modulations with diminished seventh chord pivots. Make analysis, including function of pivot in each key.

Devising Modulations Using Diminished Seventh Chords   When choosing a diminished seventh chord as a pivot, the easiest and most practical procedure is to first choose the diminished seventh chord to be used as a function in the new key. The chosen chord will always have a satisfactory function in the old key, as shown in Table 2.1. After making the choice, careful consideration must be given to the pivot chord's voicing and inversion, if any, in order to provide smooth melodic lines from its preceding chord and to its chord of resolution, as well as satisfactory resolution of the secondary leading tone and the seventh of the diminished seventh chord.

As an example we will modulate from C major to B♭ minor, choosing the vii°⁷/iv in the new key as pivot. Spelled D F A♭ C♭, it is enharmonic with the vii°⁷, B D F A♭, of C major. Should we choose to show both functions in the music, the score would appear as in Figure 2.44. Note that because of the enharmonic spelling, the vii°⁷ of C major appears in first inversion.

Fig. 2.44

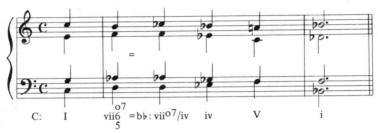

Most commonly, however, the pivot is shown as it functions in the new key only. Figure 2.45*a* is the same as Figure 2.44 without showing the pivot function in C. Figure 2.45*b* shows the same modulation except that we have chosen to place the vii°⁷/iv of the new key in first inversion, causing the vii°⁷ of C to be in second inversion. Both versions are correct, though *b* is somewhat better as it eliminates the need for the two unequal fifths found in version *a*. Version *c* modulates to A♯ minor, the enharmonic equivalent of B♭ minor. The same harmonic formula is used, only spelled in A♯ minor. The sounds of versions *b* and *c* are identical.

Fig. 2.45

Awkwardness in any one or more of the melodic lines in these modulations can often be lessened or eliminated by judicious use of nonharmonic tones. Figure 2.46 is the same as Figure 2.45a, with several nonharmonic tones added.

Fig. 2.46

Assignment 2.15. Writing modulations with a diminished seventh chord as pivot, with the pivot specified.   Indicate in the analysis the function of the diminished seventh chord in both keys. Use nonharmonic tones when necessary to improve melodic lines.

a) Write a modulation between the two given keys using the diminished seventh chord listed as the pivot as it functions in the *new key*.

b) Repeat this project using the diminished seventh chord listed as the pivot as it functions in the *old key*.

c) Repeat this project by choosing a different diminished seventh chord as pivot for each pair of keys listed.

1.	C major to A♭ major	vii°7
2.	C major to F major	vii°7/V
3.	G minor to F major	vii°7/iv
4.	B minor to D minor	vii°7
5.	A major to G♭ major	vii°7/ii
6.	D♭ major to E♭ major	vii°7
7.	F♯ minor to C minor	vii°7/iv
8.	E♭ minor to F minor	vii°7/V
9.	F♯ major to A major	vii°7/ii
10.	A♭ minor to B♭ major	vii°7

Assignment 2.16. Writing modulations making use of the "premature" resolution of the root, third, or fifth of the diminished seventh chord.   In our example, Figure 2.47, we have used the vii°7/ii in C major (C♯ E G B♭) and shown the process, as well as the possibilities of progressing to both major and minor versions of the new key center and to any key enharmonic with these.

Using Figure 2.47 as a model, choose a beginning key, a diminished seventh chord in that key, and modulate by lowering in turn the root, third, and fifth of the diminished seventh chord.

Fig. 2.47

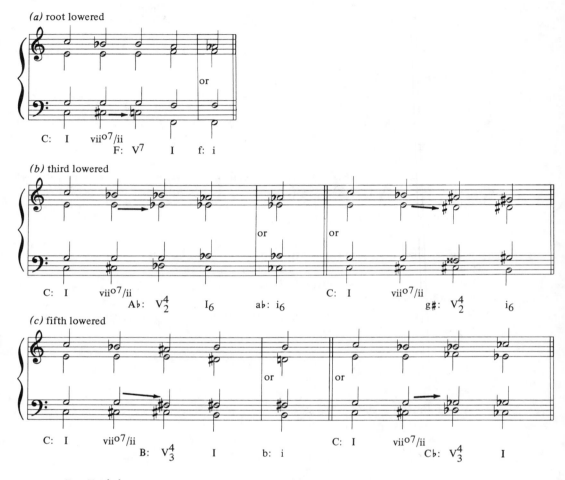

Ear Training

Singing Diminished Seventh Chords

   Exercise 2.1. Sing these progressions with letter names in any key indicated by the instructor. Sing each chord from its root, unless otherwise indicated, as in this example. G major, progression I vii°⁷/V V I:

Fig. 2.48

1. I vii°⁷/V V I
2. I vii°/V V I
3. I vii⁰⁷/V V I
4. I vii°/ii ii V I
5. I vii°⁷/ii ii V I
6. I vi vii°⁷/IV IV V I
7. I vi vii°⁷/iii iii IV V I
8. I V vii°⁷/vi vi ii V I
9. i vii°/V V i
10. i vii°⁷/V V i
11. i vii°⁷/iv iv V i
12. I ♯ii°⁷ I₆ IV V I
13. I vi ♯vi°⁷ V₆ I
14. i iv vii⁰⁷/VI VI iv V i

Harmonic Listening   Identifying a diminished triad or diminished seventh chord by ear is easiest done by first identifying the chord of resolution. When the diminished sonority is used as a secondary leading tone chord, its symbol is simply vii°/, vii°⁷ or vii⁰ ⁷ of the chord that follows. For example, when hearing a vi triad preceded by a diminished seventh chord, the latter is vii°⁷/vi. But keep in mind the two exceptions, the nondominant diminished seventh chords ♯ii°⁷ and ♯vi°⁷ in major keys. When the diminished seventh chord contains a note a *half step below the third of the tonic triad*, it is ♯ii°⁷; when the diminished seventh chord contains a note a *half step below the third of the dominant chord*, it is a ♯vi°⁷. In the progression of a diminished seventh chord to tonic six-four, there is no way to tell by ear whether the spelling of the vii°⁷/V is that based on the raised second scale degree (♯ii) or on the fourth scale degree (♯iv). Review Figure 2.26.

When the resolution is irregular, that is, when the root of the chord of resolution is not preceded by its leading tone, it can be assumed that the composer probably spelled the chord with the bass note as its root. For example, if you heard the progression of Figure 2.28, you would not hear a leading tone (F♯) progressing to the root (G) of the ii⁶₅ chord. Therefore, the bass note (B) of the diminished seventh chord is assumed to be the root of a vii°⁷/V.

Many students find it helpful in listening to take advantage of the fact that there are only three possible diminished seventh chord sounds (not spellings) as described on page 35. This fact implies that every diminished seventh chord must contain one of these notes: the leading tone, the tonic, and the raised tonic, or its enharmonic equivalent, the lowered supertonic. If one of these tones can be heard, then the *most frequently used* diminished seventh chords can be identified as follows:

Note heard	Major key	Minor key
leading tone	vii°⁷	vii°⁷
	vii°⁷/vi	
tonic	vii°⁷/V	vii°⁷/V
	♯ii°⁷	
raised tonic	vii°⁷/ii	
	♯vi°⁷	
lowered supertonic		vii°⁷/iv

Exercise 2.2. Harmonic dictation.   Harmonic dictation exercises will now include examples of the secondary leading tone triads and seventh chords.

Listening for the Diminished Seventh Chord Pivot   When hearing a modulation with a diminished seventh chord as its pivot, listen first to the complete exercise to identify the tonic of the new key. Next, listen to the chord of resolution following the diminished seventh chord and identify its function in the new key. Knowing its use in the new key will make clear its function in the old key.

Fig. 2.49

In Figure 2.49, the diminished seventh chord resolves to I_4^6 of the new key. Therefore, it is vii°⁷/V. This is confirmed by the fact that the tonic of the new key is included in the pivot. Relating the pivot to the old key, the diminished seventh chord contains the raised tonic tone, indicating vii°⁷/ii as its function in the old key. You should also be able to spell the pivot in both keys. In this case, the spelling of the pivot is enharmonic: vii°⁷/ii in G = G♯ B D F, while vii°⁷/V in F = B D F A♭.

Exercise 2.3. Harmonic dictation. Listen to examples of modulation using a diminished seventh chord as pivot. In addition to identifying the progression by Roman numeral symbols, also be prepared to spell the pivot in both keys.

Keyboard Harmony

Playing Diminished Triads and Chords

Exercise 2.4. Play Assignments 2.9 and 2.10 at the keyboard.

Exercise 2.5. Play chord progressions from Exercise 2.1 at the keyboard in any key, as directed.

Exercise 2.6 Play these additional progressions in keys as assigned.

1. I vii°⁷/V V$_2^4$ I₆ vii°₆ I

2. I vii°⁷/V vii$_4^{°7}$ I₆ vii°₆ I
    3

3. I ii ♯ii°⁷ I₆ vii°₆/V I$_4^6$ V I
    5

4. I vi ♯vi°⁷ V$_5^6$ I vii°₆⁷/V V⁷ I
    5

5. I ♯vi°₆⁷ V$_3^4$vii°⁷/iii iii I₆ vii°₆⁷/vi vi₆ vii°⁷/ii ii V I
    5 5

6. I vii°⁷/V V$_5^6$/V V vii°₆ 27/ii V$_3^4$/ii ii₆ vii°₆⁷ V$_3^4$ I₆ vii°⁷/V I$_4^6$ V I
    5 5

7. i vii°₆⁷/iv iv₆ vii°₆⁷/V V i₆ vii$_4^{°7}$ vii°⁷/V V i
    5 5 3

8. i i₆ vii°⁷/iv V$_5^6$/iv iv vii°⁷/V V$_5^6$/V V i

Modulation with a Diminished Seventh Chord as Pivot   When improvising modulations at the keyboard, establish the old key with a simple progression (I–IV–V–I or I–ii$^6_5$–V–I, and so forth). Follow this with the diminished seventh chord required in the new key and a short progression to establish the new key. Figure 2.50 is the first problem of Assignment 2.15 (page 71) using vii^{o7} as the pivot in the new key.

Fig. 2.50

C: vii^{o7}/ii =
Ab: vii^{o7}

Exercise 2.7.   At the keyboard, improvise modulations listed in Assignment 2.15.

Exercise 2.8.   Improvise modulations between any two keys chosen at random, using any diminished seventh chord as pivot.

Modulation Using the "Premature" Resolution of the Seventh   Figure 2.51 shows the three possibilities of modulation when using a diminished seventh chord in root position and lowering successively its root, third, and fifth.

Fig. 2.51

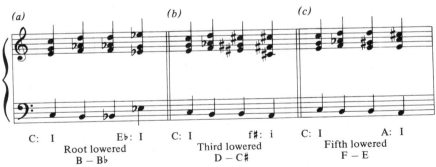

C: I   Eb: I   C: I   f#: i   C: I   A: I
Root lowered   Third lowered   Fifth lowered
B – Bb   D – C#   F – E

In addition to the above, these possibilities exist:

a)   V^7–i in Eb minor
     V^7–i in D# minor (V^7: Bb D F Ab = A# C× E# G#)

b)   V$_{\substack{4 \\ 2}}$ I in F♯ major

V$_{\substack{4 \\ 2}}$ I in G♭ major (V^7: C♯ E♯ G♯ B = D♭ F A♭ C♭)

c)   V$_{\substack{4 \\ 3}}$-i in A minor

Figure 2.52 uses the same harmonic progressions, but the diminished seventh chord is placed in that inversion which will allow the bass note to resolve to the root of the following chord.

Fig. 2.52

Alternate keys are the same as for Figure 2.51.

Exercise 2.9.   Improvise modulations. Choose a key and then any diminished seventh chord in that key. Resolve the root, third, and fifth in turn, down by half step, using the resulting chord as a V^7 in the new key. Use Figure 2.51 as a guide.

Exercise 2.10.   Improvise modulations as in Exercise 2.9, but place the diminished seventh chord in an inversion which will allow the bass note to resolve to the root of its following chord. Use Figure 2.52 as a guide.

CHAPTER THREE

Binary and Ternary Forms

Chapters 3, 4, and 5 are independent presentations. They may be interpolated in any order and at any time between other chapters of this text. The presentation of harmonic materials resumes in Chapter 6.

The study of music form, begun in *Elementary Harmony, Theory and Practice,* should be reviewed at this time (in Chapter 6, phrases and periods, and in Chapter 14, the phrase group, the double period, phrase extension, and thematic development). The formal structures, *binary* and *ternary*, are also known as *two-part forms* or *two-part song forms* and *three-part forms* or *three-part song forms*.

The terms binary and ternary refer simply to formal structures that may be divided into two or three parts respectively. By this definition, forms already studied might be so identified; for example, a contrasting period would be binary as it is composed of two different phrases, or a phrase group made up of three phrases could be considered ternary. But the terms binary and ternary imply certain conditions which differentiate them from the forms already studied: (1) each part of a binary or ternary structure in itself consists of one of the smaller forms, such as period, phrase group, or double period; (2) the succession of parts is characterized by a relationship of keys, often tonic and dominant or tonic and relative major or minor (particularly true in ternary form); and (3) a definite contrast in the nature of the thematic material between the first and second parts, and in ternary form, a return to the original material in the third part.

Binary Form

Each of the two sections of binary form concludes with a strong cadence, usually perfect. The cadence of the first part may be in a closely related key. Each of the two parts will be any one of the smaller forms previously studied, very often the same in each part. At least one and usually both parts are larger than a phrase. Extensions will often be found, including (particularly in instrumental music) a prelude or introduction to the first part and a concluding section or codetta after the second part. One or both parts will often be set apart by repeat signs to em-

phasize the binary structure. In analysis, the two parts are often designated as A and B, where B indicates a contrast to A. Figure 3.1 could then be analyzed as A   B,   the small letters referring to phrases.
a a'   b c

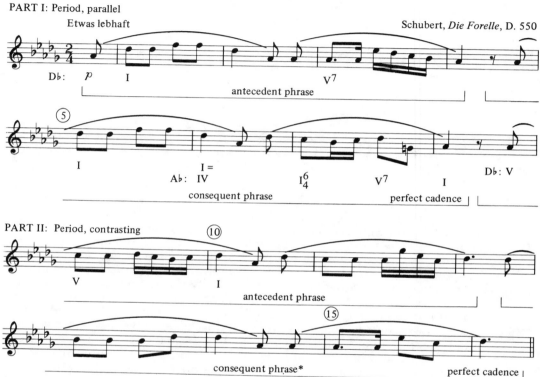

PART I: Period, parallel

Etwas lebhaft

Schubert, *Die Forelle*, D. 550

Db: *p*   I   V⁷

antecedent phrase

(5)

I

Ab: IV   I   I₄⁶   V⁷   I   Db: V

consequent phrase   perfect cadence

PART II: Period, contrasting   (10)

V   I

antecedent phrase

(15)

consequent phrase*   perfect cadence

*In the original, this phrase is repeated. No change of analysis results.

In contrast to the formal balance between the two parts of the previous example, Figure 3.2 shows parts of unequal length. Part I is a period, while part II is a phrase group, the last phrase with extension. (In Brahms' original score, the tenor voice is written in the bass clef an octave lower, and the voices are accompanied by two pianos. Most of the eighteen waltzes of this opus are in binary form and are worthy of study.)

Fig. 3.2

Brahms, *Liebeslieder Wälzer*, Op. 52, "O die Frauen"

PART I

Im Ländler Tempo   (5)

Soprano
Tenor

O die Frau-en,   o die Frau-en   wie sie Won - ne, Won - ne   la - den!

Bb: I   ii₅⁶   V   I   ii₅⁶   V   I   vi   V⁹   V⁷   I

PART II

Wä - re lang ein Mönch ge - wor - den, wä - re lang ein Mönch ge -
V/vi   vi   V/vi   vi   V/V   V   V/V

wor - den, wä - ren nicht die Frau - en, die Frau - en.
V   V/iii   v9   I   V   I

Assignment 3.1. Analyze these examples of binary form, as assigned, from sight singing texts (see Assignment 3.4 for music examples).

Music for Sight Singing: 165, 212, 220, 234, 288, 294, 295, 317, 422, 430, 432, 437, 443, 444, 448.
More Music for Sight Singing: 372, 387, 646, 658, 695, 698, 701, 702, 703, 709, 735, 737, 797, 798, 811, 873, 877.

Ternary Form

In ternary form, the second part furnishes a contrast to the first part, while the third part is similar to, or even exactly the same as, the first part. The result is an ABA form; this three-part structure consisting of statement, contrast, and restatement occurs with considerable frequency in all varieties of music, ranging from folk songs and popular songs to symphonic movements.

The *first part* of a ternary form may be any of the smaller forms, usually larger than a phrase. It ends on a strong cadence in the tonic key or a closely related key.

The *second part* offers a contrast, usually by different thematic material, though at times by using material similar to the first part but in a related key. Any small form may be used and it usually ends on a weak cadence, often on the dominant, which serves as a bridge to the return of the original idea.

The *third part*, the return of the original idea, may be a literal repetition of the first part, either written out or indicated in a *da capo* (D.C.) at the end of the second part, or it may show strong similarity to the first part without being exactly the same.

Any of the parts may be found with extensions, codettas, or irregular phrase lengths.

A short and very simple example from Grieg shows an A B A form consisting only of a period (A), a repeated phrase (B), and a D.C. as the return to A.

Grieg, *Holberg Suite*,
Op. 40, "Gavotte"

Fig. 3.3

Allegretto

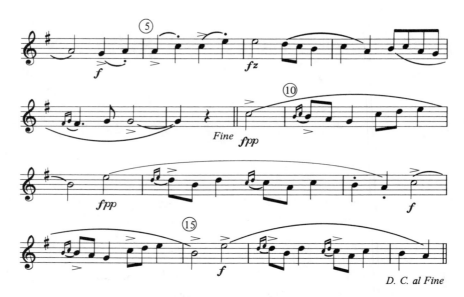

Slightly more complex is Figure 3.4, showing extensions in each part of the composition. When used as a vocal solo in a large work, as here, the ternary form using a D.C. is often known as a "da capo aria."

Fig. 3.4

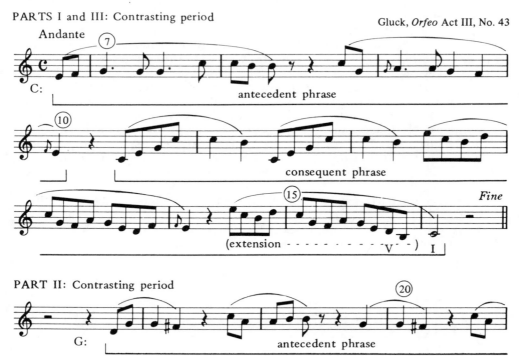

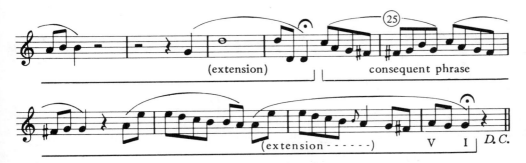

In contrast to the simplicity of form in the preceding examples, Figure 3.5 demonstrates a few of the possibilities in expanding a ternary form into a major musical expression. While maintaining the A B A format, each of the parts can include numerous extensions of various lengths, and part B often includes two or more ideas in contrast to part A. Figure 3.5 can be diagrammed

A	B	A
ab	cd ef	a'

as indicated in the following score.

Fig. 3.5

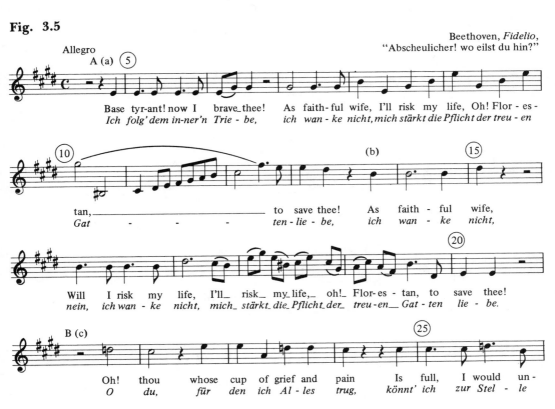

(d) ③⓪

chain thee! I come to break thy fet - ters, now,___ And in___
drin - gen, wo Bos - heit dich in Fes - seln schlug,___ und sü -

③⑤ (e)

___ thy woe sus - tain___ thee! Oh! thou whose cup of___
- ssen Trost dir brin - - gen! O du, für den ich___

④⓪ (f)

grief___ and woe Is full,___ I___ would un - chain thee! I come to
Al - les trug, könnt' ich___ zur Stel - le drin - gen, wo Bos - heit

④⑤ 3

break thy fet - ters now, and___ in___ thy woe___ sus - tain thee.
dich in Fes - seln schlug, könnt'_ ich___ zur Stel - le drin - gen!

⑤⓪ A (a')

Base ty - rant, now I brave_ thee! As faith - ful wife, I'll ven - ture
Ich folg' dem in - ner'n Trie - be, ich wan - ke nicht, mich stärkt die

⑤⑤

life Oh! Flor - est - an! _____ to
Pflicht der treu - en Gat - - - - - - ten -

⑥⓪

save thee! Base ty - rant, now I brave_ thee! As faith - ful wife, Now
lie - be, ich folg' dem in - ner'n Trie - be, ich wan - ke nicht, nein,

⑥⑤

will I yield my life, I'll yield my life, oh! Flor - es -
nein, ich wan - ke nicht, mich stärkt die Pflicht der treu - en

tan! _____ to   save thee!
Gat - - - - - - - - *ten   lie - be.*

The Three-Part Period

A smaller form incorporating the three-part idea is often known as a *three-part period*. This consists of only three phrases, the first of which may or may not end with a strong cadence, and the third of which may or may not be written as a *da capo*.

Fig. 3.6*

Schubert, *Die Schöne Müllerin*, D. 795, "Wohin"

phrase 1 (A)

phrase 2 (B)

phrase 3 (A)

*Repeated sections are written out in the original, and the opening measure of phrase 3 differs slightly in the repeat.

Assignment 3.2. Analyze these examples of ternary form, as assigned, from sight singing texts (see Assignment 3.4 for music examples).

Music for Sight Singing: 115, 194, 208, 268, 274, 282, 287, 309, 347, 351, 383, 425.
More Music for Sight Singing: 298, 312, 357, 437, 654, 672, 682, 697, 699, 724, 726, 729, 734, 799.

For extended examples, as in Figure 3.5, see:

Brahms, Three Intermezzi, Op. 117
Mozart, *The Marriage of Figaro*, Act II, "Voi che sapete"
Tschaikowski, Violin Concerto, second movement

Rounded Binary or Incipient Ternary

These two names refer to a single type of formal structure. This problem in terminology is caused by the fact that music written in this form displays both binary and ternary characteristics. Figure 3.7 appears obviously to be in two parts, each consisting of a single period. But upon examination, the second phrase of Part II is seen to be a return to the idea first presented at the beginning of Part I. The fact that the return is modified alters the analysis only to the extent (in this case) of identifying it as a″.

Thus, this excerpt can be considered binary because it consists of two equal parts (even marked with repeat signs), with cadences considered usual for a two-part form. But the return of the opening material at the end of the form is definitely ternary in character. Hence, both terminologies aptly describe the situation, as can be seen in the formal diagram of Figure 3.7

$$A \quad \|: \| : B \quad :\|$$
$$a \quad a' \quad\quad b \quad a''$$

Fig. 3.7

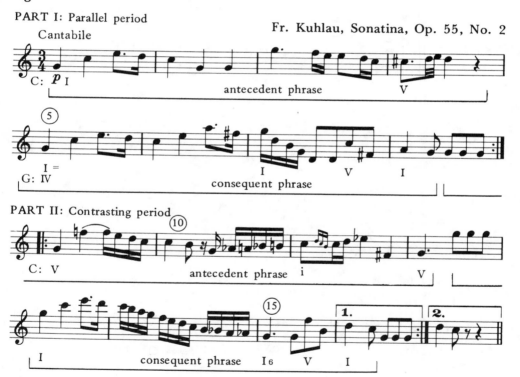

PART I: Parallel period

Cantabile

Fr. Kuhlau, Sonatina, Op. 55, No. 2

A more common use of this form shows Part II consisting of three or more phrases, the last two of which comprise a return to the original period as A or A′. In Figure 3.8, the formal diagram is

$$A \quad \|: \| : B \quad :\|$$
$$a \quad b \quad\quad c \quad a \quad b''$$

$$or, \quad A \quad\quad B \quad\quad A$$

Fig. 3.8

Haydn, Sonata in D Major for Piano,
second movement

Part II of Figure 3.9 includes four phrases

```
A  :‖: B        :‖
a  b    c  d  a  b'
or,  A      B    A
```

Fig. 3.9

Schubert, *Adagio and Rondo*, D. 506

It might be argued that the preceding example is an undisputed three-part form, with three equal eight-measure periods. This it certainly would be if the repeat signs were removed. The aural effect when played with the repeat signs, as intended by the composer, is that of binary form with a ternary inflection, as contrasted to an A B A composition performed without repeats.

Assignment 3.3.   Analyze these examples of rounded binary (incipient ternary) forms, as assigned, from sight singing texts (see Assignment 3.4 for music examples).

Music for Sight Singing: 139, 198, 417, 420, 438.
More Music for Sight Singing: 288, 338, 442, 477, 656, 705, 713.

Assignment 3.4.   These excerpts include examples of binary, ternary, and rounded binary (incipient ternary) forms. Analyze the form of each, including locations of phrases, periods, extensions, and the outer limits of each of the parts (two parts in the binary forms and three parts in the remaining forms).

Haydn, Sonata for Piano in D Major,
second movement

(3)

(4)

Mozart, Quintet for Strings,
K. 593, third movement

(5) Observe how the cadence chord of each phrase functions also as the first chord of the following phrase.

Elgar, *Enigma Variations* (Theme)

Extract from Elgar's ENIGMA VARIATIONS (piano reduction) reproduced by permission of Novello and Company Limited.

Brahms, *Neue Liebeslieder*,
Op. 65, "An jeder Hand"

An je - der Hand die Fin - ger hatt ich be - deckt mit Rin -

CHAPTER FOUR

Less Common Chord Progressions—
Extended Part-Writing Procedures

Theory and Analysis

Review of Commonly Used Progressions

Up to this point, our study of harmonic progression has been limited to the "commonly used progressions," so called because they make up the vast majority of all the chord progressions used in music in the period of common practice. These progressions were first discussed in Chapter 12 of *Elementary Harmony*, and listed there as Table 12.1. They can be compressed into a flow chart, where any given chord gravitates towards the tonic, from left to right in the diagram. Below the diagram are listed the remaining common progressions: those that skip in the direction of tonic (sometimes called *elision*) and those that progress away from tonic (sometimes called *retrogression*).

Fig. 4.1

Major:		iii	→	vi →	ii or IV	→	V or vii°	→	I
Minor:	VII→	III →	VI →	ii° or iv	→	V or vii°	→	I
Others[1]:	iii or vi → V;iii → ii₆ or IV, V → vi, vi → iii → IV

Major: iii →   vi →   ii or IV   →   V or vii°   →   I
Minor: VII→   III →   VI →   ii° or iv   →   V or vii°   →   I
Others[1]:   iii or vi → V;iii → ii$_6$ or IV, V → vi, vi → iii → IV

Any triad may progress to I when interrupting any progression above, for example, ii-I-V.

The choice of bass tone (root in bass or inversion) for each of these triads can be summarized as follows:

     a Root in bass
        All triads except diminished triads are commonly found with root in bass.

[1]Roman numerals are for chords in major keys but apply equally to minor keys.

   b First Inversion
1. Diminished triads are usually in first inversion.
2. I, ii, IV and V are commonly used in first inversion.
3. iii and vi ordinarily are found in first inversion only when the preceding triad has the same bass note and it is the root of its triad (V-iii$_6$, I-vi$_6$), or when functioning as a temporary tonic (i$_6$) following its secondary dominant.

   c Second Inversion

The triad in second inversion is ordinarily used only in these special situations:
1. the cadential six-four chord
2. the passing six-four chord
3. the pedal six-four chord
4. the arpeggiated six-four chord

   d Seventh Chords

Any seventh chord may be found with any one of its members in the bass.

Review of Commonly Used Exceptions

In addition to the pairs of triads listed in Figure 4.1 we have also seen that in certain situations, other progressions may also be identified as commonly used progressions.

   1. Triads in first inversion in succession, the bass describing a scalar line as in Figure 4.2 (review *Elementary Harmony,* Chapter 16).

Fig. 4.2

2. Harmonic sequence. The harmonic sequence can be identified by a regularly recurring pattern of root movements (review *Elementary Harmony,* Chapter 16). In Figure 4.3, the regularly recurring pattern of roots is down a second, up a fourth.

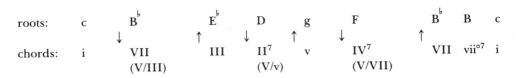

roots:	c	B♭		E♭	D	g	F		B♭	B	c
		↓		↑	↓	↑	↓			↑	
chords:	i	VII		III	II⁷	v	IV⁷		VII	vii°⁷	i
		(V/III)			(V/v)		(V/VII)				

Fig. 4.3

Weber, *Der Freischütz,*
"Overture"

    3. A common progression interrupted by the secondary dominant or secondary leading tone chord of the second chord of the progression (review *Elementary Harmony,* Chapter 18).

    Example: The progression IV-ii, interrupted by the secondary dominant of ii: IV-V/ii-ii.

    4. Diminished seventh chords in succession (review Chapter 2 in this text).

Harmonic Progressions that Include a Chromatic Melodic Line

In addition to those situations just reviewed, the use of a melodic chromatic line (a line proceeding by half steps) provides another opportunity for use of chord progressions not ordinarily found elsewhere. In a passage containing such a line, (usually the bass voice, but possible in any voice), any chord progression may result, including chromatic chords to be studied in later chapters of this text. The analysis may show common progressions, or there may be few or many progressions not found in Figure 4.1. In the latter case, and in Figure 4.4, the use of Roman numerals is often meaningless, because the progression is under the control of the chromatic line, rather than a system of root movements.

Fig. 4.4

Mozart, Symphony No. 40 in G Minor,
K. 550, second movement

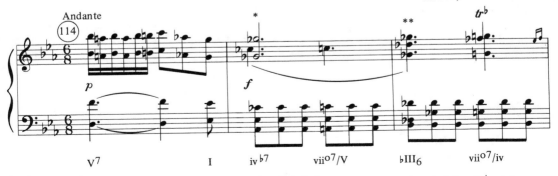

    V⁷   I   iv♭⁷   vii°⁷/V   ♭III₆   vii°⁷/iv

*iv♭⁷: the seventh above the root is lowered in relation to the key (G♭ of A♭ C♭ E♭ G♭ is a chromatically lowered tone in the key of E♭ major).
**The flat preceding a chord number indicates that the sonority is built on a lowered scale step. ♭III in E♭ major indicates a major triad built on the lowered third scale step, G♭.

$\text{iv}_6 \qquad \text{vii}^{o7}/\text{V} \qquad \qquad \text{I}^6_4 \qquad \qquad \text{V}^7 \qquad \qquad \text{I}$

One of the best known examples of the descending chromatic bass line, this one of ten measures' duration, is Chopin's Prelude in E Minor, the first part of which is shown as Figure 4.5. It should first be recognized that the right-hand "melody" is probably a pedal point on B, with an upper neighbor, in measures 1–4, and on A until measure 8. The beginning harmony and that of the cadences is clear:

e: i ⸺ I⁷ ⸺ iv ⸺ V iv V iv V ⸺ i
measure   1   4   9   10 11 12   13

Between these points, the harmonic succession is controlled by the chromatic bass line, and where this is static, as in measures 4–5, by the chromatically descending inner voice. No chord-by-chord analysis can be meaningful in progressions such as these.

Fig. 4.5

Chopin, Prelude in E Minor, Op. 28, No. 4

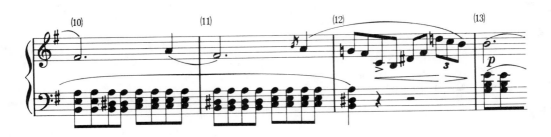

Other Less Common Progressions

The remaining chord progressions are those which appear in pairs (and rarely in groups of three or more) during a passage of music, and which are not found in the chart, Figure 4.1, or in the special situations just described. Although these progressions represent but a minute percentage of the total musical output of the period, they appear frequently enough to demand attention.

A few representative examples of these progressions follow, certain characteristics of which are:

a) the less common progression usually consists of two successive chords, though sometimes three or even four may be found.

b) in a less common progression, the soprano and bass are ordinarily found in contrary or oblique motion.

c) a less common progression rarely occurs more than once in a phrase.

Fig. 4.6

Chopin, Nocturne, Op. 15, No. 3

Fig. 4.7

Hymn: Gaudeamus Pariter

In Figure 4.8, the root movement pattern of measures 3–6 is of interest. The root movement of a third down, fifth up (IV-ii-vi) is followed by its inversion, third up, fifth down (iii-V-I).

Fig. 4.8

Dvořák, *Biblical Songs*, Op. 99, No. 9

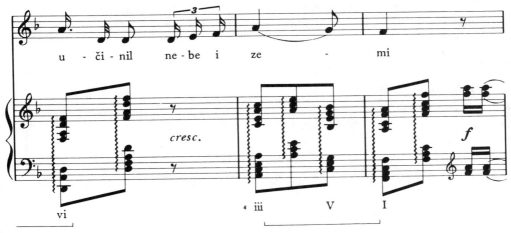

Fig. 4.9

Brahms, Intermezzo,
Op. 118, No. 2

Fig. 4.10

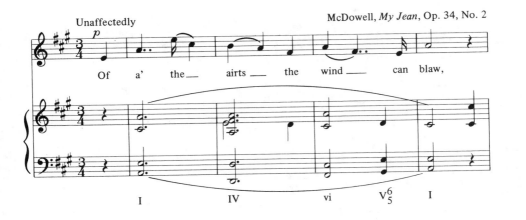

McDowell, *My Jean*, Op. 34, No. 2

After a half cadence, a new phrase sometimes begins with a chord which otherwise would not ordinarily follow V. The V-IV of Figure 4.11 illustrates one such possibility.

Fig. 4.11

Mozart, *Haffner* Symphony, K. 385

Assignment 4.1. Harmonic analysis.   Analyze the harmony of each of these excerpts. Locate the less common progression by bracketing the appropriate Roman numerals, for example: C major, progression EGB-DFA would be indicated iii-ii.

Chopin, Mazurka,
Op. 56, No. 1

(1)

(2)   Etwas bewegt   Reger, *Valet will ich dir geben*

(3) Andante sostenuto ㉚

Berlioz, *The Damnation of Faust*, Scene IX

on sent i - ci S'en - vo - ler le____ sou -

ci! Que j'ai - me ce si - len - ce, et

(4) Zeimlich langsam

Brahms, *An die Nachtigall*, Op. 46, No. 4

Geuss' nicht so laut der lieb - ent - flamm - ten

Lie - der ton - rei - chen Schall vom

Purcell, *Amphitryon*, "Saraband"

Rachmaninoff, Symphony No. 2 in E Minor, third movement

Extended Part-Writing Procedures

Review of Basic Procedures   We have emphasized from the beginning of this couse of study that good part-writing is the result of the successful superimposition of several good melodic lines, which when sounded together produce an acceptable harmonic movement. To facilitate the accomplishment of this goal, we have presented a set of part-writing procedures called "rules,"[2] based on practices of composers of the historical period under study. Along with these we have presented a number of commonly used exceptions, but with the qualification that exceptional practices should not prevail over a common practice when no particular gain in musical quality is realized.

In a very simple example, Figure 4.12, you will quickly observe that the unnecessarily doubled fifth in the IV triad leads to no particular improvement in the musical texture, and, in fact, in this case forces the alto and tenor voices into somewhat more awkward melodic lines. Therefore, while *a* is not "wrong" the progression at *b* is definitely better.

Fig. 4.12

Less Common Procedures   When part-writing situations arise in which there is good and valid reason for not following the suggested rules, alternate proce-

---

[2]These rules are listed in Appendix 1, "The Essentials of Part-Writing," page 397. Also, review the article, "Rules? Why Rules?" in *Elementary Harmony*, page 97.

dures must be devised to fit the particular problem. We cannot catalogue these as we did the common procedures, as it would be virtually impossible to list all the situations in which a less common procedure would be required. We can, however, list those "deviations" which usually occur when not folllowing the basic procedures. They are:

1. Unusual doubling—any doubling in any triad or seventh chord other than that listed under "Usual Doubling" in Appendix 1 (page 397).
2. Crossed voices—the normal pitch relationship of two voices is reversed. For example, the alto line may descend to a pitch lower than that of the tenor sounding at that time.
3. Abnormal distance between voices—more than an octave between soprano and alto or between alto and tenor.

The necessity for the use of these three practices can be placed into two categories: (1) solving technical part-writing problems, and (2) creating voice lines of greater melodic interest.

Solving Technical Part-Writing Problems   Figures 4.13 and 4.14 are two excerpts from Mozart containing doubled thirds and a doubled fifth in major triads, roots in bass.

In Figure 4.13, avoiding a parallel fifth requires the doubled third at the *. Placing the usual E♭ in the tenor at this point would create a parallel fifth between it and the alto voice in progressing to the next chord.

Fig. 4.13

Figure 4.14 displays three less common doublings. Observe in measure 2 the contrary soprano and tenor lines, B♭ C D and D C B♭. The superior sound of this contrary motion justifies the doubled third in the chord of the first beat. Then note that this sonority could not have been approached from the chord of measure 1 without parallel octaves had the first measure displayed usual root doubling (E♭). The doubled fifth of measure 1 allows the contrary motion of measure 2. All this has been carefully worked out by the composer for this special situation, while the remainder of the phrase exhibits only common part-writing procedures.

The doubled third of measure 6 (G in the E♭ major triad) exists to make possible a most effective suspension on the next beat. With usual doubling, no approach to the suspended note would be possible. The importance of the suspension outweighs the disadvantage of the doubled third.

Fig. 4.14

Mozart, *Requiem*, "Hostias et preces"

Hos - ti - as   et   pre - ces   ti - bi   Do - mi - ne,

ti - bi,   Do - mi - ne   laud - is   of - fe - ri - mus

In Figure 4.15*a*, the F major triad with a doubled third (at *) is found between a triad in closed position and a triad in open position. Open position is necessary at this point to separate the alto and tenor voices in the last half of the measure, and, since none of the options of Rule 7 ("The Essentials of Part-Writing," *Elementary Harmony*) is available, a triad earlier in the phrase must be chosen for unusual doubling. Figure 4.15*b* shows the part-writing dilemma with usual doubling.

The doubled fifth of the B major triad in measure 2 of Figure 4.15*a* is another example using this doubling to avoid a parallel fifth.

Fig. 4.15

Bach, *Von Gott will ich nicht lassen* (No. 191)

(a)

(b)

Creating Voice Lines of Greater Melodic Interest   In using the part-writing rules, we are often satisfied with the resulting melodic lines. But we can also consider the creation of melodic lines of more sophistication and interest than would be possible within the confines of the usual part-writing procedures. In doing so, the part-writing procedures must be carefully modified, or even replaced, while maintaining the objectives of a successful four-voice texture.

A fragmentary example of such melodic manipulation was shown in Figure 4.14, measure 2, where the soprano and bass voices used the same three pitches in contrary motion. Figure 4.16 displays a more complex melodic situation. (To appreciate fully the musical features discussed in this example, it is necessary to hear the music as it was intended to be performed, that is, by singing rather than at the piano.) Observe first the descending six-note alto line, its first note at *, in contrary motion to the soprano and bass voices ascending in tenths. Such a combination is impossible without part-writing accomodations: (1) the doubled third (at *) approached by overlapping voices, followed by (2) the incomplete A major triad (a complete triad with E in the tenor would have created parallel fifths), and (3) on the next beat, the tenor and the bass approached by overlapping voices from the unison A.

This feature alone would have created an outstanding phrase, but as the alto scale line ends, Handel shifts the interest to the tenor voice, which leaps up to G above the alto (crossed voices) in order to prepare a suspension in the tenor voice's most effective range, preparing an exciting climax to an exceptional phrase of music.

Fig. 4.16

Handel, *Messiah*, "Let All the Angels of God Worship Him"

Let all   the   an - gels of God.____ wor - ship Him.

For comparison, we show in Figure 4.17 how this passage might have appeared using conventional part-writing procedures.

Fig. 4.17

Fig. 4.18

Bach, *Sei Lob und Ehr dem Höchsten Gut*
(No. 248)

G: V₆   I   V   I =
           C: V   IV₆(vii°⁷) I   V   I

In our final example, the wide distance between the soprano and alto voices at the * in Figure 4.18 allows the bass and tenor voices to form a short "duet" in tenths. The resulting doubled third (A) followed by another doubled third (E) in the next chord is overshadowed by the effectiveness of the moving lines.

You will, of course, occasionally find examples of part-writing contrary to any examples in this course of study. It should be remembered that the course in part-writing as presented is the result of observation of the usual practice of composers, and that any further differences that exist are not necessarily incorrect simply because they do not conform with this presentation.

For the student, deviations from common part-writing principles should be used sparingly and only for *good musical reasons.* While you are encouraged to use more freedom in your part-writing efforts, you should be able to explain why any use of a less common procedure improves the musical score you have written.

Assignment 4.2. Analysis of part-wrtiting procedures.   Each of these excerpts contains one or more examples of less common part-writing procedures. Locate these examples and write out, or be prepared to discuss, the reasons these procedures were used.

(1)   Bach, *Gottes Sohn ist kommen* (No. 18)

(2)   Bach, *Liebster Jesu, wir sind hier* (No. 131)

Bach, *Eins ist Not! Ach Herr, dies Eine* (No. 280)

(3)

Allegro maestoso

(4)   Mendelssohn, *Elijah* (No. 22)

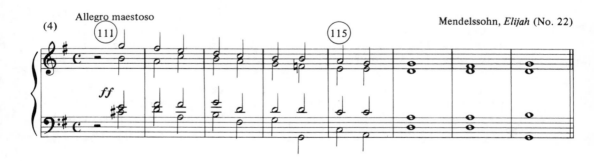

(5) Adagio   Haydn, Mass in C, "Paukenmesse"

A - gnus De - i,   A - gnus De - i,   A - gnus De - i,   qui

tol - lis pec - ca - ta   mun - di, pec - ca - ta   mun - di,

(6) Andante   Brahms, *Sankt Raphael*

Application

Written Materials

The arranger or writer of music is constantly confronted with the problem of choosing effective chord progressions. He or she must determine whether the progression sounds well, not only by itself, but also in the context of the entire phrase of music. Experimentation with different chord progressions is highly desirable, so that the final choice is technically correct in addition to being musically interesting and aesthetically acceptable.

This process of experimentation, rejection, and acceptance plays a major part in the efforts of the composer. The music of any composer lives or dies according to the public acceptance or rejection of his or her choices. Since the chord choices indicated as regular progressions in this chapter are those which the accepted composers of the eighteenth and nineteenth centuries found most useful, they will also be most useful to the student at this time. The same is true of the common part-writing procedures. However, the student is encouraged to experiment with the less common progressions and procedures, and to use them sparingly where they are musically effective. Results of such experimentation cannot be judged objectively, but only from the opinions of your teacher and other students, and from comparison of your work with that of the best composers of the period.

In working with less common devices in the following assignments, two basic principles should be kept in mind.

1. When using less common chord progressions, oblique or contrary motion between outside voices will help to insure a good aural effect.

2. Use less common part-writing procedures only to make specific improvement in the four-part texture.

Assignment 4.3.   Write the following progressions in four voices in keys as assigned. Chords may be used in inversion where desirable. Choose a time signature and create a rhythmic pattern which will insure acceptable harmonic rhythm.

I V iii ii V I V I   i iv III VI V i V i
I ii vi V I ii⁷ V I   i v III iv i V i
I vii° vi ii iii IV I V I   i vi° vii° i i ii°⁷ V i

Assignment 4.4.   Harmonize melodies in four voices. Use examples of less common chord progressions and part-writing procedures where effective. Make harmonic analysis and edit the finished composition for tempo and dynamic markings. Melodies from Assignment 1.5 may also be used.

Assignment 4.5.   Write original exercises making use of the less common chord progressions and/or the less common part-writing procedures. Edit your composition and make harmonic analysis.

Ear Training

Exercise 4.1.   Harmonic dictation will now include examples of the less common progressions. By being able to recognize the common progressions of Figure 4.1, as studied in ear training from the beginning of this course of study, the presence of any other chord progression should be markedly noticeable. Identify the progression through its root movement.

Keyboard Harmony

Exercise 4.2.   Play progressions from Assignment 4.3 in any major or minor key.

CHAPTER FIVE

Application of Part-Writing Procedures to Instrumental Writing

Theory and Analysis

In the study of part-writing, the four-voice chorale style[1] of writing has been used to illustrate procedures and to serve as a medium for student effort. There are, of course, many compositional styles other than the four-part vocal style, for example, piano solo, vocal or instrumental solo with accompaniment, three part women's chorus, string quartet, and so on. The procedures already learned are, in general, applicable to any style of harmonic writing within the historical period under consideration. Exceptions will be found, as they were in four-part writing, while additional practices not in four-part writing will be found in other styles because of the characteristics of the instrument or voice for which the music is written.

Part-writing procedures of the seventeenth to nineteenth centuries were derived from even earlier compositional practices. In these earlier centuries, vocal music was predominant and was written with the superimposition of melodic lines as its compositional basis (review in *Elementary Harmony,* Chapter 6, "Another Metrical Concept," and Chapter 9, "The Theory of Inversion"). Much of this music, particularly secular vocal music, was intended also for instrumental use. In performance practices of the time, instruments could double the voice lines, substitute for voice lines, or play the composition exclusively with instruments, ignoring the vocal text. As a result of this practice, much of the early music written specifically for instruments looks and sounds like vocal music without vocal texts.

Techniques for instrumental writing changed as composers gradually departed from writing "vocal" lines and wrote more and more with the unique

---

[1]The meaning of term "style" in reference to music is not constant. In the following paragraphs, style refers to various vocal and instrumental groupings, such as "piano style," "chorale style," and so on. For discussion of the various definitions of style see Willi Apel, *Harvard Dictionary of Music,* "Style" and "Style Analysis."

characteristics of each of the instruments in mind. Instrumental music no longer looked like vocal music on paper, or sounded like it in performance. In spite of this difference in appearance and sound, the basic principles of vocal part-writing were never abandoned in instrumental music. It is the purpose of the following illustrations to show how the traditional part-writing is maintained in instrumental composition (particularly for the piano), while at the same time exploiting the capabilities of the instrument. The discussion of extended part-writing procedures (Chapter 4, page 107) applies equally well to writing for orchestral and band instruments, taking into consideration their pitch ranges, timbre, and technical characteristics.

Similarities Between Vocal and Instrumental Writing

In the following excerpts, applications of the principles of harmony and part-writing procedures (chord movement, doublings, use of nonharmonic tones, and so on) will be shown.

Although the first excerpt (Figure 5.1) appears to be in three voices, the inner voice actually functions as two voices by means of the arpeggio device.

Fig. 5.1   Beethoven, Sonata for Piano, Op. 13,
                                                             second movement

Note carefully these details.

measure 1, beat 1—major triad, normal doubling
        beat 2—V_2^4, no note doubled, the seventh resolves down normally in the next measure
measure 2, beat 1—major triad, first inversion, normal doubling (soprano doubled).
        beat 2—another major triad in first inversion with normal doubling: the passing seventh resolves down normally.
measure 3, beat 1, similar to previous measures.
        beat 2—second half of beat (b♭dfa♭ chord) in which the seventh resolves normally, down by step.

Figure 5.2a shows an excerpt in broken chord (Alberti bass) style while Figure 5.2b shows the same music arranged in four-part vocal style. Study of Figure 5.2b in comparison with 5.2a will disclose the careful consideration given to voice leading when the chord progressions are written in instrumental style. Note also the use of correct doublings and resolutions.

a) minor triad with doubled third, measures 1, 3.

b) first inversion with doubled soprano, measure 1.

c) no doubling of note of resolution when accented non-harmonic tones are used, measures 2, 5, 6.

d) no note doubled and correct resolution of seventh in seventh chords, all of which are complete, measures 2, 4, 5.

Fig. 5.2   Mozart, Sonata in C Major for Piano, K. 330,
(a) Allegro moderato   first movement

In Figure 5.3*a*, arpeggiation of a chord for more than an octave, as seen in each measure, produces notes which must be considered duplicates of those in the four-part texture. Implied in measure 5 is the presence of the seventh of V^7 (D) one sixteenth note before its actual appearance. These small adjustments do not diminish the validity of the analysis.

In the arrangement, Figure 5.3b, the nonharmonic tones and duplicated tones of the original have been deleted to show the remaining four-voice texture.

Fig. 5.3

Schumann, *Dichterliebe*, Op. 48, "Im wunderschönen Monat Mai"

Differentiating Instrumental from Vocal Writing

1. *Extended Harmonies.*   In harmonic chorale style, chord changes are frequent, very often on each beat of the measure. In other styles, particularly instrumental, a single harmony is often of a longer duration, such as the three measures of the tonic triad in Figure 5.4.

Fig. 5.4

Extended harmonies such as these are effective when written in conjuction with other compositional features that highlight the continuous single harmony. A few of these are:[2]

a) Striking melodic motive or theme (B. Op. 2, No. 1, first movement, measures 1–4)

b) Strong rhythmic pattern (B. Op. 14, No. 2, "Scherzo," last 17 measures)

c) Change in inversion of chord during duration of single harmony (B. Op. 7, third movement, measures 1–4)

d) In passages of rapid tempo (B. Op. 31, No. 2, last movement, measures 1–4)

e) Long melodic line implying a single harmony (M. Op. 53, No. 2, measures 1–2; also, Figure 5.4 above)

[2]In this section (*Differences*), musical excerpts cited but not quoted will be found in three sources: B—Beethoven, Sonatas for Piano; M—Mendelssohn, *Songs Without Words;* S—Schumann, *Album for the Young*, Op. 68.

f) Melodic line in which the interest lies in the use of non-harmonic tones or chromatic scale passages (B. Op. 2, No. 2, fourth movement, measures 57–58)

g) In introductions, codettas, or cadenzas (B. Op. 7, first movement, measures 1–4; M. Op. 62, No. 4, measures 1–4, and last four measures)

2. *Free Voicing.* In keyboard music, it is not necessary that a given number of voice lines be maintained throughout a composition. A glance at any keyboard composition of the eighteenth and nineteenth centuries will show a vertical texture of any number of voices from one to as many as eight or more, and a constant change in the number of voice lines as the composition progresses.

Fig. 5.5

Mozart, Sonata in B♭ Major for Piano, K. 281, third movement

3. *Sonority Doubling.* Voice lines in keyboard music (as well as in orchestrations) are often doubled at the octave to produce a richer sound. At the keyboard, the octave naturally fits the hand position, so the device is used frequently in either or both hands. In instrumental ensemble music, two or more different instruments may play in parallel unisons or octaves, producing a combined sound differing from that of any of the individual instruments.

A sonority doubling is always an octave reinforcement of a single voice line, such as a bass line or a soprano line. Octaves between two different voice lines can never be considered sonority doubling; these are simply undesirable parallel octaves.

a) Bass line doubled in octaves.

Fig. 5.6

Mozart, Sonata in F Major for Violin and Piano, K. 377, second movement

Andante

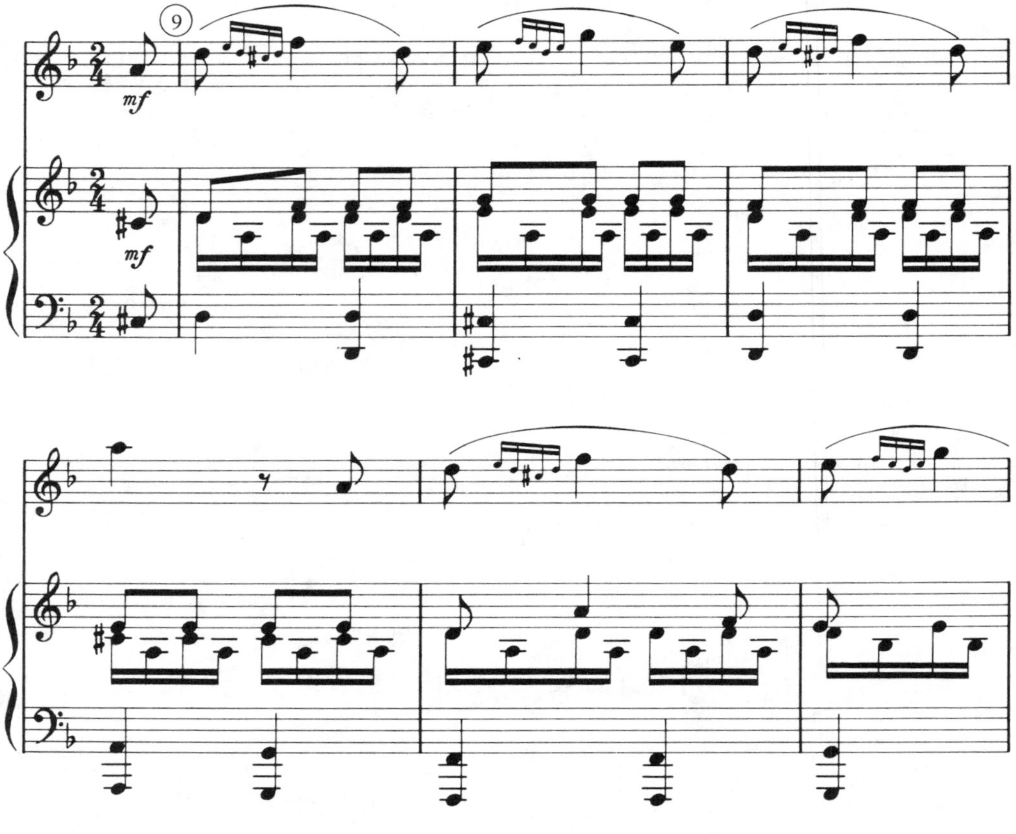

b) Doubling in inner voices.

Fig. 5.7

Andante

Brahms, Romanze, Op. 118, No. 5

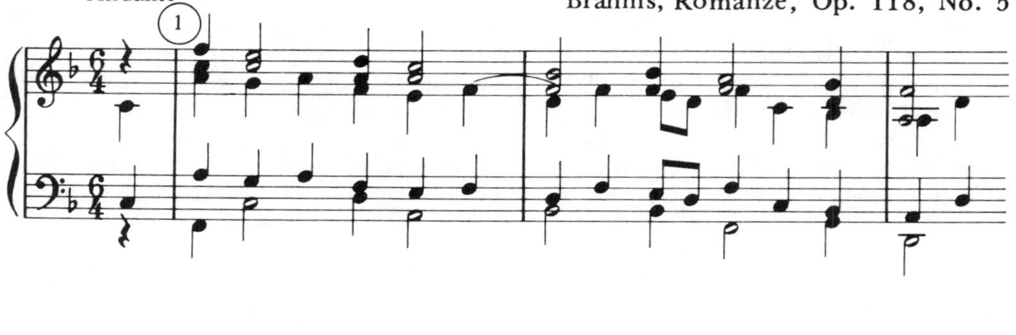

c) Soprano voice doubled.

Fig. 5.8

Brahms, Romanze, Op. 118, No. 5

4. *Arpeggiated Harmonies.* This very common device is used most often in piano music. It helps keep the music in motion when a single triad or a series of chords is being used. Almost any piano composition of the eighteenth and nineteenth centuries will provide an example of this device, ranging from simple arpeggiation of the basic triad to extended arpeggiation over a wide range (see Figure 5.19). The use of common part-writing procedures in arpeggiated harmonies has been described in connection with Figures 5.2 and 5.3.

5. *Pedal Point.* This device is common in instrumental music. Several varieties of the pedal point exist; these are among them.

a) Single pedal tone in the bass (see also Figure 5.17).

Fig. 5.9

Schubert, *Wanderers Nachtlied*, D. 768

Ü - ber al - len Gip - feln ist Ruh,   in al - len Wip - feln

b) Double pedal in the bass, usually the interval of a fifth.

Fig. 5.10

Andante con moto

Schubert, *Rosamunde*, D. 797, "Romanze"

Der Voll-mond strahlt auf Ber - ges-höhn wie hab ich dich ver - misst!

c) Inverted pedal (pedal in the upper voice).

Fig. 5.11

Tempo di minuetto, un poco allegretto

Mozart, Sonata in F Major for Violin and Piano, K. 377, third movement

d) "Interrupted pedal," in which the pedal tone is repeated at frequent (and usually regular) intervals of time to help create the effect of a sustained pedal tone.

Fig. 5.12

Bach, *Well-Tempered Clavier*, Vol. 1, Prelude No. 2

For examples showing pedal points of longer duration, see:

B. Op. 22, "Allegro con brio," measures 4–7
M. Op. 19, No. 6, measures 7–14
Op. 102, No. 3, last 12 measures (decorated pedal and inverted decorated pedal)
S. No. 31, measures 34–40
No. 18, measures 1–4

See also Chopin, Prelude, Op. 28, No. 15; the entire piece is built on a pedal tone A♭ and G♯, alternating in the keys of D♭ major and C♯ minor.

6. *Melody in a voice line other than the soprano.* The melody line can be found as an inner voice (see Figure 5.4), as the lowest voice line (Figure 5.13), or can be divided between two voice lines (Figure 5.14).

Fig. 5.13   Schumann, *Album for the Young*, No. 10

Allegro animato

Fig. 5.14

Beethoven, Sonata in C Minor for Piano,
Op. 13, first movement

Allegro di molto

7. *Melody doubled in thirds or sixths.*

a) Melody doubled at the tenth (an octave plus a third).

Fig. 5.15   Mendelssohn, *Songs Without Words,* Op. 85,
                                                                                          No. 2

b) Melody doubled in thirds, plus additional sonority doubling.

Fig. 5.16   Mozart, Sonata in A Major for Piano, K. 331,
                                                                                first movement, Var. IV

c) Melody doubled in sixths.

Fig. 5.17

Chopin, Mazurka, Op. 67, No. 3

8. *Range and spacing of voices.* In four-part chorale style, the upper and lower limits of each vocal line were determined by the average range of the human voice. Similarly, in instrumental music the range of the instrument determines the upper and lower limits of the music it plays. Most orchestral and band instruments have a much wider range than the human voice; the keyboard has a very wide range, allowing a melodic line to extend over a large compass.

Spacing between voices is often determined by technical possibilities of the instrument. On the keyboard, for example, the two hands of the player are sometimes far apart, resulting in wide spacing between the inner voices. (See Figure 5.2, measures 73 to 76.)

A Note on Compositional Style

We have observed many times on previous pages that the harmonic concepts and part-writing procedures presented in this book are those of the historical period *c.* 1650–*c.* 1900. An analysis of almost any piece of music written in this period would show, in general, application of the materials thus far studied—principles of chord succession, use of nonharmonic tones, procedures of part-writing, principles of harmonic rhythm, and so on. For this reason, this historical era is often designated by the term "common practice period." The question may then arise, why does not all the music of this period sound alike? Why does the music of Bach sound different from that of Mozart? Haydn different from Brahms? Schubert different from Berlioz?

Although all composers of this period generally made use of the same basic material, results from the pens of various composers differ because of the differing ways individual composers use given harmonic material and the frequency of use of one type of material in comparison with the frequency of use of other types. The following illustrations may clarify these two concepts.

a) Differing ways of using like harmonic material. Compare the chorale excerpt in Figure 5.18 with the excerpt from Beethoven in Figure 5.14.

Fig. 5.18

Bach, *Ach Gott von Himmel sieh darein* (No. 253)

Both these excerpts use the triads i and V only, but note how differently they serve as a basis for musical composition. Bach uses one triad per melody note, alternating V and i; Beethoven uses each triad for four consecutive measures. Bach's bass line is melodic; Beethoven uses the same bass note for twelve measures. Bach's melody is always in the upper voice; in Beethoven, the melody alternates between soprano and bass, and has a much wider range. In Bach, the triad is stated simply and all notes simultaneously; in Beethoven the triad is divided and presented in broken chords.

Even the manner of presenting a simple arpeggiated triad can vary greatly with different composers as can be seen in the four excerpts of Figure 5.19, each for the left hand of the piano.

Fig. 5.19

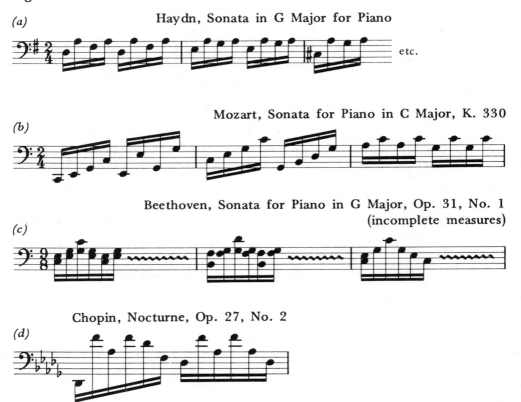

(a)   Haydn, Sonata in G Major for Piano

(b)   Mozart, Sonata for Piano in C Major, K. 330

(c)   Beethoven, Sonata for Piano in G Major, Op. 31, No. 1
        (incomplete measures)

(d)   Chopin, Nocturne, Op. 27, No. 2

    b) Frequency of use of material.   Inherent in the harmonic tonal system is such a great variety of harmonic, nonharmonic, melodic, and rhythmic possibilities that only by remote chance might two composers use the same theoretical material in the same way, or differing materials in the same proportions. Comparison could be made between a typical Bach chorale and a typical modern church hymn. Each is a succession of chords, usually with a chord change on each beat, but the hymn will contain only a few nonharmonic tones, while the Bach chorale will contain so many non-harmonic tones that each voice line almost becomes a melody itself. This difference in the frequency of use of non-harmonic tones is the major difference between the sound and effect of the two compositional styles. Figures 5.2 and 5.15 are both based on arpeggiation, the former using simple arpeggios in the left hand, while in the latter the bass note of each arpeggio is a member of the bass melodic line.

These contrasts illustrate the principle of different frequencies of usage of any technical device. Similar comparisons can be made between pieces of music on the basis of frequency of use of modulations, various triads, various seventh chords, rhythmic patterns, and so on.

It is not the intention of this text to study specific stylistic differences between composers or between pieces of the same composer. The importance of the foregoing discussion is that the differing styles of various composers in the historical period under study are founded on the same basic materials—those which have been presented to this point, and those which will be found in the remainder of the volume. The student will be able, with this knowledge of technical materials and stylistic differences, to investigate a given piece of music by observing what technical materials are used or omitted by the composer, the manner in which these materials are used, and the frequency or infrequency of their use.

Application

Written Materials

To put into practical effect the principles outlined in this chapter, a series of writing projects will be presented, each including directions and explanations appropriate to the specific project. In subsequent chapters, applications of new principles and materials will be applied to projects similar to these, and the directions and explanations given here will also apply to such subsequent assignments.

Project I.   Realization of seventeenth- and eighteenth-century figured basses.   Figured bass is used almost universally today as an aid in teaching part-writing. Its original function was quite different. In music of the seventeenth and early eighteenth centuries which included a keyboard part (such as sonata for violin, flute, or oboe, song or aria with accompaniment, string trio with keyboard part, and so on), the keyboard part was written as a single melodic line in the bass, together with a figured bass. (This practice is also known as *thorough bass;* the bass melodic line is often termed *continuo*.) It was the responsibility of the keyboard player to *improvise* an accompaniment from this figured bass line. There is very little demand for such skill today; since about 1750, keyboard parts have been written out by the composer, and modern editions of earlier compositions supply a keyboard part based on the composer's bass line. Composing such a part is known as "realizing the figured bass." No two persons will realize a figured bass line in exactly the same way, since the figured bass does not indicate chord position or the character of any of the melodic lines above the bass. Figures 5.20 and 5.21*a* each show an excerpt from a violin sonata by Handel. Parts *b* and *c* of each figure show two different realizations of Handel's figured bass as found in current publications of these sonatas.

It is obvious from study of these two figures that various styles of keyboard

Fig. 5.20

Handel, Sonata in G Minor for Violin and
Figured Bass, Op. 1, No. 10

Fig. 5.21

Handel, Sonata in D Major for Violin and Figured Bass, Op. 1, No. 13

Realization by A. LeMaitre from Haendel, *Sonates pour Violon et Piano*, Paris. © Copyright Heugel et Cie. Permission granted by the publisher. Theodore Presser sole representative in the United States, Canada and Mexico.

Realization by Johann Hinnenthal from *Hallische Händel-Ausgabe*, Serie IV, Band 4, "Sechs Sonaten für Violine," Kassel, Bärenreiter-Verlag, 1955.

writing can be employed in the realization. Note the simple use of block triads in Figures 5.20*b* and 5.21*b;* in Figure 5.20*c,* note the counter melody provided in the realization and in figure 5.21*c* observe that the realization contains a melodic line when the solo plays a broken chord line (measures 1–2) and becomes chordal when the solo plays a melodic line (measures 3–4). Further ideas for the development of an accompaniment can be seen in Figure 5.22, where the given bass is doubled in thirds, and in Figure 5.23, which shows a four-part texture much like the four-voice chorale style.

Fig. 5.22

Telemann, Partita 5

Fig. 5.23

Lully, *Cadmus et Hermione* (1673), Act III, Scene 6

mer   mil-le fleurs   sous ses   pas

Triads in the piano accompaniment for a solo voice or instrument are usually complete, even if this means the simultaneous use of the third of the triad or the leading tone in both the melody and the accompaniment (see Figure 5.22, measure 2, and Figure 5.23, measure 3). In a dominant seventh chord, the leading tone may be omitted in the accompaniment when it is found in the melody.

Any good pianistic device, as discussed in the earlier portion of this chapter, may be used in a realization. For further study of basic methods of realization, see the figured bass examples in the *Historical Anthology of Music,* Vol. 2, by Archibald T. Davison and Willi Apel (Cambridge, Massachusetts: Harvard University Press, 1950). To study realizations of greater complexity and more sophistication, consult collections of works by individual composers of the Baroque era, both in performing editions (such as those credited in Figure 5.20*b* and *c*) and in scholarly editions of complete works of these composers (such as credited in Figure 5.21*c*).

Assignment 5.1. Copy this example on three staves, as in Figures 5.20–5.23, and write accompaniment on treble and bass staff, following the figured bass directions. The long line in the figured bass, as in measures 2 and 4, indicates the upper parts are to be held, or at least the same harmony to be maintained, while the bass moves.

Telemann, Sonata für Blockflöte und Basso Continuo,
No. 1, "Largo"

Assignment 5.2.   In this example, much of the figured bass has not been indicated, on the assumption by the composer that the performer will understand from the context of the music what figured bass is required. In measure 3, below the C♯ is understood a "6"; the B natural is a passing tone, and below the A is understood a "7." In measure 18, and similar subsequent measures, a single triad per measure is appropriate above the florid bass line.

Allegro
Violin   Vivaldi, Concerto in Fa, "Allegro alla Francese"

Assignment 5.3.   There is no figuration in the original. Supply a figured bass and add your realization.

Purcell, Song: *I Envy Not a Monarch's Fate*

I   en - vy   not_____ a   mon - arch's

fate,   Nor   the vain   hon - ors,   nor   the vain   hon - ors___

Assignment 5.4. This is the second half of a binary form. The first half started in G minor and modulated to D minor.

Marcello, Sonata in G Minor for Flute or Violin

Project II.   Harmonizing folk songs and traditional songs as vocal solo with accompaniment.   Harmonizing a folk song combines the skill of choosing a harmonic background for a melodic line (as studied throughout this course starting in early chapters of *Elementary Harmony*) and the skill of writing an accompaniment as just studied in Project I. Following are three examples of published folk song arrangements, ranging from easy to moderate in difficulty.

Figure 5.24 shows a common procedure in harmonizing folk tunes, that of including the melody in the accompaniment. Parts *a* and *b* of this figure are the first and last phrases of the setting, showing changes in the accompaniment to avoid monotony when the tune is repeated.

Fig. 5.24

Welsh Folk Song, "The Ash Grove,"
arr. Robert Ottman

From BASIC REPERTOIRE FOR SINGERS by Robert Ottman and Paul Krueger. Copyright 1959 by Southern Music Company, San Antonio, Texas. Used by permission.

In Figure 5.25, the folk tune melody is modified when placed in the accompaniment. Observe also the piano interlude which appears between stanzas.

Fig. 5.25

German Folk Song, "Soll sich der Mond,"
arr. Johannes Brahms

Figure 5.26 is the third stanza of the folk song setting. In the first, the melody is included in the piano part, while for this stanza, the soprano line of the accompaniment is a completely independent melody.

Fig. 5.26

Russian Folk Song, "The Jackdaw and the Falcon,"
arr. Kurt Schindler

The preceding examples show but a few of the countless ways of creating a keyboard harmonization for a melodic line. Before embarking upon assignments in Project II, the student should examine, play, and sing many additional accompanied folk songs. Numerous volumes of this type of material are usually available in most libraries, while the following collections of folk songs are particularly recommended because they include a large number of accompaniments to folk songs from diverse geographical areas.

One Hundred Folk Songs of All Nations, edited by Granville Bantock, Bryn Mawr, Pa., Theodore Presser Co. Also in this series, other volumes containing folk songs of a single country, such as *One Hundred English Folk Songs,* edited by Cecil Sharp, *Sixty Folk Songs of France,* edited by Julien Tiersot, etc.

Das Lied der Volker, 13 volumes, edited by Heinrich Möller, Mainz, B. Schott's Söhne.

Brahms, Johannes, *48 German Folk Songs* and *28 German Folk Songs,* in volume 26 of the complete works of Brahms (Sämtliche Werke, Leipzig, Breitkopf & Härtel).

Botsford Collection of Folk Songs, 3 volumes, New York, G. Schirmer, Inc.

Assignment 5.5.   Copy out a melody from those following or from another source, as assigned. Using three staves, as in Figures 5.24–5.26, harmonize the folk tune with a keyboard accompaniment. The following steps will be helpful in planning the harmonization.

a) Sing or play the melody; read the text carefully. Folk songs usually have no tempo indication; a tempo should be chosen appropriate to the character of the melody and the text.

b) Choose a harmonic progression, just as was done in harmonizing a chorale or a melody at the keyboard in earlier chapters. Be sure that each melody note is either part of a triad or a nonharmonic tone as previously defined.

c) Choose a style of accompaniment (arpeggiated, block chord, and so on) appropriate to the melody being harmonized. It is not necessary that the same style be maintained throughout the composition, but there should not be an abrupt change from one style to another.

d) Give special attention to the movement between the soprano and bass lines, just as in harmonizing a chorale.

e) Consider the possibility of adding a short (two- or four-measure) introduction and/or coda to your harmonization.

f) Edit your manuscript. This includes tempo markings, dynamic markings, and phrasing in the piano score. Phrasing marks are used to indicate melodic motives and places where *legato* is desired. Study Figures 5.24–5.26 and examples from published harmonizations.

(1)   English Folk Song

How plea - sant   is   it   in   the   blos - som   of   the   year   to

stray and   find   a   nook   Where   naught doth   fill   the hol - low

of   the   list' - ning   ear,   ex - cept   the   mur - m'ring brook   or

bird   in   neigh - b'ring grove, that   in   sol - i - tude doth love   to

breathe his   lone - ly   hymn.   Lost   in   the   min - gled song, I

care - less   roam   a - long   from morn to twi - light   dim.

(2)   English Folk Song

A   North Coun - try   lass   up   to   Lon - don did pass,   Al   -

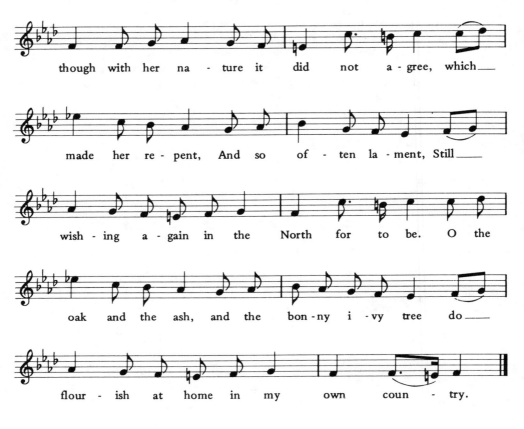

though with her na - ture it did not a - gree, which___

made her re - pent, And so of - ten la - ment, Still___

wish - ing a - gain in the North for to be. O the

oak and the ash, and the bon -ny i -vy tree do___

flour - ish at home in my own coun - try.

(3)   English Folk Song

Love me lit - tle, love me long,___ is the___ bur - den

of__ my__ song, Love that is too hot and strong___

(4)   German Folk Song

Es blies__ ein__ Jä - ger wohl in sein__ Horn, wohl

in sein___ Horn, und al - les was er blies___ das___

war___ ver - lorn. Hol - lal - la, tra - ra - ra - ra, und

al - les was er blies, das___ war ver - lorn.

Project III. Composing an original melody and accompaniment to a given text. Composing an original song combines the skill of writing a good melodic line, as studied in previous chapters, and the ability to write an accompaniment, as studied in projects I and II. In addition, knowledge of combining a text with a melodic line is necessary.[3]

a) Meter. A poem, which, like music, has meter and rhythm, is usually chosen as a text for a song. The melodic line is composed with the metrical considerations of the poem in mind. Scansion of the poem is necessary to determine the accented and unaccented syllables of the poem; these will generally occur simultaneously with musical accents.

Sleep my child and peace at- tend thee, All through the night.

Fig. 5.27

Sleep my child and peace at - tend thee, All through the night.

The meter of a poetic line does not necessarily indicate a specific musical meter. In Figures 5.28 and 5.29 the same poetic lines have been set in both simple and compound time, but in both cases, the metrical accents of music and poetry coincide.

I walk in the gar- den ear- ly.

Just at the break of the day.

The flow- ers all whis- per to- geth- er.

Nev- er a word I say.

[3]See *Harvard Dictionary of Music,* "Text and Music."

Fig. 5.28

Schumann, *Dichterliebe,* Op. 48,
"Am leuchtenden Sommermorgen"

I walk in the gar - den ear - ly,   Just   at   the break of the
Am leuch- ten-den Som - mer -mor- gen   geh' ich   im Gar - ten her-

day,   The flow - ers all whis - per to-
um.   Es flü - stern und spre - chen die

geth - er,   Nev - er   a word____ I   say.
Blu - men;   ich   a - ber wand - le   stumm.

Fig. 5.29

Franz, *Am leuchtenden Sommermorgen,*
Op. 11, No. 2

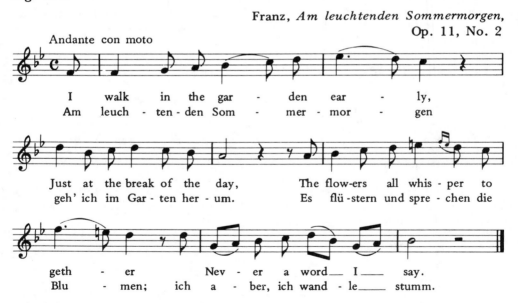

Andante con moto

I   walk   in   the gar - den ear - ly,
Am   leuch - ten - den Som - mer - mor - gen

Just at the break of the   day,   The flow-ers all whis - per to
geh' ich im Gar - ten her - um.   Es flü -stern und spre - chen die

geth - er   Nev - er   a word__ I __ say.
Blu - men;   ich a - ber, ich wand - le__ stumm.

Figure 5.30 shows three different settings of the first line of *Nur wer die Sehnsuch kennt,* each with a different time signature. Note again how the accents in the melodic line conform to the accents in the poetic line.

Fig. 5.30

Schubert, D. 877

Schumann, Op.98a, No.3

Tschaikowski, Op.6, No.6

None   but the   ach - ing heart,   knows all   my   an - guish!   A -
Nur   wer die   Sehn - such kennt,   weiss, was ich   lei - de,   al -

b) Form. The form of a song is usually dictated by the form of the poem being set. In simple poetry, where the meter is constant and each line of equal length, a simple setting may result—one phrase of music (regular) for each line of poetry. Such well-known songs as "Auld Lang Syne" and "The Blue Bell of Scotland" illustrate this procedure. Any of the forms previously studied can be utilized: phrases, periods, double periods, and so on.

In addition, the devices of extension may be used. In Figure 5.31, part of the last line of the poetic stanza is repeated to extend the phrase.

Fig. 5.31

Etwas bewegt   Schubert, *Winterreise,* D. 911, "Frühlingstraum"

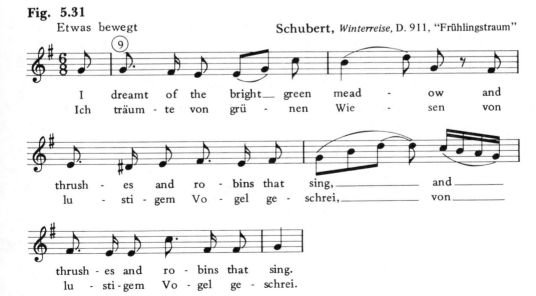

I   dreamt   of   the   bright___   green   mead   -   ow   and
Ich   träum - te   von   grü - nen   Wie   -   sen   von

thrush - es   and   ro - bins that   sing, _____   and _____
lu - sti - gem   Vo - gel ge - schrei, _____   von _____

thrush - es and   ro - bins that   sing.
lu - sti - gem   Vo - gel ge - schrei.

In Figure 5.32, phrase 1, a short poetic line is extended to make a full four-measure musical phrase; in phrase 2, the same short line is extended to make a five-measure phrase:

> The post brings you no note today,
> my heart,
> So now why act in this strange way,
> my heart?

Fig. 5.32

Etwas geschwind   Schubert, *Winterreise*, D. 911, "Die Post"

The post brings you no note to - day, my
Die Post bringt kei - nen Brief für dich, mein

heart,_____ my heart,_____ so now why act in
Herz,_____ mein Herz,_____ was drängst du denn so

this strange way, my heart,_____ my heart?____
wun - der - lich, mein Herz,_____ mein Herz?____

c) Syllabic and Melismatic methods of text setting. When one syllable of the text is set to one note of the melody, the result is known as a *syllabic* setting. (See Figures 5.26–5.28.) When more than one note is assigned to a single syllable, the result is *melismatic,* and the group of single notes sung to a single syllable is called a *melisma.* Most art songs use syllabic settings with occasional short melismas, usually two or three notes, but sometimes longer, as in Figure 5.31.

d) Strophic and through-composed songs. In the *strophic* songs, each stanza of the poem is sung to the same melody. Most church hymns are strophic. See also Schubert, *Die Schöne Müllerin,* Op. 25, Nos. 1, 7, 8, 9, 10, 13, 14, 16, 20. In the *through-composed* song, new music occurs in each stanza. Most art songs are through-composed.

e) Vocal notation. The notation of the music of the vocal line differs from instrumental notation. When the setting is syllabic, notation of eighth notes and smaller are not "beamed"; each note carries its own separate flag.

Spring is come not Spring is come

However, in a few very recent editions of music, the latter method can be found. In a melisma, the beam extends the length of the melisma (when eighth notes and shorter are used) and a phrase mark extends from the first to the last note of the melisma.

Spring ——— is   come

All these procedures are illustrated in the last four measures of Figure 5.31.

Assignment 5.6.   A number of poems are here provided to set to music with piano accompaniment. (The student may find other poems more to his or her liking.) The finished composition should be fully edited, including tempo markings, phrasing, dynamic markings, and so on. Be sure to follow the procedures of vocal notation.

> Ye flowery banks o' bonny Doon.
> > How can ye blume sae fair?
> How can ye chant, ye little birds,
> > And I sae fu' of care?
>
> Thou'll break my heart, thou bonny bird,
> > That sings upon the bough;
> Thou minds me o' the happy days,
> > When my fause love was true.
>
> —*Robert Burns*

> Of a' the airts the wind can blaw;
> > I dearly like the west,
> For there the bonnie lassy lives,
> > The lassie I lo'e best;
> There wild woods grow, and rivers row,
> > And mony a hill between;
> But day and night my fancy's flight
> > Is ever wi' my Jean.
>
> —*Robert Burns*

> The sun, above the mountain's head,
> A freshening lustre mellow
> Through all the long green fields has spread,
> His first sweet evening yellow.
>
> —*William Wordsworth*

> Pack clouds away, and welcome day,
> > With night we banish sorrow;
> Sweet air, blow soft; mount, lark, aloft,
> > To give my love good morrow.

Wings from the wind to please her mind.
   Notes from the lark I'll borrow;
Bird, prune thy wing, nightingale, sing,
   To give my love good morrow.

          —Thomas Heywood

Ask me no more where Jove bestows,
When June is past, the fading rose;
For in your beauties orient deep,
These flow'rs as in their causes sleep.

Ask me no more whither do stray
The golden atoms of the day;
For in pure love heaven did prepare
Those powders to enrich your hair.

Ask me no more where those stars light
That downwards fall in dead of night;
For in your eyes they sit, and there
Fixed become as in their sphere.

          —Thomas Carew

Away delights, go seek some other dwelling,
For I must die.
Farewell false love! thy tongue is ever telling
Lie after lie.
Forever let me rest now from thy smarts;
Alas, for pity, go
And fire their hearts
That have been hard to thee! Mine was not so.

          —John Fletcher

Four ducks on a pond,
A grass-bank beyond,
A blue sky of spring,
White clouds on the wing;
What a little thing
To remember for years—
To remember with tears!

          —William Allingham

Jenny kissed me when we met,
   Jumping from the chair she sat in.
Time, you thief! who love to get
   Sweets into your list, put that in.

Say I'm weary, say I'm sad;
   Say that health and wealth have missed me;
   Say I'm growing old, but add—
      Jenny kissed me!

          —Leigh Hunt

Keyboard Harmony

Exercise 5.1. Assignments 5.1–5.4 may be played at the keyboard. Two students should participate, one to sing the melody or play it on an instrument, the other to play an accompaniment by realizing the figured bass.

CHAPTER SIX

Diatonic Seventh Chords

Theory and Analysis

Diatonic seventh chords based on each of the scale steps of major and minor keys are shown in Figure 6.1. Those marked with an * have been presented in earlier chapters: the V^7, ii^7, and $ii^{\phi7}$ in *Elementary Harmony*, Chapter 17; the vii^{o7} and $vii^{\phi7}$ in *Advanced Harmony*, Chapter 3; the VII^7 (V^7/III) in *Elementary Harmony*, Chapter 18 and reviewed in *Advanced Harmony*, Chapter 1.

Fig. 6.1

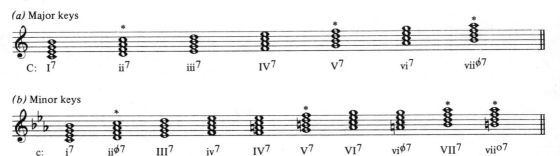

(a) Major keys

C: I^7 ii^7 iii^7 IV^7 V^7 vi^7 $vii^{\phi7}$

(b) Minor keys

c: i^7 $ii^{\phi7}$ III^7 iv^7 IV^7 V^7 VI^7 $vi^{\phi7}$ VII^7 vii^{o7}

The Major Seventh Chord

Although Figure 6.1 contains many new chords, as based on their Roman numeral identification, only one new type of chord needs to be accounted for. This type is the major-major seventh chord (usually called, simply, a major seventh chord), consisting of a major triad and the interval of a major seventh between the root and the seventh of the chord. Major seventh chords are used as I^7 and IV^7 in a major key, and as III^7 in a minor key.

Fig. 6.2

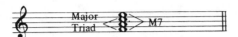

Assignment 6.1. Spell each diatonic seventh chord in each major and minor key.

The Single Diatonic Seventh Chord

The chords of Figure 6.1 that are new to this chapter (not marked with an *) are infrequently used other than in a harmonic sequence. The most common of these rare single seventh chords is the subdominant seventh in its resolution to the dominant, as shown in Figure 6.3, IV^6_5/V^6_5 in major; see also Figure 1.15, Figure 6.4 (iv^7-V in minor), and Figure 6.5 (IV^4_2-vii^o_6 in minor).

Fig. 6.3

Handel, *Messiah*, "Surely He Hath Borne
Our Griefs"

Fig. 6.4

Schumann, *Auf einer Burg,* Op. 39,
No. 7

Fig. 6.5

Johann Crüger (1658), *Jesus, meine Zuversicht*

The IV^7 in minor has a dual function. Not only can it resolve to the dominant as in Figure 6.5 and in measure 2 of Figure 1.15, but can also function as a secondary dominant, V^7/VII as listed in Figure 1.2 and shown in the next example.

Fig. 6.6

Handel, *Messiah,* "How Beautiful Are the
Feet of Them"

The vi^{ø7} in a minor key can occur as the sonority located over the raised sixth scale step in a descending chromatic scale line.

Fig. 6.7

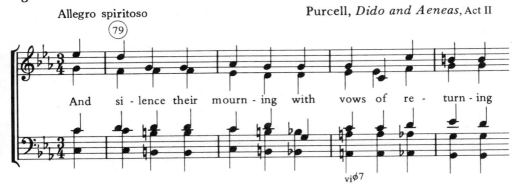

Allegro spiritoso

Purcell, *Dido and Aeneas*, Act II

And   si - lence their   mourn - ing   with   vows of   re - turn - ing

vi^{ø7}

Most other single uses of these sonorities strongly suggest analysis of the seventh as the simple use of an ordinary nonharmonic tone. In Figure 6.8, the apparent seventh is probably better analyzed as a lower neighbor tone.

Fig. 6.8

Andantino

Fauré, *Les Roses d'Ispahan*, Op. 39, No. 4

I^7(?)

Diatonic Seventh Chords in Sequence

In contrast to the paucity of individual uses of these chords, the frequency of their use in the harmonic sequence is very high. Most often they appear in that sequence whose successive roots are up a fourth and down a fifth. In this progression, a chain suspension in each of two voices creates a seventh above each root. The seventh alternates between each of the two voices and in each case resolves to the third of the next chord, which becomes the preparation for the next seventh. Notice that in minor, these descending lines require the use of the descending minor scale. The v^7 thus produced (F minor: C E♭ G B♭) is rarely encountered in any other context.

Fig. 6.9

This same three-voice structure is seen in Figure 6.10, where each seventh is decorated by a four-note melodic figure.

Fig. 6.10

An interesting variation of this three-voice texture is seen in Figure 6.11. In measures 1–3, each quarter rest in the bass voice appears to have replaced an expected bass note of the sequence. By supplying the notes A, F♯, and D for these rests, the sequence structure is complete. In measures 7–8, the composer has held the bass notes A and G for two beats each, instead of dropping down a fifth to the expected notes D and C, respectively. Note the use of v⁷ in measure 2.

Fig. 6.11

Telemann, Partita 5, "Aria 2"

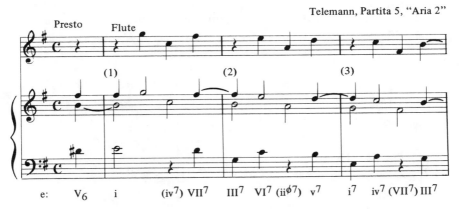

e: V₆   i   (iv⁷) VII⁷   III⁷ VI⁷ (ii∅⁷) v⁷   i⁷ iv⁷ (VII⁷) III⁷

vi∅⁷ ii∅⁷   V⁷   i   iv⁷ =

a: i⁷   iv⁷   VII⁷   III   IV₂⁴ vii°₆   i =   e: iv   ii∅⁷

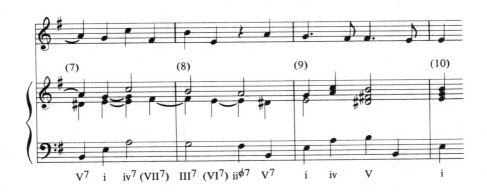

V⁷   i   iv⁷ (VII⁷)   III⁷ (VI⁷) ii∅⁷ V⁷   i   iv   V   i

In four voices with roots in the bass, seventh chords in succession are usually alternately complete and incomplete. Either the third or root may be doubled in the incomplete chord, except that the third should not be doubled in the V^7 at the cadence point.

Fig. 6.12

Bach *O Ewigkeit, du Donnerwort* (No. 26)

All seventh chords, whether used in a sequence or used singly, are commonly found in any inversion. In inversion, these chords are invariably complete. In figure 6.13 the root in the bass alternates with the fifth in the bass in alternate seventh chords.

Fig. 6.13

Grieg, *Holberg* Suite, "Musette"

A sequence may consist of a pattern of root movements different from the one shown so far, and any sequence may be found with the seventh chord alternating with a triad. Both of these possibilities are shown in Figure 6.14 where the root movement describes the sequence, down a third and up a second, with alternating seventh chords and triads in first inversion.

Fig. 6.14

Bach, Prelude in D Major (organ)

Sequences of seventh chords may, of course, be of mixed types. Though Figure 6.15 shows a sequence primarily of secondary dominant chords alternating with triads, a diatonic seventh chord is required when the following triad is diminished.

Fig. 6.15

Mozart, Concerto in F Major for Piano and Orchestra, K. 459, first movement

In instrumental style, there may seemingly be more freedom in the treatment of the seventh. In Figure 6.16 the circled sevenths resolve on the second eighth note following.

Fig. 6.16

Brahms, Ballade, Op. 118, No. 3

Assignment 6.2. Harmonic Analysis.   Analyze each example, taking particular note of the use of the seventh in both single seventh chords and in sequences.

(4) In addition to the analysis, write out the basic chain suspension figures, as in Figure 6.9, for both of the sequences in the next example.

Schumann, *Dichterliebe*, Op. 48,
"Das ist ein Flöten und Geigen"

(6) In measure 8 of the next excerpt consider the D♭ and its duplication in the arpeggio as a nonharmonic tone against A C E♭ G♭. Note its resolution at the end of measure 9.

Brahms, Intermezzo, Op. 117, No. 2

(7) This excerpt from a twentieth-century work includes a harmonic sequence markedly similar to the typical earlier sequence. Locate the sequence, describe its root movement, and explain the function of tones that are not members of the harmonic sequential pattern.

Application

Written Materials

Procedures for writing the dominant seventh and supertonic seventh chords are equally valid for writing the remaining diatonic seventh chords. Particular attention must be paid to the introduction and resolution of the seventh, as described in Part-writing Rule 9, page 397.

These seventh chords are usually found complete, and in inversion they are almost invariably complete. When seventh chords with roots in the bass are found in sequence, they are usually found alternately complete and incomplete. In constructing a sequence, roots in the bass a fifth apart, the incomplete chord will have either the third or seventh in the soprano. If the soprano is the third, either the root or the third may be doubled. If the soprano is the seventh, only the root is doubled. Each incomplete seventh chord in the sequence is found with the same doubling as the first incomplete seventh chord.

An exceptional part-writing procedure is necessary in the progression IV⁷-V when the seventh of the chord is above the third of the chord. In this position the resolution to V may easily produce parallel fifths as in Figure 6.17 (When the third of the chord is above the seventh, there is no particular problem.)

Fig. 6.17

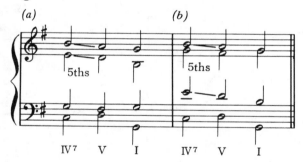

Several solutions are possible, including

Fig. 6.18

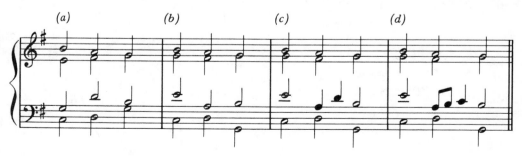

Fig. 6.19

Bach, *Nimm von uns* (No. 292)

The parallel fifth may also be avoided by progressing IV^7-V^7.

Fig. 6.20

Hymn: Mendelssohn

Assignment 6.3. Complete the exercises by filling in alto and tenor voices. Make harmonic analysis. Check each seventh chord to see that the seventh is correctly approached and resolved. Note that in most music, seventh chords are usually not so heavily concentrated as in the few measures of these exercises; they are heavily concentrated here to provide a maximum of part-writing experience. Overuse of seventh chords can produce a texture overly rich and even cloying; ordinarily, they should be sparingly used.

(1)

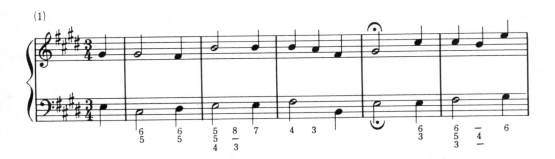

Assignment 6.4. Realization of a figured bass.   Using three staves, write a
piano accompaniment based on the composer's bass line and figuration. The
first example is the first part of a binary form.

Corelli, Concerto IX, "Corrente"

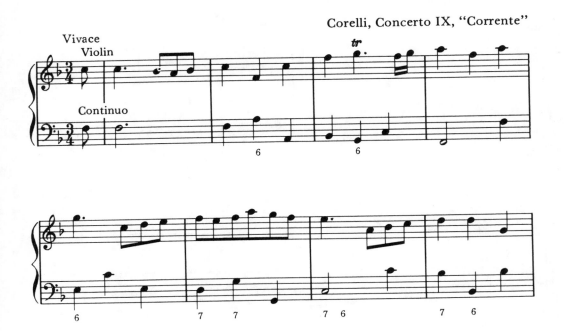

Bach, Sonata No. 1 in C Major for Flute and Continuo

Adagio

Ear Training

Singing the Major Seventh Chord

Exercise 6.1. Using any given note as the root, sing the major seventh chord, using numbers (1-3-5-7) or letter names.

Fig. 6.21

| 1 | 3 | 5 | 7 | 5 | 3 | 1 | or | D | F♯ | A | C♯ | A | F♯ | D |

Exercise 6.2. Repeat Exercise 6.1, but begin on the third, fifth, or seventh of the major seventh chord.

Fig. 6.22

Exercise 6.3. Sing the tonic triad in a given key, followed by one of the diatonic seventh chords, as directed. Use letter names in singing.

Major keys	*Minor keys*
I – I⁷	i – i⁷
I – iii⁷	i – III⁷
I – IV⁷	i – iv⁷
I – vi⁷	i – IV⁷
	i – vi°⁷
	i – VI⁷

Fig. 6.23   Sing i-iv⁷ in B♭ minor.

i   iv⁷

Singing Progressions of Seventh Chords

Exercise 6.4. Sing the following chord progressions, using letter names in various keys as directed.

Major keys	*Minor keys*
I IV⁷ V I	i iv⁷ V i
I I⁷ IV V I	i IV⁷ V i
I iii⁷ vi ii V I	i VI⁷ ii° (or iv) V i
i vi⁷ ii (or IV) V I	i i⁷ iv V i

Exercise 6.5. Sing a sequence of seventh chords in each major and minor key, singing from the root of each chord and using letter names.

Major key: I-IV^7-vii^{ø7}-iii^7-vi^7-ii^7- V^7-I
Minor key: i-iv^7-VII^7-III^7-VI^7-ii^{ø7}-V-I

Harmonic Dictation

Exercise 6.6. Harmonic dictation will now include examples of all diatonic seventh chords.

Keyboard Harmony

Playing Harmonic Progressions.

Exercise 6.7. Play the following progressions in keys as directed by instructor. The Arabic numeral over the opening tonic triad indicates soprano note of the triad.

Major keys	*Minor keys*
1 or 5	1 or 5
I I^7 IV V (or vii$^{o}_6$) I	i i^7 iv V i
1 or 5	1
I I$^6_5$ IV V (or vii$^{o}_6$) I	i i$^6_5$ iv V i
1	1
I vi iii^7 IV V I	i VI III^7 iv V i
1 or 5	1, 3, 5
I IV^7 V I	i iv^7 V i
3	1, 3, 5
I IV$^6_5$ V$^6_5$ I	i IV$^6_5$ V$^6_5$ i
5	3 or 5
I V$_6$ vi^7 ii$^4_3$ V I	i v$_6$ VI^7 ii$^{ø}_{4\atop3}$ V i
5	1 or 5
I V vi$^4_2$ ii$^6_5$ V I	i V VI$^4_2$ ii$^{ø}_{6\atop5}$ V i

Exercise 6.8. Play the following exercises in keys as directed by the instructor.

Major key: 1
       I I$_6$ IV$^4_2$ vii$^{o}_6$ iii$^4_2$ vi$_6$ ii V I

Major key: 5 or 3
       I   iii vi^7 ii V I$^6_5$ IV vii$^{o}_6$ I

Major key: 1
       I ii$^4_2$ V$^6_5$ I I$^6_5$ IV vii$^{ø}_{6\atop5}$ I$_6$ vi^7 ii$^4_3$ V^7 I

Minor key: 1

$$\text{i} \quad \text{ii}^{\o}_{\substack{4\\2}} \quad \text{V}^6_5 \quad \text{i} \quad \text{i}^6_5 \quad \text{iv} \quad \text{vii}^{\o 7}_{\substack{6\\5}} \quad \text{i}_6 \quad \text{VI}^7 \quad \text{ii}^{\o}_{\substack{4\\3}} \quad \text{V}^7 \quad \text{i}$$

Minor key: 1, 3, or 5

$$\text{i} \quad \text{vii}^{\o 7}_{\substack{6\\5}} \quad \text{v}_6 \quad \text{vi}^{\o 7} \quad \text{ii}^{\o 7}_{\substack{4\\3}} \quad \text{V} \quad \text{i}$$

Playing Harmonic Sequences When playing the common harmonic sequence, roots up a fourth and down a fifth, using diatonic seventh chords, observe these details:

1. When each chord has its root in the bass, the complete chord (all members present) progresses to an incomplete chord (fifth omitted), which in turn progresses to a complete chord and so on.

2. When inversions are used, chords are complete.

3. In a major key, to continue the sequence past the cadence, play $\text{V}^7\text{-I}^7$ instead of $\text{V}^7\text{-I}$.

4. In a minor key, the lowered seventh and sixth scale steps are used until a cadence is desired when $\text{V}^7\text{-i}$ is played. To continue the sequence past the tonic triad, play $\text{v}^7\text{-i}^7$.

Exercise 6.9. *Playing the Harmonic Sequence, All Chords with their Roots in the Bass.* Play these patterns in all major and minor keys. Include practice in continuing past the authentic cadence.

Fig. 6.24

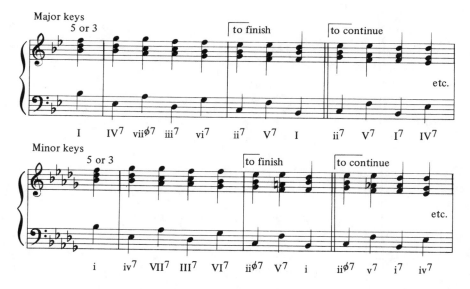

This sequence need not always start with the progression I-IV^7. The opening tonic may progress to a different seventh chord, for example, I-ii^7-V^7-I^7 etc., or another chord may progress to a seventh chord, as I-V-vi^7-ii^7 etc. There are almost limitless possibilities for experimentation.

Exercise 6.10. Playing the Sequence with Chords in Inversion. Each of these exercises may be played in either a major or minor key by making an appropriate change in the key signature. Comments at the close of Exercise 6.9 also apply here.

Fig. 6.25

Improvising an Accompaniment from a Figured Bass In the example by Handel, Figure 6.26, a keyboard accompaniment is begun for you. The figured bass examples in Assignments 5.1–5.4 and 6.4 may also be used for this purpose.

As an alternate procedure, two students may participate, one playing the melodic line, the other playing a harmonic progression similar to the exercises immediately preceding this one.

Exercise 6.11. Improvise an accompaniment from the given figured bass.

Fig. 6.26

Handel, Sonata in **B** minor for
Flute and Continuo

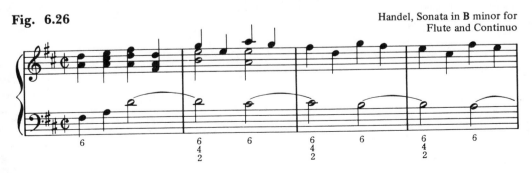

CHAPTER SEVEN

Borrowed Chords,
The Neapolitan Sixth Chord,
Augmented Triads

Theory and Analysis

Borrowed Chords

Very common is the practice of using a chord as spelled in the minor mode as part of a progression in a major mode, such as the use of ii°, D F A♭, or VI, A♭ C E♭ of C minor in the key of C major. Chords used thus are usually termed *borrowed* chords. Chords in a minor key borrowed from a major key, however, are limited, since the raised sixth and seventh scale degrees of minor already account for several spellings diatonic in both modes: C minor, ii = D F A, IV = F A C, V = G B D, and vii° = B D F.[1]

Figure 7.1 shows those chords from a minor key that are commonly used in its parallel major key. Only one seventh chord, the ii⌀7, is commonly found; others of these chords with sevenths are sometimes found in harmonic sequences.

Fig. 7.1

C major: i   ii°   ii⌀7   ♭III   iv   ♭VI   ♭VII   vii°7
                                     (V/♭VI)   (V/N)   (V/♭III)

[1]Some theorists prefer to identify all chords whose roots belong to the same basic scale system as diatonic in that system. Hence, all chords in C major and in C minor, for example, are diatonic in the tonality of C.

Assignment 7.1. Spell each of the chords of Figure 7.1 in each major key.

The major triads of Figure 7.1 often function as secondary dominant chords, as indicated in parentheses (N = Neapolitan or ♭II, explained later in this chapter). When used as secondary dominants, these chords will be identified with V/- symbols. The vii°[7] has already been presented as a chord of dominant function, but at the same time it can be considered borrowed from its diatonic counterpart in minor.

A borrowed chord with a diatonic root (i, ii°, ii°[7], and iv) is often introduced by its unaltered version, as in Figure 7.2, where IV progresses to iv. Following iv is a sonority spelled as ii°, G B♭ D♭. Whether to so identify it because of the slow tempo, or simply to consider the note G as an upper neighbor is a subjective decision.

Fig. 7.2

Just as frequently, borrowed chords are introduced independently of the parallel major chord, as in the progressions of Figure 7.3, I-ii$^6_5$ and I$_6$-iv.

Fig. 7.3

The last iv triad (third chord from the end) can also be considered a iv^7, analyzing the A in the upper voice as a seventh rather than as an appoggiatura.

Figures 7.4 and 7.5 show two uses of the $\flat$VI, the first in the progression I-$\flat$VI-V and the second as its use in the deceptive cadence.

Fig. 7.4   Brahms, *Liebeslieder Walzer*,
                                                                 Op. 52, No. 14

blickt der Mond her - nie - der!

♭VI   (iv₆)

Fig. 7.5   Bach, *Vater unser im Himmelreich* (No. 267)

vi   ii₅⁶ V ♭VI

Tonicizing the Borrowed Chord

The borrowed chord, like any other major or minor triad, may be tonicized by its preceding secondary dominant. In Figure 7.6, measures 37–40, the harmonic sequence, roots up a fourth and down a third, includes the borrowed chords ♭VI and ♭VII, each tonicized by its preceding secondary dominant chord.

Fig. 7.6

Chopin, Polonaise in A Major,
Op. 40, No. 1

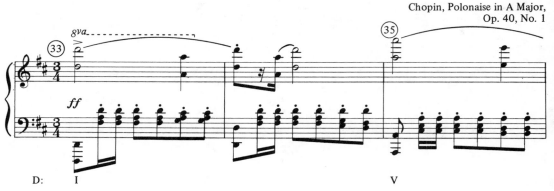

D: I   V

In Figure 7.7, the sequence in B♭ major produces the borrowed chords v and iv, preceded by V/v and V/iv, respectively. By considering the vii°⁷/vi to include the implied root, D, the root movement of the sequence can be said to start at that point. Note also at the beginning of the phrase the series of chords in first inversion, their chromaticism adding to the intensity of the phrase.

Fig. 7.7

Bach, *Ach Gott und Herr* (No. 279)

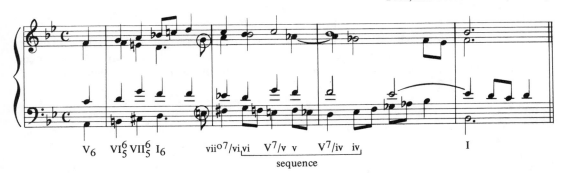

Temporary Change of Mode

Sufficient use of borrowed chords in a passage can lead to the effect of a temporary change of mode, usually major to minor, or an uncertainty as to which mode is predominant. In the preceding example, Figure 7.7, the progression V⁷/v-v-V⁷/iv-iv gives the impression of B♭ minor within the key of B♭ major. In Figure 7.8, the alternation of I and i triads has the effect of confusing the mode until the ♭VI seems to confirm a minor key, only to end in the original key of G major.

Fig. 7.8

Brahms, Symphony No. 2 in D Major, Op. 73

The opposite change of mode, from minor to major, is far less common, though the change in either direction is frequently used by Schubert, as in Figure 7.9, where the tonality changes from minor to major and back to minor within a single 8-measure period.

Fig. 7.9

Schubert, *Die schöne Müllerin*, D. 795, "Die liebe Farbe"

Modulation by Change of Mode

Since the key signature of a major key and its parallel minor differ by three accidentals, use of chords from the opposite mode will often conveniently and dramatically expedite a modulation from a major key to one of its remote keys. In Figure 7.10, progressing from I to i in the key of F makes possible an easy transition to the key of D♭, whether the modulation is analyzed as common chord (F: i = D♭: iii), or as a direct modulation at the beginning of the new phrase. In Figure 7.11, by spelling the borrowed i chord enharmonically, the key of E (4 sharps) is easily reached from the key of D♭ (5 flats).

Fig. 7.10

F major to
D♭ major

Beethoven, Symphony No. 3, Op. 55,
first movement

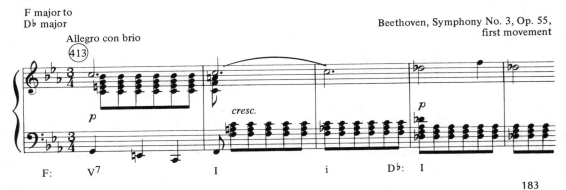

Fig. 7.11

D♭ major, i, D♭ F♭ A♭ =
E major, vi, C♯ E G♯   second spelling shown

Beethoven, Sonata for Piano, Op. 110,
first movement

In Figure 7.12, the borrowed ♭VI in the deceptive cadence becomes the new tonic in modulating from B♭ major to G♭ major.

Fig. 7.12

Chopin, Prelude, Op. 45

Assignment 7.2. Harmonic Analysis. Analyze these excerpts and describe the use of the borrowed chords in each.

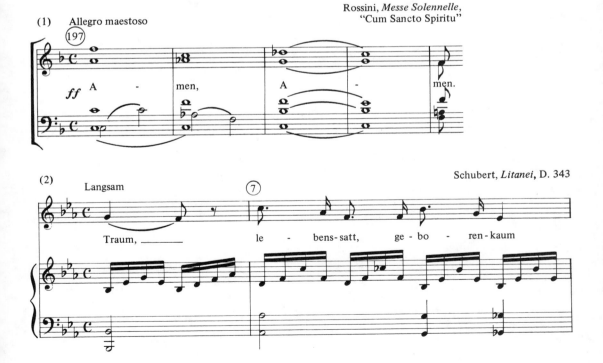

aus   der Welt   hin - ü - ber - schei - den

Andante con moto

Mozart, *Don Giovanni*, K. 527,
Act I, No. 4

(3)   ⑧⑤

del — le___ vec-chie   fa___con-qui-sta   pel   pia - cer___

de por - le in li - sta,   sua pas-sion pre-do-mi - nan - te _____ è la gio-vin prin-ci-

Schubert, *Jägers Liebeslied*, D. 909

(4) Mässig geschwind

Bach, *Orgelbüchlein*,
"O Mensch, bewein dein sünde gross"

(5) Adagio assai

Schubert, Sonata in A Major for Piano, D. 664,
second movement

(6) Andante

Massenet, *Manon*, Act I

Eh! j'i - ma - gi - ne Que cet - te bel - le en-fant

c'est Ma-non! ma cou-si - ne!

Je suis Les - caut.

Brahms, *Ein deutsches Requiem*, Op. 45,
"Ye Now are Sorrowful"

The Neapolitan Sixth Chord

The term *Neapolitan sixth* refers to a major triad built on the lowered second scale degree in either major or minor (C: D♭ F A♭). How this chord came to be named Neapolitan is not known. The inclusion of "sixth" reflects its almost exclusive use in first inversion, at least until the mid-nineteenth century, by which time use of the chord with its root in the bass had become more frequent. For analysis, the Roman numeral ♭II₆ identifies the sonority, though an alternate symbol, N₆, is now widely accepted and will be used in this text. When found with its root in the bass, the symbols N and ♭II and the term Neapolitan identify this chord, although the expression "Neapolitan sixth with root in bass" is still often seen and heard.

C major: N (♭II)   N₆ (♭II₆) c minor: N (♭II)   N₆ (♭II₆)

Assignment 7.3. Spell the Neapolitan sixth chord in each major and minor key.

The Neapolitan sixth chord functions exactly as the diatonic ii₆ in major or ii°₆ in minor, progressing easily either to tonic six-four or to the dominant. The progression N₆-V always includes a melodic interval of the diminished third, lowered second scale degree to leading tone, as in Figure 7.13, measures 136–137, D♭-B.

Fig. 7.13

Fig. 7.14

Among other possible resolutions of the N_6, half-step movement in the bass is fairly common, as in Figure 7.15, half step up to a diminished seventh chord, Figure 7.16, half step down to a diminished seventh chord, and Figure 7.17, half step up to a secondary dominant chord.

Fig. 7.15

Fig. 7.16

Fig. 7.17

Schumann, Quartet, Op. 41, No. 3,
second movement

The Neapolitan chord in root position (N or ♭II) is shown in Figure 7.18, the chord in this instance followed by the unaltered supertonic triad, ii°.

Fig. 7.18

Brahms, Symphony No. 3, Op. 90,
fourth movement

The Secondary Dominant of the Neapolitan Chord

VI in a minor key and ♭VI in a major key serve as the secondary dominant function to the Neapolitan chord, and when so used are symbolized V/N or V/♭II. As a triad, it is seen in Figure 7.19, while its use as an embellishing seventh chord between N_6 and N is shown in Figure 7.20. Note that the V^7/N requires a lowered seventh to become a major-minor seventh chord.

Fig. 7.19

Fig. 7.20

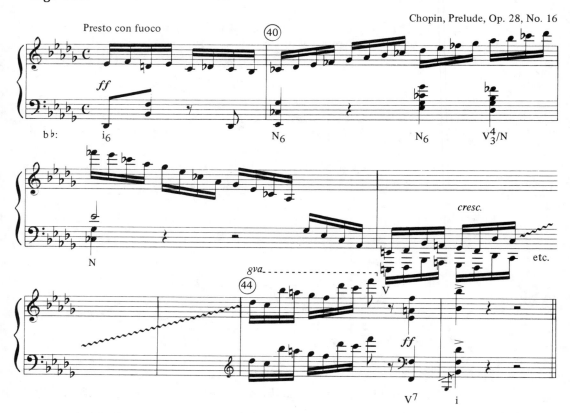

Using the principle of the common progression, I-vii°$_6$-I$_6$, a diminished triad can similarly be used between N and N$_6$ (vii°$_6$/N). In Figure 7.21, N is preceded by its secondary dominant, the four chords constituting a short progression on the level of N.

Fig. 7.21

Chopin, Prelude, Op. 28, No. 12

g#:   i   iv   V   V   I   vii°₆   I₆   i⁶₄   V   i

The Neapolitan Chord in a Sequence

This chord is frequently found in a harmonic sequence. When arriving at the supertonic sonority, that chord is simply altered to become an N or N₆.

Fig. 7.22

Brahms, Quartet, Op. 51, No. 2,
fourth movement

e: V⁷/N N V⁷

The Neapolitan as a Pivot Chord

The Neapolitan chord can be effective in modulation, acting as a function in either the old key or the new key at the pivot point. In Figure 7.23, the N_6 is spelled enharmonically to function as IV_6 in the new key, representing a change of key from five flats to six sharps.

Fig. 7.23

B♭ minor, N_6, C♭ E♭ G♭ =
F♯ major, IV, B D♯ F♯   second spelling shown

Mozart, Symphony No. 39 in E♭ Major, K. 543,
fourth movement

The Augmented Triad

An augmented triad is composed of two major thirds; the resulting distance from root to fifth of the triad is an augmented fifth, the inversion of which is the diminished fourth.

Fig. 7.24

Assignment 7.4. Spelling the augmented triad. a) Spell an augmented triad when any pitch name is given as the root. An augmented triad cannot be spelled from a root whose pitch name includes a double sharp. The fifth of the triad would then be a triple sharp.

b) Spell an augmented triad when any pitch name is given as the third.

c) Spell an augmented triad when the pitch name is the fifth.

Assignment 7.5. Intervals. a) Spell the interval of an augmented fifth from any given note (except a note with a double sharp). b) Spell the interval of a diminished fourth from any given note.

The Augmented Triad in a Key

In a major key, all augmented triads are altered chords, the fifth of the triad being raised in each case. The most commonly used augmented triads in major are I+, IV+, and V+ (Figure 7.25a). In a minor key, only the III+ (Figure 7.25b) is regularly encountered. Its fifth is the leading tone of the key. All of these triads are used freely with root in bass or in first inversion; examples in second inversion are rare.

Fig. 7.25

Assignment 7.6. Spell the I+, IV+, and V+ in each major key. Spell the III+ in each minor key.

In a major key, the augmented triad is approached in one of two ways:
1. A major triad is followed by a triad with the same root but with its fifth raised one half step, as in Figure 7.26. When the alteration is of such short duration, its analysis as a chromatic passing tone is justified. As the duration of the chromatic tone increases, positive identification as an augmented triad becomes more likely. The triad identified as I+ in Figure 7.27 is found on a strong beat and is of two beats duration. The following IV+ is of one beat only and on a weak beat. Are either or both actually augmented triads or simply major triads with passing tones? Only a subjective evaluation by the individual listener is really valid.

Wolf, *Auf einer Wanderung*

Fig. 7.27

I+, IV+

2. When the augmented triad is approached and followed by a different chord or chords, its identity is more secure. Approach to the altered tone by neighbor tone is common in these instances.

The approach as a neighbor tone is common when the augmented triad is preceded and followed by a different chord, as in Figure 7.28 (E♯-D×-E♯ in I-V+ - I).

Fig. 7.28

Dvořák, Concerto for Violin in A Minor, Op. 53, third movement

Resolution of the augmented triad is determined by the necessity of resolving the altered tone. Therefore, some augmented triads resolve by root movement of a fifth, such as I+ - IV and V+ - I, while others resolve by root movement of a third, such as IV+ - ii$_6$ or V+ - iii$_6$ (usually retaining the same bass note).

In a minor key, the fifth of the augmented triad III+ is the leading tone of the key, and is usually approached and resolved stepwise. The progression III+ - VI is most frequent (Figure 7.29), though others are possible (Figure 7.30). In Figure 7.29, observe the ascending chromatic scale line in the bass, accounting for some uncommon chord progressions.

Fig. 7.29

Bach, *Wir Christenleut* (No. 321)

g: II III$\frac{+}{6}$ VI IV$_6$ VII V$_6$ i

Fig. 7.30

Bach, *O Ewigkeit, du Donnerwort* (No. 26)

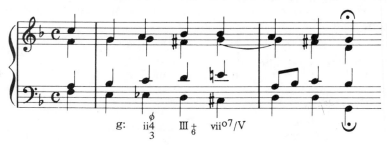

g: ii$\overset{\phi}{\underset{3}{4}}$ III$\frac{+}{6}$ vii^{o7}/V

Other Augmented Sonorities

On occasion, other augmented triads will be encountered, some functioning as those already described, while others contain features making other analyses more desirable. In Figure 7.31, the apparent ♭VI+, though of two beats duration, does not resolve as a typical augmented triad. The E♭ as a passing tone is a better analysis.

Fig. 7.31

Grieg, *Letzter Frühling*, Op. 34, No. 2

Andante

G: vi (♭VI+) I$\frac{6}{4}$ V^7 I

The sound of the first chord of measure 2 in Figure 7.32 is clearly augmented, yet appears to be simply a suspension in the V triad.

Fig. 7.32

Lento

Chopin, Nocturne, Op. 15, No. 3

The excerpt from the Schumann Concerto, Figure 7.33, appears to show a III+$^6_4$ and VI+$^6_4$ preceding VI$_6$ and N$_6$ respectively. The short duration of these augmented sonorities suggest that the third and fifth of each are simply appoggiaturas to the triads which follow.

Fig. 7.33

Schumann, Concerto in A Minor for Piano and
Orchestra, Op. 54, first movement

Allegro affetuoso

a: (III+) VI$_6$ (I) iv$_6$ (VI+) N$_6$ (V) i$_6$ iv   i$^6_4$ V   i

Again, and as demonstrated many times in similar situations in earlier chapters, the importance in analysis lies not in the identification of a sonority with an indisputable symbol, but in the understanding of the function of the sound in the musical context.

   Assignment 7.7. Harmonic Analysis.   These excerpts contain examples of both the Neapolitan sixth chord and various augmented triads.

(1) Adagio

Rossini, *Comic Duet for Two Cats*

mia   -   u,   mi   -   au,

mia - - - - - - - u,

Vivaldi, Concerto Grosso,
Op. 3, No. 10

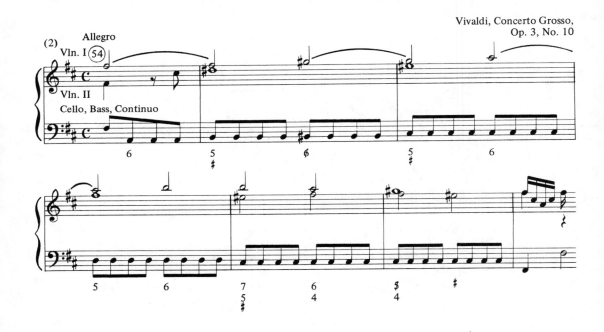

(2) Allegro
Vln. I (54)
Vln. II
Cello, Bass, Continuo

Beethoven, Concerto in C Minor for Piano and Orchestra,
Op. 37, first movement

(3) Allegro con brio
⑨

Beethoven, Quartet, Op. 59, No. 2,
first movement

Brahms, Intermezzo, Op. 118, No. 2

Mussorgsky, *Pictures at an Exhibition*,
"The Old Castle"

Application

Written Materials

Writing Borrowed Chords, Neapolitan Chords, and Augmented Triads   All previous part-writing procedures apply to the writing of these chords. Additional considerations are:

1. When the root of a triad is an altered note, that note may be doubled, as in C major, ♭VI, A♭ C E♭, or N, D♭ F A♭.
2. In the Neapolitan sixth chord, the third is commonly doubled, because both the root and the fifth (lowered second and sixth scale steps) ordinarily require a downward resolution.
3. The augmented triads are found with root or third in the bass. The fifth, the altered tone, progresses up by half step.

Assignment 7.8. Part-Writing Borrowed Chords.   Fill in alto and tenor voices. Make harmonic analysis.

Assignment 7.9. Part-Writing the Neapolitan Chord. Fill in alto and tenor voices. Make harmonic analysis.

Assignment 7.10. Part-Writing Augmented Triads. Fill in alto and tenor voices. Make harmonic analysis.

Assignment 7.11. Part-Writing Extended Exercises, Using Various Altered Chords. Fill in alto and tenor voices. Make harmonic analysis.

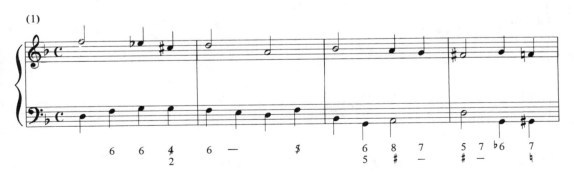

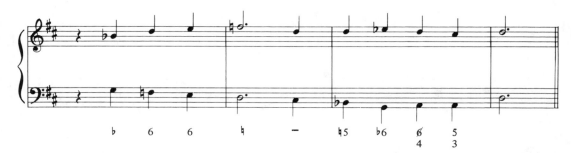

Assignment 7.12. Write the following progressions in four voices. Choose a meter and rhythmic pattern which will insure good harmonic rhythm at the cadences. Unaltered chords may be repeated, with change of soprano and/or inversion, if necessary.

a) D minor: i III+$_6$ VI ii$^{\varnothing 6}_{5}$ i$^6_4$ V i

b) F minor: i v$_6$ VI N$_6$ V^7 i ii$^o_6$ V i

c) E major: I I+ ii$_6$ V^7 V$^6_5$ vi V V+ I

Assignment 7.13. Figured Bass Realizations. Copy out these examples on three staves and write a part for keyboard based on the composer's figuration.

Telemann, Sonata in F Minor for
Flute and Figured Bass

This excerpt begins with the V/ii in G major.

C.P. E. Bach, Sonata in G Major for
Flute and Figured Bass

Ear Training

Borrowed Chords

Exercise 7.1. Sing the following progressions, using letter names in major keys indicated by the instructor.

I IV V I; I iv V I   I vi IV V I; I ♭VI iv V I

I ii V I; I ii° V I

I ii⁷ V I; I ii⌀⁷ V I

I V vi; I V ♭VI

The Neapolitan Sixth Chord

Exercise 7.2. Sing, with letter names, the Neapolitan sixth chord in any major or minor key. Listen for the tonic note of the key and sing a note a half step higher, followed by singing a major triad on that note.

Exercise 7.3. Sing the progression I N₆ V I in any major key and the progression i N₆ V i in any minor key. Sing the N₆ from its third (fourth scale step), for example, in C major: C E G E C, F A♭ D♭ A♭ F, G B D B G, C E G E C.

The Augmented Triad

Exercise 7.4. Singing Augmented Triads. *a*) To sing an augmented triad from its root, sing two major thirds in succession. To sing an augmented triad from its third requires that the major third be followed by the diminished fourth. This latter interval is enharmonic with a major third and can be sung as a major third.

Fig. 7.34

b) Sing augmented triads as in *a*, but sing with letter names when the name of the root or third is given.

Exercise 7.5. Intervals in the Augmented Triad Identify aurally the intervals of the augmented fifth and the diminished fourth. These two intervals are enharmonic with the minor sixth and the major third, respectively. To identify them as the augmented fifth or the diminished fourth, it is necessary that the augmented triad be heard at the same time. Follow this procedure:

a) Listen to the interval played at the piano. Sing the interval on la.

b) Listen to the chord played at the piano. The instructor will indicate whether the root or third is in the bass.

c) Sing the triad from the root, using 1, 3, 5, 3, 1.

d) Sing the interval with the correct numbers.

e) Identify the interval by name. 1 up to 5 or 5 down to 1 will be an augmented fifth. 5 up to 1 or 1 down to 5 will be a diminished fourth.

Fig. 7.35

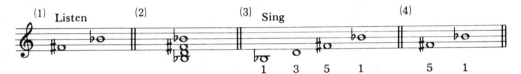

Exercise 7.6. Spelling Augmented Triads and Intervals in the Augmented Triad from Dictation.

a) The letter name of the bass tone will be given; whether the bass is root or third will also be given. Spell the triad, then spell the interval.

b) The letter name of one note of the interval will be given; whether the bass is the root or third will also be given. Spell the triad and the interval. An example, in which F is the first note of the interval and the bass note is the third of the triad, follows.

Fig. 7.36

Exercise 7.7. Singing the I+, IV+, V+, and III+ triads. *a*) The tonic tone will be given, together with its letter name. Sing the tonic triad with letter names, followed by the I+ triad with letter names. Repeat this procedure with the IV+ and V+ triads.

b) Follow directions in *a* above; after the minor tonic triad sing the III+ triad.

Fig. 7.37

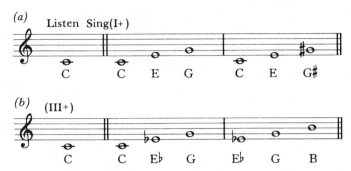

Exercise 7.8. Singing the Augmented Triad in a Harmonic Progression. Sing the following progressions, using letter names, in keys as indicated by instructor.

I I+ IV V I

I V V+ I

I IV IV+ ii V I

i III+ VI iv V i

Exercise 7.9. Harmonic Dictation. Exercises will now include examples of borrowed chords, augmented triads, and the Neapolitan sixth.

Keyboard Harmony

Borrowed Chords

Exercise 7.10. Play these progressions in all keys. The progression in major is followed by the same progression substituting borrowed chords.

I IV V I; I iv V I
I ii V I; I ii° V I
I ii⁷ V I; I ii°⁷ V I
I V vi: I V ♭VI
I vi IV V I; I ♭VI iv V I

The Neapolitan Sixth Chord
Exercise 7.11.   Play these progressions in all keys.

Major keys	*Minor keys*
I N_6 I_4^6 V I	i N_6 i_4^6 V i
I N_6 V I	i N_6 V i
I $\flat$VI N_6 I_4^6 V I	i VI N_6 i_4^6 V i
I N_6 V_2^4 I_6 vii$_6^o$ I	i N_6 V_2^4 I_6 vii$_6^o$ I
I N_6 vii^{o7}/V V I	i N_6 vii^{o7}/V V i

Augmented Triads
Exercise 7.12.   Play the progressions from Exercise 7.8 at the keyboard.

CHAPTER EIGHT

Augmented Sixth Chords

Theory and Analysis

Chords of the augmented sixth differ in intervallic construction from any chord previously presented in that they contain the interval of an augmented sixth. Two such chords are present in Figure 8.1, both of which contain the augmented sixth interval, B♭ up to G♯.

Fig. 8.1

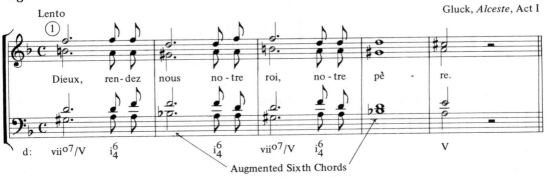

Lento

Gluck, *Alceste*, Act I

Dieux, ren-dez nous no - tre roi, no - tre pè - re.

d: vii°⁷/V i⁶₄ i⁶₄ vii°⁷/V i⁶₄ V

Augmented Sixth Chords

Characteristics of the Interval of the Augmented Sixth

Before considering the complete chord, we will note the basic characteristics of the interval itself. The spelling, B♭ up to G♯, as used in the augmented sixth chords of Figure 8.1, is used as a basis for this discussion and for illustration in Figure 8.2.

1. The interval is one half step larger than a major sixth (Figure 8.2a).
2. Its lower tone is ordinarily the lowered sixth scale step of the key, while the upper tone is ordinarily the raised fourth scale degree (Figure 8.2b).

217

3. The lowered sixth scale step is usually the lowest sounding tone of the chord, while the upper tone may be found in any higher voice.

4. The interval resolves to an octave, the upper tone ascending one half step, and the lower tone descending one half step, each to the dominant tone of the key (Figure 8.2c).

5. The interval is enharmonic with the interval of a minor seventh: A6 = B♭ up to G♯; m7 = B♭ up to A♭. When heard out of context, they sound identically, but as part of a chord, each resolves differently (Figure 8.2c, d). As a minor seventh the interval usually outlines a seventh chord, requiring a downward resolution of its upper note, while as an augmented sixth, the upper note is the raised fourth scale degree, which must ascend.

Fig. 8.2

Derivation of the Augmented Sixth

In their most common usage[1], chords containing an augmented sixth are of subdominant function, resolving to the tonic six-four (Figure 8.1, measure 2) or to the dominant (Figure 8.1, measures 4–5). It is easy to see how the interval developed in such simple progressions as iv$_6$-i$_4^6$ or ii$_4^ø$-V when a passing tone from the fourth scale degree to the raised fourth scale degree momentarily creates the interval of the augmented sixth between it and the bass tone (Figure 8.3).

Fig. 8.3

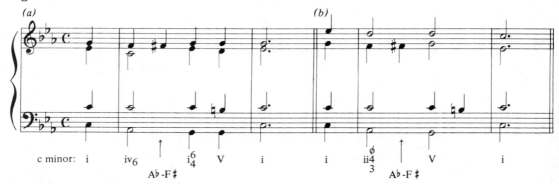

[1]Other uses of the augmented sixth interval and chords will be discussed beginning on page 224.

The process can be seen in the Bach chorale of Figure 8.4 where, in measure 2, contrary passing tones create a momentary augmented sixth inverval, F-D♯.

Fig. 8.4

Bach, *Wer nur den lieben Gott lasst* (No. 146)

Types of Augmented Sixth Chords

Augmented sixth chords, when spelled in thirds, always contain the interval of a diminished third (Figure 8.5*a*). Each chord is commonly found in the inversion that will display the interval of the augmented sixth. There are three such structures, each popularly known by a geographical name.[2]

The Italian sixth—a triad consisting of a diminished third and a major third. To display the interval of the augmented sixth, the triad is found in first inversion (see Figure 8.5*b*). The chord symbol is It6.

The German sixth—a seventh chord consisting of a triad identical to the Italian sixth, plus the interval of a minor third above the fifth of the triad. To display the interval of the augmented sixth, the chord is found in first inversion (see Figure 8.5*c*). The chord symbol is Gr6.

The French sixth—a seventh chord consisting of the intervals of a major third, a diminished third, and a major third. To display the interval of the augmented sixth, the chord is found in second inversion (see Figure 8.5*d*). The chord symbol is Fr6.

Fig. 8.5

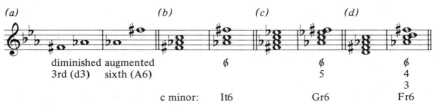

	(a)	(b)	(c)	(d)
	diminished augmented 3rd (d3) sixth (A6)	♯6	♯6 5	♯6 4 3
	c minor: It6		Gr6	Fr6

These chords are also often known by their figured bass symbols: the augmented sixth chord (Italian sixth), the augmented six-five chord (German sixth), and the augmented six-four-three chord (French sixth), as indicated in Figure 8.5.

---

[2]The sources or meanings of these geographical terms are unknown.

Conventional Use of Augmented Sixth Chords in a Minor Key

It is likely that augmented sixth chords were first used in minor keys, as only one alteration in a chord of subdominant function was necessary. By raising the fourth scale degree one half step in each of the iv, iv^7, and ii^{ø7} chords and inverting to display the interval of the augmented sixth, the three augmented sixth chords are achieved. To illustrate in C minor, F is raised to F♯ in each chord.

iv F A♭ C   add F♯: F♯ A♭ C   invert to It6: A♭ C F♯
iv^7 F A♭ C E♭ add F♯: F♯ A♭ C E♭   invert to Gr6: A♭ C E♭ F♯
ii^{ø7} D F A♭ C add F♯: D F♯ A♭ C   invert to Fr6: A♭ C D F♯

Assignment 8.1. Spell the Italian, German, and French sixth chords in each minor key. Spell each by interval, as discussed in a previous paragraph, or, first spell the diatonic chord in the key and then raise the fourth scale degree. *Examples:* (1) Spell the Italian sixth chord in D minor. The iv triad is spelled G B♭ D; raise the fourth scale step, G♯; the Italian sixth is G♯ B♭ D. (2) Spell the French sixth in G♯ minor. The ii^{ø7} chord is spelled A♯ C♯E G♯; raise the fourth scale step, C×; the French sixth is spelled A♯ C× E G♯. Follow each spelling by spelling it in its conventional inversion.

Figure 8.6 shows the two resolutions, to V and to tonic six-four, of each augmented sixth chord. Note the parallel fifths in the progression Gr6-V. Although avoided by earlier composers, the use of this progression became more common in the nineteenth century, as seen in Figure 8.23.

Fig. 8.6

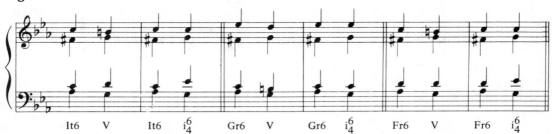

Looking back at Figure 8.1, we can now identify the first of the two augmented sixth chords as the German sixth and the second as the Italian sixth. The It6 was undoubtedly chosen by Gluck instead of the Gr6 to avoid the fifths in progressing to V.

Avoiding the parallel fifth is also shown in Figure 8.7, where Haydn, at the last thirty-second note, changes the Gr6 to an It6. Use of the remaining augmented sixth chord, the Fr6 is shown in Figure 8.8.

Fig. 8.7

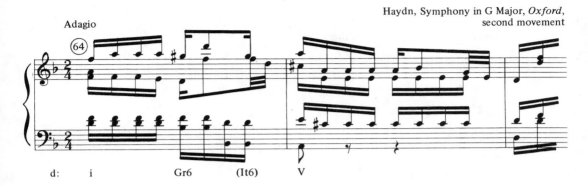

Haydn, Symphony in G Major, *Oxford*, second movement

Fig. 8.8

Verdi, *Il Trovatore*, Act II, "Stride la vampa"

Conventional Use of Augmented Sixth Chords in a Major Key

The three augmented sixth chords just presented also appear in major keys, built on the same roots and with spellings identical to those in minor keys. To achieve this identical spelling, additional tones must be altered.

Fig. 8.9

As in minor keys, the fourth scale step is raised in each chord. In addition, the sixth scale step is lowered in each chord, and, in the German sixth, the third scale step is also lowered. Resolution of the interval of the augmented sixth is identical to that in minor keys.

Assignment 8.2. Spell the Italian, German, and French sixth chords in each major key. An augmented sixth chord in a major key is spelled the same as in the parallel minor key.

Example: Fr6 in B major is identical to Fr6 in B minor, C♯ E♯ G B. When there is no parallel minor (D♭, G♭ and C♭ major), chords must be spelled by interval.

Fig. 8.10
Beethoven, Sonata in A Major for Piano, Op. 101, first movement

Fig. 8.11
Mozart, Symphony in D Major, *Prague*, K. 504, second movement

Fig. 8.12   Beethoven, Sonata in A Major for Violin and Piano
Op. 47, "Kreutzer," first movement

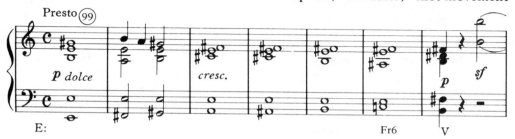

Alternate Spellings of the German Sixth Chord in a Major key.   In a major key, the seventh of the Gr6 is a lowered third scale step. In resolving to I_4^6 this note progresses upwards (Figure 8.13a). A number of composers prefer to spell this note enharmonically as a chromatically raised note which will then continue upwards in its resolution, as in Figure 8.13b, where D♯ has replaced E♭. In so doing, the D♯ becomes the root of the chord on the raised second scale degree when spelled in thirds, and the chord is found in second inversion to display the interval of the augmented sixth. The function of these chords is identical, so both may be symbolized by Gr6. If differentiation is desired, the alternate spelling may be symbolized Gr6(♯ii).

The chord in its alternate spelling is sometimes known as a doubly augmented six-four-three. In Figure 8.13b, the interval A♭-D♯ is a doubly augmented fourth.

Fig. 8.13

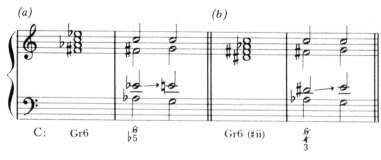

Fig. 8.14   Schumann, *Dichterliebe*, "Am leuchtenden
Sommermorgen," Op. 48, No. 12

Assignment 8.3.   Spell the alternate form of the German sixth in each major key. Spell the Gr6 as in Assignment 8.2, then substitute the enharmonic equivalent of the seventh of the chord, using this note as the root, with other members of the chord retaining their original spelling. For example, for the alternate spelling in F♯ major, spell B♯ D F♯ A, change A to G× and spell G× B♯ D F♯.

A more unusual spelling is that shown in Figure 8.15, where the German sixth chord A♯ C E G is spelled C E G B♭ in conformity with its major-minor seventh chord sound.

Fig. 8.15

Brahms, Sonata in E Minor for Violoncello and Piano, Op. 38, first movement

C E G B♭ =
A♯ C E G

Augmented Sixth Chords with Bass Notes Other than the Sixth Scale Step

These chords are occasionally found with root in bass, or in some inversion other than previously described. In these, the interval of the diminished third usually appears, resolving to a unison. Previous symbols will suffice, although, if desired, adding the figured bass symbol will completely identify the sonority, for example Gr$\frac{5}{3}$, or Fr$\frac{6}{5}$.

Fig. 8.16

Wagner, *Die Walküre*,
Act III, Scene 3

Figure 8.17 includes a number of augmented sixth sonorities: (1) a "normal" German sixth chord; (2) the German sixth with root in bass; (3) a descending melodic line which creates a series of differing augmented sixth sonorities, German, French, and Italian in order, all with the raised fourth scale step in the bass, finally ending with an interval of a diminished third resolving to a unison; and (4) two additional augmented sixth chords, which will be discussed in the next section.

Fig. 8.17

Tschaikowski, *Eugene Onegin*,
Act I, No. 9

The German sixth chord at the * in Figure 8.18 is not only in second inversion, but is spelled both as a Gr6, D F♭ A♭ C♭, and as a Gr6(♯ii) B D F♭ A♭. The enharmonic pitches B and C♭ are both used as part of the chord spelling.

Fig. 8.18

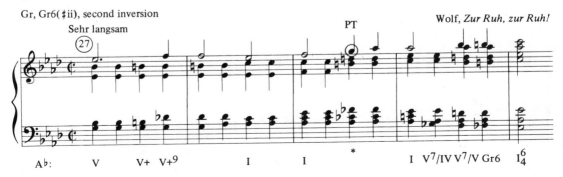

Wolf, *Zur Ruh, zur Ruh!*

In Figure 8.19, the pedal point gives the aural effect of the German sixth in third inversion. The interval of the augmented sixth, B$\flat\flat$-G, resolves normally to the octave A$\flat$.

Fig. 8.19

Dvořák, Symphony No. 9 in E Minor, Op. 95, *New World*, second movement

D$\flat$:   vi   iv$^6_4$ Gr   I

Augmented Sixth Chords Built on Scale Steps Other Than ii, ♯ii, or ♯iv

The interval of the augmented sixth in these infrequent chords resolves out to an octave on a scale step other than the dominant. In Figure 8.20 (the final measures of this composition) the interval D$\flat$-B resolves out to the octave C, the tonic note. Its symbol, vii It6, indicates the scale step of the root as spelled in thirds. The Fr6 of Figure 8.22 (iii Fr6) acts as a "secondary augmented sixth" to its following chord, so it could be symbolized as Fr6/VI. In addition to the following examples, two other such chords are located in Figure 8.17, measures 5 and 6.

Fig. 8.20

Fauré. *Au bord de l'Eau,*
Op. 8, No. 1

Andante quasi allegretto

c: I   vii It6   I   vii It6

I

Fig. 8.21

W.F. Bach, Sonata in G Major for Piano,
second movement

Fig. 8.22   Beethoven, Sonata in A Minor for Violin and Piano,
Op. 23, third movement

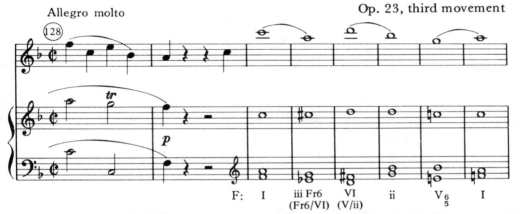

Augmented Sixth Chords in which the Interval of the Augmented Sixth Does Not Resolve to the Octave

Avoidance of traditional resolution of the interval of the augmented sixth becomes quite frequent in music of the later nineteenth-century composers.

Fig. 8.23

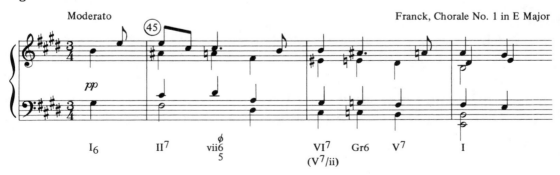

Franck, Chorale No. 1 in E Major

The German sixth chord of Figure 8.23 resolves to V^7 requiring the upper note of the interval of the augmented sixth to resolve downwards (A♯-A♮). Perfect parallel fifths become unavoidable in this progression; Franck emphasizes this effect by preceding the progression with the VI^7, creating the aural effect of a succession of three parallel major-minor seventh chords.

In Figure 8.24, the arpeggiated F♭ A♭ C♭ chord in the accompaniment looks like a ♭VI triad in A♭ major; the augmented sixth chord is created by the addition of D in the voice part. Resolution of the chord is interrupted by the secondary dominant, V/V.

Fig. 8.24

Wolf, *Und willst du deinen Liebsten sterben sehen*

Augmented Minor Seventh Chords

These are augmented triads with an additional interval of a minor seventh above the root.

Fig. 8.25

C: I+♭7
V+7
c: VI+♭7

These chords are infrequently used in music. Of the three, the first two are by far the more common; the VI+$^{\flat 7}$ is shown here to illustrate a use of an augmented seventh chord which might occasionally be encountered.

Assignment 8.4. Spell the I+$^{\flat 7}$ and the V+^{7} in each major key.

In each of these chords, the voices are usually arranged to show the interval of the augmented sixth rather than the diminished third. They differ from the augmented sixth chords in that the lower note of the interval of the augmented sixth is usually in an inner voice, as will be observed in the following illustrations.

Fig. 8.26 Mendelssohn, *Songs Without Words,* Op. 38, No. 1

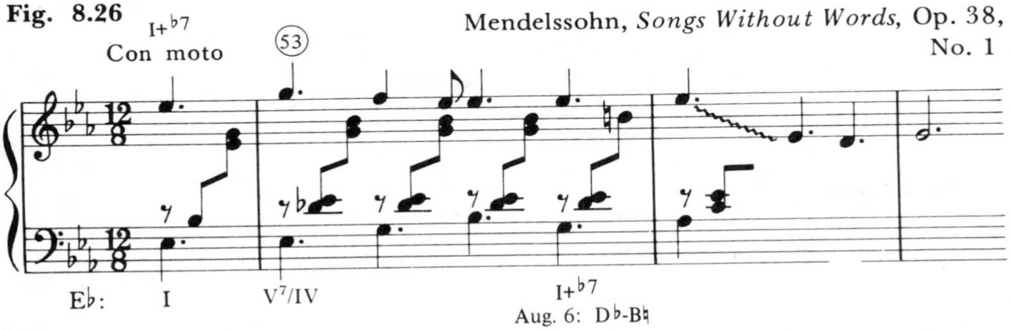
I+♭7
Con moto
53
E♭: I
V7/IV
I+♭7
Aug. 6: D♭-B♮

Fig. 8.27 d'Indy, *La Rêve de Cinyras,* Act II

Assez vite
6
F: I
V+7

Fig. 8.28 Franck, Chorale No. 2 in B Minor

VI+♭7
Largamente
g: i 6 4
VI+ ♭7
N6
vii°6 5
Gr6
I 6 4

V⁷   i

Assignment 8.5. Harmonic Analysis.

Make a harmonic analysis of each example. Locate the interval of the augmented sixth in each case and describe its resolution.

Beethoven, Sonata in D Major for Violin and Piano, Op. 12, No. 1, third movement

Beethoven, Sonata in G Minor for Cello and Piano,
Op. 5, No. 2, second movement

(2) Allegro molto

Mozart, Symphony in G Minor, K. 550,
first movement

(3) Allegro molto

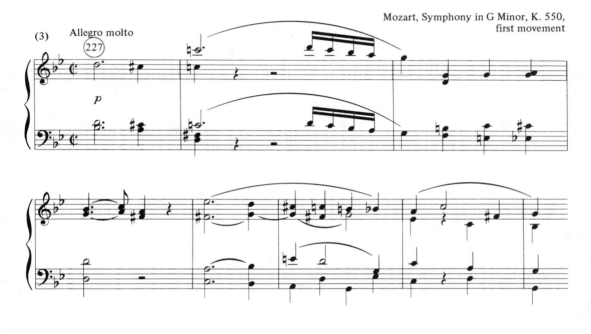

Schumann, Concerto for Piano and Orchestra,
Op. 54, third movement

(4) Allegro vivace

Beethoven, Quartet, Op. 127,
second movement

(5)   Adagio molto espressivo

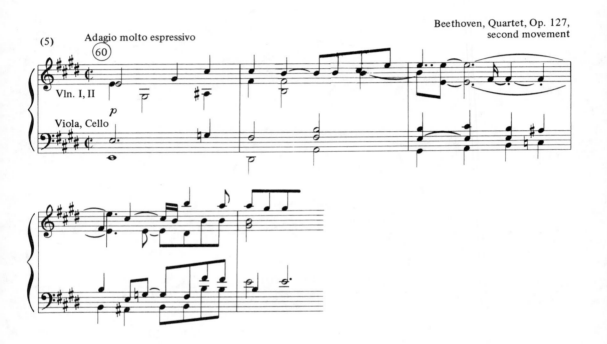

Franck, Symphony in D Minor,
first movement

(6)   Allegro non troppo

Brahms, Piano Quintet, Op. 26,
first movement

(7)

Franck, Chorale No. 3 in A Minor

(8)

Gounod, *Faust*, Act II

(9)

Schubert, Symphony in B Minor, "Unfinished," second movement

Strauss, *Till Eulenspiegels lustige Streiche,* "Epilog"

The German Sixth Chord as a Pivot in Modulation

Since the sound of a German sixth chord is enharmonic with that of a major-minor seventh chord, it is a convenient chord to use in a modulation. As a pivot, it may equal any function characteristic of a major-minor seventh chord, or, any major-minor seventh chord may become an augmented sixth chord.[3] The majority of such pivots include these three specific uses: Gr6 = V^7; V^7 = Gr6; V^7/IV = Gr6.

Figure 8.29 shows examples of each of these possibilities. Observe that the spelling of the pivot in the new key is sometimes the same as that of the original key with an enharmonic change of one note (spelled root of the Gr6 is enharmonic with the seventh of the major-minor seventh chord, as in Figure 8.29 *a, c,*

---

[3]The Italian sixth may equal an incomplete major-minor seventh chord, but such pivots are not common.

and *e*), or the pivot in the new key may be the enharmonic spelling of three tones of the chord in the old key, as in Figures 8.29*b*, *d*, and *f*.

Fig. 8.29

Gr6 = V^7: modulation up one half step

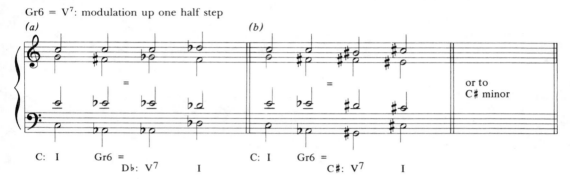

V^7 = Gr6: modulation down one half step

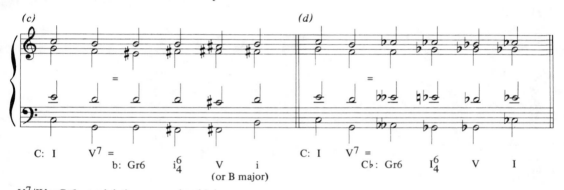

V^7/IV = Gr6: modulation up a major third

Figure 8.30 is a rare example in which both spellings of the pivot are shown by the composer. Ordinarily, a pivot with any enharmonic change is spelled as found in the new key. Figure 8.31 shows the pivot as spelled with the single enharmonic change, while Figure 8.32 shows the triad spelled enharmonically.

Fig. 8.30

B major, V^7/IV,   B D♯ F♯ A =
E♭ major, Gr6,   A C♭ E♭ G♭   both spellings shown

Chopin, Mazurka, Op. 56, No. 1

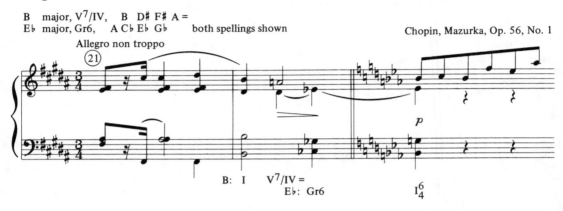

B: I   V^7/IV =
         E♭: Gr6   I$^6_4$

Fig. 8.31

B♭ major, V^7 F A C E♭ =
A minor, Gr6, D♯ F A C   second spelling shown

Schubert, Sonata in A Minor for Piano,
D. 845, first movement

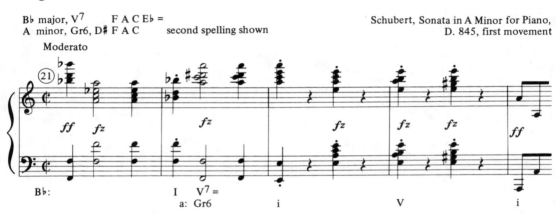

B♭:   I   V^7 =
                    a: Gr6   i   V   i

Fig. 8.32

C minor, Gr6, F♯ A♭ C E♭   =
C♯ minor, V^7,   G♯ B♯ D♯ F♯   second spelling shown

Beethoven, Sonata for Piano, No. 27, Op. 90,
second movement

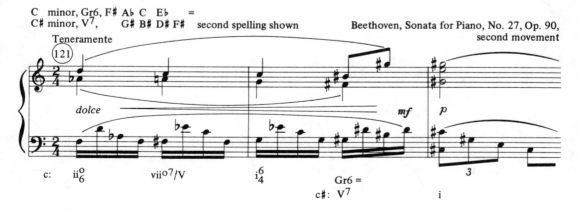

c: ii$^o_6$ vii^{o7}/V   i$^6_4$
                                        Gr6 =
                                    c♯: V^7 i

Occasionally, a pivot will be seen as spelled in the original key, as in Figure 8.33, where V^7 as spelled in D♭ major acts as the augmented sixth pivot in modulating to C major.

Fig. 8.33

Berlioz, *Les Nuits d'Été*,
Op. 7, "L'Ille inconnue"

D♭ major, V^7,   A♭ C E♭ G♭ =
C major, Gr6, F♯ A♭ C E♭   first spelling shown

Other pivotal uses of the German sixth are represented by Figure 8.34 in which V^7/IV = vii Gr6. Although the resolution of the augmented sixth seems momentarily like a common Gr6 resolution to D minor, any such impression is nullified immediately by V^7 in A major.

Fig. 8.34

Schubert, Sonata in D Major for Piano,
D. 850, second movement

Assignment 8.6. Spell augmented sixth chords as enharmonic equivalents in these pivots: Gr6 = V^7, V^7 = Gr6 and V^7/IV = Gr6.

Examples:

A♭ or a♭: Gr6, D F♭ A♭ C♭ = A or a: V^7, E G♯ B D

B or b: V^7, F♯ A♯ C♯ E = B♭ or b♭: Gr6, E G♭ B♭ D♭

= a♯; Gr6, D× F♯ A♯C♯

D or d: V^7/IV, D F♯ A C = F♯ or f♯: Gr6, B♯ D F♯ A

= G♭: C E♭♭ G♭ B♭♭

Observe that in each case the seventh of V^7 or V^7/IV is the same pitch as the root of the German sixth chord.

Assignment 8.7. Harmonic Analysis.   Each of these examples contains a modulation in which an augmented sixth chord is a pivot. Remember that there are two spellings for such a pivot, one for the old key and a different one for the new key, and that ordinarily only one spelling will be found in the music. As part of your analysis, spell the pivot in both keys.

Mendelssohn, Piano Trio in D Minor, Op. 49
third movement (piano score only)

Beethoven, Sonata for Cello and Piano, Op. 102, No. 1,
first movement

Mussorgsky, *Boris Gudonov*,
Act III, Scene 1

Schubert, Symphony in B Minor, "Unfinished,"'
D. 759, second movement

Mozart, Sonata for Violin and Piano, K. 454, second movement

Application

Written Materials

The writing of an augmented sixth chord is based upon the approach and resolution of the interval of the augmented sixth.

Approach by step. Most frequently, each note of the interval is approached by whole step, by half step, or by same note. Oblique motion and contrary motion in approaching and leaving the interval are, as might be expected, most common, while similar motion is sometimes useful.

Fig. 8.35

Approach by leap. The lower note of the interval may be approached by leap from the tonic note (see Figures 8.7 and 8.8). The upper note may be approached by leap occasionally (see Figure 8.11). Both voices are not approached by leap at the same time.

Resolution. The interval of the augmented sixth resolves outwards to the octave.

Exceptional practices may be summarized as follows:

a) The interval of the diminished third resolves to the unison (see Figure 8.17).

b) The progression Gr6-V always produces perfect parallel fifths. Earlier composers usually employed the It6 when progressing to V (see Figure 8.1); with the Gr6, some evasive device was used such as is shown in Figure 8.7, where the tone located a fifth above the bass moves quickly to a tone a third above the bass, creating an Italian sixth of very short duration. Late nineteenth-century composers allowed the parallel fifths to stand (see Figure 8.23).

c) Members of the augmented seventh chord are so arranged that the interval of the augmented sixth is present, and this interval resolves normally (review Figures 8.26 to 8.28). The chord of resolution will contain a doubled third.

In the four-note chords (German and French sixths) no tone is doubled or omitted. In the three-note chord (Italian sixth), the fifth of the triad is doubled, since the root and third comprise the interval of the augmented sixth.

Assignment 8.8. Part-Writing Augmented Sixth Chords. These exercises contain examples of the conventional augmented sixth chords and the German sixth with alternate spelling, as described on page 223. Fill in inner voices and make harmonic analysis below the staff.

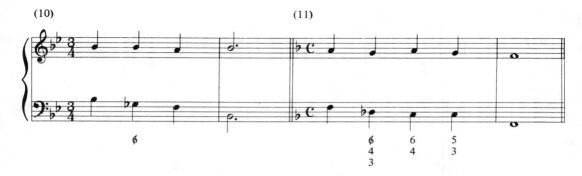

Assignment 8.9. Part-Writing Augmented Sixth Chords.

Assignment 8.9. Part-Writing Augmented Sixth Chords. These exercises contain examples of those varieties of augmented sixth chords described on pages 224–228. Fill in inner voices and make harmonic analysis below the staff.

Assignment 8.10. Part-Writing Augmented Sixth Chords: 1–4 Soprano and Bass Given; 5–6 Bass Only Given. These exercises contain representative examples from all the augmented sixth chords. Complete missing voices and make harmonic analysis below the staff.

Assignment 8.11. Melody Harmonization. The following melodies are taken from songs by Franz Schubert and can be found in Volume One of the songs (C. F. Peters edition or G. Schirmer edition) as follows:

a) *Die Winterreise,* "Rast," D. 911, measures 26–31.

b) *Die Winterreise,* "Der Wegweiser," D.911, last line of melody.

c) Ständchen, "Horch, horch, die Lerch," D.889, measures 23–30.

d) Der Wanderer, D.493, last line of melody.

Harmonize each melody with piano accompaniment, using an augmented sixth chord at some point. Compare your results with Schubert's accompaniment.

Assignment 8.12. Part-Writing. In these examples, the German sixth chord is used as a pivot in a modulation. Be sure to describe the function of the pivot chord in both keys.

Assignment 8.13. Writing Modulations Using the German Sixth Chord as a Pivot. Write in four parts the chords given and continue to a cadence in an appropriate key. In most cases, there will be a choice of reaching either a major key or its parallel minor key. Write each in several keys, as assigned.

For practice, write the pivot as spelled in both keys, shown in Figure 8.30 and in Assignment 8.12 (1) and (3).

a) i V VI Gr6 = V⁷ - - -
   I V vi Gr6 = V⁷ - - -

b) i V i V⁷/iv = Gr6 - - -
   I V I V⁷/IV = Gr6 - - -

c) i iv V⁷ = Gr6 - - -
   I IV V⁷ = Gr6 - - -

Ear Training

The interval of the augmented sixth is enharmonic with the interval of the minor seventh (Figure 8.36*a*). In listening to chords containing the interval of the augmented sixth, confusion with chords containing the interval of the minor seventh may easily result. This is particularly true in the case of the Italian and German sixth chords, each of which has a sound enharmonic with a major-minor seventh chord (Figure 8.36*b* and *c*).

Fig. 8.36

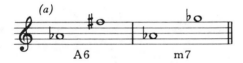

Less confusion exists with the French sixth because of the dissonant character of the sonority caused by the presence of both a major third and an augmented fourth above the bass note.

Differentiation between the augmented sixth chord sound and the major-minor seventh chord can be made by listening to the resolution of the interval in question. If the interval is an augmented sixth, the upper tone will progress *up* by half step. If the interval is a minor seventh, the upper note will progress *down* by half step.

Exercise 8.1. Singing the Interval of the Augmented Sixth. *a)* Sing, using letter names, the interval of a minor seventh; then sing the same interval with the spelling of an augmented sixth.

Fig. 8.37

b) Sing intervals as in *a* above, and add the resolution of each interval.

Fig. 8.38

Sing: D   C   D   B   D   B♯ C♯ C♯

Exercise 8.2. Singing Augmented Sixth Chords. *a)* Sing, using letter names, each of the three augmented sixth chords. Instead of singing from the root, as has been done previously, sing these chords from the bass tone usually found in an augmented sixth chord—sixth scale step in minor and lowered sixth scale step in major.

Fig. 8.39

A minor

Sing: F   A   C   D♯   C   A   F   F   A   D♯   A   F

F   A   B   D♯   B   A   F

b) Sing augmented sixth chords as in *a* above, but follow each chord with the dominant chord or tonic six-four, as directed, for example:

Fig. 8.40

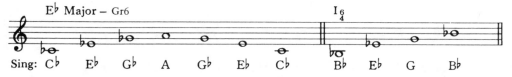

Sing: C♭   E♭   G♭   A   G♭   E♭   C♭   B♭   E♭   G   B♭

Exercise 8.3. Harmonic Dictation. Exercises in harmonic dictation will now include examples of augmented sixth chords. The following points will be helpful in identifying augmented sixth chords.

a) The German sixth sound is enharmonic with that of a complete major-minor seventh chord. Listen for the resolution of the interval of the augmented sixth. When this interval resolves out to the octave on the dominant, the chord is the Gr6.

When the outward resolution is to some tone other than the dominant, the Gr6 is spelled (in thirds) on the scale step below the note of resolution. For example, if the augmented sixth interval resolves to tonic, the chord is spelled in thirds from the seventh scale step.

b) The Italian sixth sound is enharmonic with that of an incomplete major-minor seventh chord with its fifth missing. Otherwise, its identification is identical to that of the Gr6.

c) The French sixth has a dissonant sound comparable to no other chord. A chord containing an interval of an augmented sixth and which does not sound enharmonic with a major-minor seventh chord is a French sixth. When the interval of the augmented sixth resolves out to the dominant tone, the chord is a Fr6. When it resolves to some other tone, the chord is spelled (in thirds) on a note a fifth above the note of resolution.

Exercise 8.4. Harmonic Dictation, Using the Gr6 as a Pivot.   Listen for a major minor seventh chord sound which does not function as a V^7 or a V^7/IV in one of the keys.

Keyboard Harmony

Exercise 8.5. Playing Augmented Sixth Chords at the Keyboard.   Follow this procedure.

a) Choose a key and a particular augmented sixth chord.

b) Spell the augmented sixth chord in the chosen key.

c) With the left hand, play the sixth scale degree (minor key) or lowered sixth scale degree (major key).

d) Play the remaining members of the chord with the right hand in any soprano position. Follow doubling rules stated on page 242.

Fig. 8.41

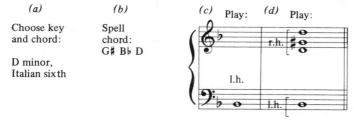

Exercise 8.6.   Play these basic progressions in each minor key. Also, (1) play each in each major key, substituting I for i, and (2) play any of these, with the opening tonic triad in the position of the third or fifth.

Fig. 8.42

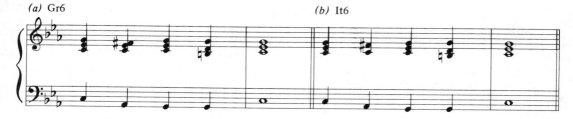

(c) Fr6

Exercise 8.7. Play the following progressions in keys as assigned. Each exercise contains a German sixth chord. Replay each exercise twice, substituting an Italian sixth and a French sixth in successive playings.

Minor keys

i VI Gr6 i$_4^6$ V i

i VI^7 Gr6 i$_4^6$ V i

i iv$_6$ Gr6 i$_4^6$ V i

i vii$_6^o$/V Gr6 i$_4^6$V i

i ii$_4^{\o}$ Gr6 i$_4^6$ V i
  $_3$

Major keys

I $^\flat$VI Gr6 I$_4^6$ V I

I IV$_6$ Gr6 I$_4^6$ V I

I iv$_6$ Gr6 I$_4^6$ V I

I vii$_6^o$ V Gr6 I$_4^6$ V I

I ii$_4$ Gr6 I$_4^6$ V I
  $_3$

Exercise 8.8. Play at the keyboard examples from Assignments 8.8 and 8.9.

Exercise 8.9. Harmonize the following melodic excerpts at the keyboard.

Exercise 8.10. Play at the keyboard in any major or minor key the progressions listed in Assignment 8.12 (modulations using the Gr6 chord as the pivot).

CHAPTER NINE

Chords of the Ninth, Eleventh, and Thirteenth

Theory and Analysis

The principle of chord construction by the addition of thirds can be continued past the triad and the seventh chord to include the ninth chord, the eleventh chord, and the thirteenth chord. Chords of greater complexity are not possible, since the fifteenth above a given note is simply a repetition of the given root two octaves higher.

Fig. 9.1

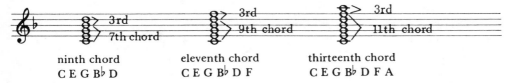

ninth chord   eleventh chord   thirteenth chord

C E G B♭ D   C E G B♭ D F   C E G B♭ D F A

Chords of the Ninth

Ninth chords of dominant and secondary dominant function are those most commonly used. Each consists of a major-minor seventh chord plus a ninth above the root. They are symbolized V^9, V^9/V, and so forth, the "9" indicating that the ninth above the root is *diatonic in the key* (Figure 9.2a, e, f). When the ninth is chromatically lowered, a typical symbol is $V^{♭9}$ (Figure 9.2b, c). Other types of ninth chords are far less frequent; two representative examples are shown as Figure 9.2d and g.

Fig. 9.2

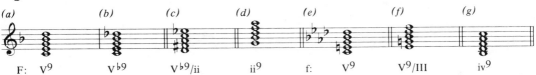

(a)   (b)   (c)   (d)   (e)   (f)   (g)

F: V^9 $V^{♭9}$ $V^{♭9}/ii$ ii^9 f: V^9 V^9/III iv^9

Assignment 9.1.   Spell the V^9 and the $V^{\flat 9}$ in each major key, and the V^9 in each minor key. Spell other ninth chords as assigned.

The ninth chord contains two dissonances, a ninth and a seventh above the root of the chord. These are treated in the same manner as already described for the seventh of a seventh chord, that is, each of these tones is introduced as a nonharmonic tone figure (passing tone, upper neighbor, suspension, or appoggiatura from below) and then resolves downwards as in Figure 9.3. Note that in four-part writing, there is an omitted note, usually the fifth or infrequently, the third.

Fig. 9.3

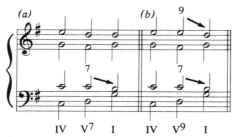

In the following discussion, ninth chords will be grouped according to the treatment of the ninth. Illustrations of particular ninth chords can be found in these figures:

Major keys	*Minor keys*
V^9, Figures 9.13, 9.14	V^9, Figures 9.5, 9.6
$V^{\flat 9}$, Figure 9.17	iv^9, Figure 9.7
$V^{\flat 9}$/ii, Figure 9.17	IV^9, Figure 9.8
V^9/iii, Figure 9.17	
V^9/IV, Figure 9.11	
V^9/V, Figures 9.10, 9.15	
V^9/vi, Figure 9.16	
ii^9, Figure 9.9	

Ninth Chords in Which the Ninth Resolves Before a Change of Chord   It is in this form that the ninth chord is most frequently found. When the ninth resolves to the octave, a seventh chord over the same root remains. This "premature" resolution is identical to that described in the discussion of the diminished seventh chord (review page 26). Analysis of this sonority as a seventh chord above which is located a nonharmonic tone is often preferable to analysis as a ninth chord, as in Figure 9.4, where at the accent (➔), the C♮ over B D♯ F♯ A can easily be considered an upper neighbor tone.

Fig. 9.4

When the ninth is held or repeated, a stronger feeling for an independent ninth chord may result, as in Figure 9.5, where six repetitions of the ninth precede its resolution to the root of V^7. As emphasis on the ninth increases, analysis as a ninth chord becomes more likely, but in any case, the decision is a subjective one at best.

Observe also in Figure 9.5 the N_5^6, created by the note E suspended from the previous chord and resolving to D♯ in measure 280.

Fig. 9.5

Beethoven, Symphony No. 3, Op. 55,
first movement

Ninth Chords in which the Ninth Resolves Simultaneously with the Chord Change. Analysis of a sonority as a ninth chord is more secure when the ninth resolves with a change of harmony. The examples following show a variety of approaches to the ninth: upper neighbor (Figures 9.7 and 9.9), suspension (Figure 9.8), appoggiatura (Figure 9.10), and passing tone (Figure 9.11). The first example, Figure 9.6, shows no note of approach because the ninth chord is the first chord of the phrase.

Fig. 9.6

The following two figures demonstrate the iv^9 and IV^9 in minor keys, the difference in the triad determined by the direction of the sixth scale step. Note also the double suspension to introduce the ninth and seventh of the IV^9.

Fig. 9.7

[1]K., when used with a work by Domenico Scarlatti, refers to the numbering system by Ralph Kirkpatrick.

Fig. 9.8

The ii⁹ of Figure 9.9 though nondominant, acts as a kind of embellishing chord to the dominant triad.

Fig. 9.9

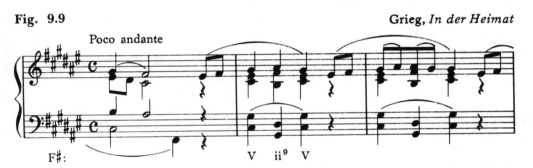

The ninth chords in each of the next two figures are examples of this sonority used as a secondary dominant function, V^9/V and V^9/IV.

Fig. 9.10

Fig. 9.11

Chopin, Nocturne, Op. 72, No. 1

Ninth Chords in which the Ninth and Seventh are Arpeggiated. The ninth may be resolved by leap to the seventh, 9–7, Figure 9.12*a,* or via a passing tone to the seventh, 9–8–7, Figure 9.12*b.*

Fig. 9.12

Figures 9.13 and 9.14 illustrate the leap 9–7. The ninth chord of the latter figure is shown in first inversion, a comparatively rare occurrence.

Fig. 9.13

Wagner, *Goetterdaemerung,* Act III

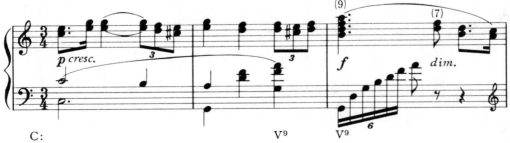

Fig. 9.14

Dvořák, Quartet, Op. 105, third movement

The pattern 9–8–7, accompanied by another voice a third lower, 7–6–5, is shown in Figure 9.15.

Fig. 9.15

Brahms, Symphony No. 2, second movement

Irregular Resolution of the Ninth. Assuming the normal resolution of the ninth to be down by step, resolutions are occasionally found in which the ninth proceeds in some other way. In Figure 9.16, the ninth, D, resolves up by step. The use of this chord in third inversion is quite rare.

Fig. 9.16

Tschaikowski, *The Nutcracker,* "Overture"

Ninth Chords in Sequence.   When found in sequence, ninth chords and seventh chords are usually found alternately. Use of sequence allows the presence of ninth chords not ordinarily encountered, such as the V^9/ii and the V^9/iii seen in Figure 9.17.

Fig. 9.17

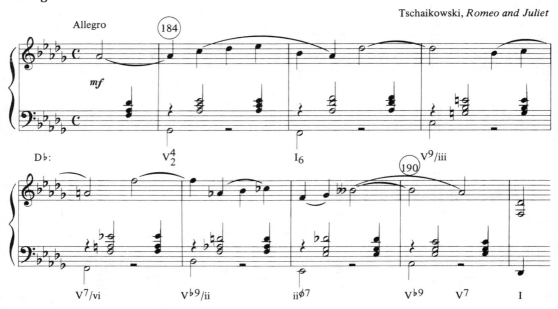

Tschaikowski, *Romeo and Juliet*

Eleventh and Thirteenth Chords

Chords of the eleventh containing a ninth and chords of the thirteenth containing an additional ninth or eleventh are comparatively rare. Most vertical sonorities containing an eleventh or thirteenth above the bass will prove to be simply a triad or seventh chord above which is a nonharmonic tone.

A sonority can more accurately be called an eleventh chord when the ninth is also present. Similarly, the thirteenth chord should also display either the ninth or eleventh. But even when a sonority is more positively identifiable as an eleventh or thirteenth chord, the dissonances in each almost invariably resolve while the root of the chord is being held ("premature" resolution), so that at the time of a change of root, only a more simple sonority, seventh or ninth, remains. Under these circumstances, it is difficult to assume the existence of any eleventh or thirteenth chord, when the simpler analysis of seventh or ninth chord plus dissonance is available.

Fig. 9.18

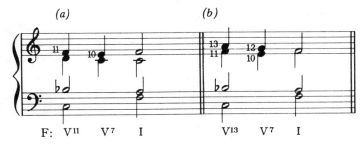

Assuming, however, the existence of these chords, their properties can be examined. In the eleventh chord, the third is omitted since this note is the eleventh's note of resolution (Part-writing Rule 8), as in Figure 9.18a and b, in Figure 9.19, and in measure 451 of Figure 9.20.

Fig. 9.19

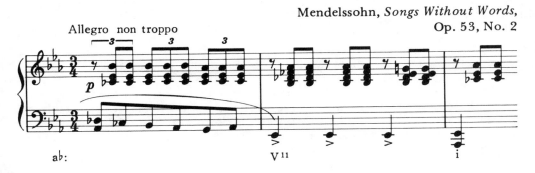

Mendelssohn, *Songs Without Words,*
Op. 53, No. 2

Fig. 9.20

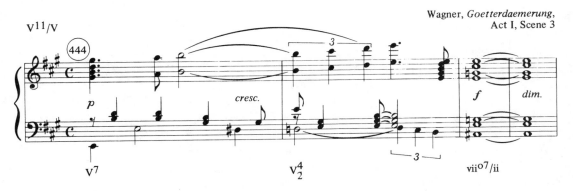

Wagner, *Goetterdaemerung,*
Act I, Scene 3

In the eleventh chord, the interval between the ninth and the eleventh may be either a third or a tenth. When the interval is a third, both the eleventh and ninth resolve down by step to a seventh chord, as in Figure 9.18a and Figure 9.19. When the interval is a tenth, the eleventh may resolve down by step, leaving a ninth chord, as in Figure 9.21.

Fig. 9.21

Duparc, *Soupir*

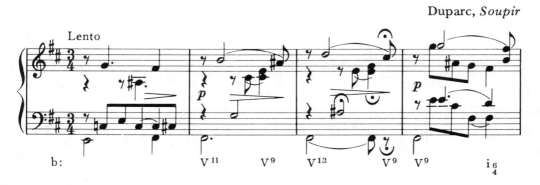

In the thirteenth chord, either the ninth or the seventh and the ninth together are usually present. In Figure 9.18b, the simultaneous resolution of the thirteenth and the eleventh produces a simple V^7 chord. The resolution of the thirteenth in Figure 9.21 leaves a V^9 sonority. In Figure 9.22, where the seventh, ninth, eleventh, and thirteenth sound simultaneously, the eleventh and thirteenth resolve in succession, leaving again a V^9 chord.

Fig. 9.22

Chopin, Nocturne, Op. 62, No. 1

Assignment 9.2. Harmonic Analysis. Analyze these examples for ninth chords, explaining the approach to and departure from the ninth. Try to determine whether the ninth acts more as a nonharmonic tone or a true chord tone.

(1)

Schumann, *Dichterliebe,* Op. 48, "Ich grolle nicht"

Brahms, Romance, Op. 118, No. 5

(5) Andante

Franck, *Symphonic Variations*

(6) Poco allegro

Mozart, Sonata in E♭ Major for Violin and Piano, K. 380,
second movement

(7) Andante

(8)

Schubert, Quartet in D Minor,
"Death and the Maiden," D. 810
Scherzo

Application

Written Materials

The ninth of the ninth chord is usually introduced and resolved in the manner of a nonharmonic tone. It usually resolves down, either stepwise or by skip to the seventh of the chord, and is introduced in one of five ways.

a) As a passing tone figure—See Figure 9.11.
b) As a suspension—See Figures 9.8 and 9.15.
c) As a neighboring tone—See Figures 9.7, 9.9, and 9.14.
d) As an appoggiatura, with skip from below—See Figures 9.10 and 9.13.

    Some attention must be given to placement of chord members in the vertical structure.
    a) The ninth of the chord is most often found in the soprano (highest) voice. This is particularly true in ninth chords other than V^9.
    b) The ninth is found at the interval of at least a ninth (rather than a second) above the root of the chord.
    c) When the ninth is not the highest note, the third of the chord is almost invariably lower than the ninth (see Figure 9.6).
    d) Examples of the chord with a note other than the root in the bass are uncommon (see Figure 9.14, third in bass, and Figure 9.16, seventh in bass).

Assignment 9.3. Writing Ninth Chords.   These may be done for practice in four-voice chorale style, as illustrated in Figure 9.23, and in keyboard style, using Figures 9.7–9.11 for examples.

Fig. 9.23

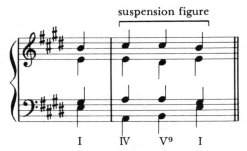

suspension figure

I   IV   V^9 I

Write the following progressions in keys, as assigned, paying particular attention to introduction of the ninth, resolution of ninth, and placement of the third and ninth of the chord.

The ninth introduced as a suspension:

I IV V^9 I   i iv V^9 i
I iv ii^9 V^7 I   i iv^9 V^7 i
I vi V^9/V V I   i IV^9 V^7 i
I $\flat$VI V$\flat^9$/V V I
I iv V$\flat^9$ V I

The ninth introduced as a passing tone:

I V^9/IV IV V I   i V^9/iv iv V i

The ninth introduced as a neighbor tone:

I V^9 I   i V^9 i

The ninth introduced as an appoggiatura:

I V V^9 I   i V V^9 i
I vi ii^9 V I   i iv^9 V^7 i
I V^9/V V I   i V^9/V V i

Keyboard Harmony

Exercise 9.1.   Play at the keyboard the progressions listed in Assignment 9.3. In the ninth chords, the fifth may be omitted for ease in playing, as in Figure 9.24.

Fig. 9.24

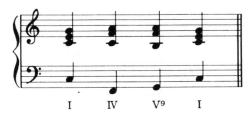

I   IV   V⁹   I

Exercise 9.2. Play diatonic harmonic sequences in major keys (Figure 9.25*a* and *b* , alternating ninth chords and seventh chords. Play in other major keys as directed.

Fig. 9.25

Exercise 9.3. continues below.

Exercise 9.3. Play the sequences of Exercise 9.2, but experiment by changing diatonic ninth chords to secondary ninth chords and/or lowering the ninth in those chords in which the diatonic resolution of the ninth is a whole step. Altered versions of the seventh chords may be included. Figure 9.26 is one possible variation of Figure 9.25*a*. Also, review the sequence in Figure 9.17.

Exercise 9.4. Play harmonic sequences in minor keys.

a) In diatonic sequences the sixth and seventh scale steps are always lowered, except at the V-i cadence (Figure 9.27).

b) A diatonic ninth chord may be altered to become a secondary dominant. The raised third may descend by chromatic half step, as in the secondary dominant triads and seventh chords. The ninth of a secondary dominant ninth chord may be lowered a half step when its normal resolution is a whole step (Figure 9.28).

Fig. 9.26

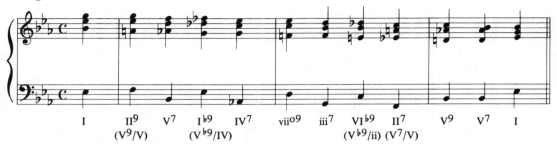

I II⁹ V⁷ I♭⁹ IV⁷ vii°⁹ iii⁷ VI♭⁹ II⁷ V⁹ V⁷ I
(V⁹/V) (V♭⁹/IV) (V♭⁹/ii) (V⁷/V)

Fig. 9.27

(a)

i iv⁹ VII⁷ III⁹ VI⁷ ii⌀⁹ V⁷ i ii⌀⁹ v⁷ i⁹ ---

(b)

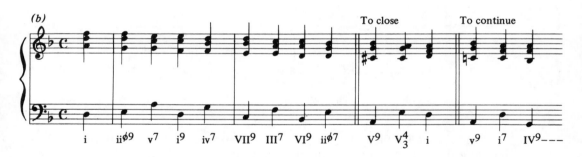

i ii⌀⁹ v⁷ i⁹ iv⁷ VII⁹ III⁷ VI⁹ ii⌀⁷ V⁹ V⁴₃ i v⁹ i⁷ IV⁹ ---

Fig. 9.28

i II⁹ v⁷ I♭⁹ IV⁷ VII♭⁹ ---
(V⁹/V) (V♭⁹/iv) (V♭⁹/II)

CHAPTER TEN

Unclassified Chord Structures and Complex Harmonic Progressions

Individual Less Common Altered Chords

Infrequently used diatonic chord structures and chord progressions were studied in Chapter 4. Individual altered chords other than those previously presented are also occasionally encountered. Such chords, and the progressions in which they are involved, can be evaluated only by their musical effectiveness in their particular musical contexts.

In Figure 10.1, the progression in A major, ii-♭VII-V/V, involves the lowered leading tone and is therefore suggestive of a key change, though no cadence in a new key ever appears.

Fig. 10.1

♭VII, major key

Haydn, *The Creation*, No. 3

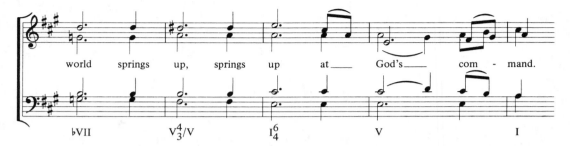

Figure 10.2 is an entirely different situation, where two triads, roots a tri-tone apart, are sounded antiphonally. The concurrent alternation of the triads i and ♭V together with the alternation of strings and brass was obviously written for its dramatic effect.

Fig. 10.2

Berlioz, *Symphonie Fantastique*, Op. 14,
fourth movement

The common harmonic sequence, roots up a fourth and down a fifth, produces a vii (minor) triad in a major key as shown in Figure 10.3. The usual IV-vii° of the sequence has been changed to V⁷/vii (♯IV⁷)-vii. The use of a secondary dominant to precede a chord built on the leading tone requires that the leading tone chord be other than diminished. The secondary dominant here establishes a legitimacy for the subsequent vii triad.

Fig. 10.3

Schumann, *Liederkreis*, Op. 39, "Waldesgespräch"

Complex Harmonic Progressions

Occurrences of less common chord progressions, as well as of individual chords, will also occasionally be encountered. These progressions, difficult to evaluate by any single analytical procedure, usually can be explained through analysis combining two or more of these already familiar devices:

1. Harmonic sequence
2. First inversions in series
3. Secondary tonal levels
4. Change of mode
5. Enharmonicism

Chord Functions Produced by Sequence and Enharmonicism

The sequence of Figure 10.4 begins and ends with the tonic of A♭ major. The sequential root movement encompasses three chords, roots up a third and down a second, beginning on the note A♭, and repeated on G♭ and F♭. Among the resulting chords are ♭III and ♭VII in a major key. More appropriate is analysis using secondary tonal levels, as shown in the lower analysis in the musical example. The chord numbers below the line reveal the first three notes of a descending minor scale line (8-♭7-♭6), continuing with the borrowed iv triad before the V-I close in major.

Fig. 10.4

Fauré, *Requiem*,
"Agnus Dei"

Chords Produced by Sequence and by Change of Mode

The music of Figure 10.5 begins and ends in C major and displays the common harmonic sequence, roots up a fourth and down a fifth. The sequence is altered by change of mode immediately after the opening tonic triad when its root is held over as a suspension, over which is the Neapolitan triad, forming an N$^4_2$ chord. The change of mode continues to the V-I cadence and includes a v$^{\varnothing 7}$ chord, rarely seen elsewhere. In this example, the lower clef is the left hand part for the piano. The omitted right hand part consists of arpeggiation of the chords shown.

Fig. 10.5

Mozart, Concerto for Piano and Orchestra,
K. 503, first movement

The example by Brahms, Figure 10.6, using the same principle, is somewhat more complex. To aid in our analysis, we will consider the diminished seventh chord as an incomplete V^9, as discussed in Chapter 2, page 36. Adding the "missing roots" to the diminished seventh chords F#A C E♭ and D F A♭ C♭ results in implied roots of D and B♭, respectively.

Our excerpt begins with iv-V in G minor. The sequence begins on the next chord, with roots moving down a fifth and up a third. The implied roots are marked * in this root movement chart and in the analysis below the music.

D* 5↓ g 3↑ B♭* 5↓ (E♭)e♭ 3↑ (G♭) F♯ 5↓ b 3↑ D 5↓ g

Note that the upward root movement is consistently a *minor third*, so that e♭ moves to (G♭) F♯ instead of G of the key. This produces a V^7/♯iii- ♯iii of G major, a change of mode from *minor* to *major*. Now observe the violin line: it is a whole tone scale[1], A♭(G♯) F♯ E D C B♭, made possible by the harmonic manipulation. Did Brahms write the harmony to fit the scale or was the scale a byproduct of the harmony? There is no way, of course, to answer this question with certainty.

Fig. 10.6

Brahms, Trio for Violin, Horn and Piano, Op. 40, first movement

Repeat of previous root movement

[1]The whole tone scale is a scale line made up entirely of whole steps. A note reaches its octave after five intervening scale steps, as in C D E F♯ (G♭) A♭ B♭ C.

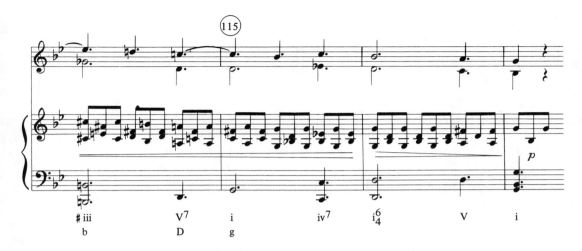

$\sharp$ iii   V⁷   i   iv⁷   i$^6_4$ V   i

b   D   g

The Interlocking Sequence

In the interlocking seqeunce, each unit of root movements is usually composed of three or more chords in which the last chord acts simultaneously as tonic of the unit and as a pivot to the next unit, such as

IV- V -I = IV-V -I = IV-*etc.*
F   G C   C D G   G

Fig. 10.7

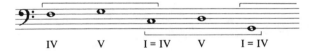

IV   V   I = IV   V   I = IV

Our example is slightly more complex as each tonic becomes alternately ii and IV: iv- V -i = ii- V-I = IV- V -i = ii-*etc.*
      f   G c   c F B♭   B♭ C f   f

Fig. 10.8

iv   V   i = ii   V   I = IV   V   I = ii etc.

Taken from a Prelude in C♯ major, our excerpt starts in A♯ minor, ending in F♯ major. We will use a secondary tonal analysis to help simplify a complex situation. The sequence begins on iv-V-i on a level of e♯; this i, e♯, equals ii of ii-V-i on the level of d♯, etc. In the diagram (Figure 10.9), the letters above the Roman numerals are chord roots, and the letters below the line are the roots of each of the temporary tonics.

Fig. 10.9

Measure	29	30	31		32	33		34	35		36	37	
Chord root	a#	E#	a#		a#	B#	e#		e#	A#	d#		d#	E#	a#
Analysis	i	V	i	=	iv	V	i	=	ii	V	i	=	iv	V	i	=
Root of I (i)	a#				e#				d#				a#		

	38	39		40	41		42	43		44	45		46	47
	a#	D#	G#		G#	A#	d#		d#	G#	C#		C#	D#	g#		g#	C#	F#
	ii	V	I	=	IV	V	i	=	ii	V	I	=	IV	V	I	=	ii	V	I
		G#				d#				C#				g#				F#

Upon completion of the analysis, we now look at the relationship of the temporary tonics (below the lines in Figure 10.9) and observe that they comprise a simple sequence, roots down a second and up a fifth:

e# ₂ d# ₅ a# ₂ G# ₅ d# *etc.*

Fig. 10.10

Bach, *Well-Tempered Clavier*, Vol. 1,
Prelude in C# Major

Secondary Tonal Level Combined with First Inversions in Series and with Change of Mode

Figure 10.11 is the opening of the first movement of Mozart's Quartet, K.465, which, because of these few measures, has been dubbed the "Dissonant" Quartet for its seemingly complex harmony. Analyzing this excerpt either in the key of its conclusion (C major) or the key of its first triad ($A\flat$ major) leads only to a series of unrelated Roman numerals. Looking ahead from measure 1, we find an imperfect authentic cadence on G_6 at measure 4, followed in measure 8 by a similar cadence on F_6. From here on, the harmony progresses as a series of first inversions, f_6-$E\flat_6$-d_6^0-c_6. Using these chords only, we find the series V_6-IV_6-iv_6-$\flat III_6$-ii_6^0-i_6, with a return from this series of borrowed chords to a V-I in C major. Thus it is logical to analyze measures 1–4 on the basis of its cadence on G. Doing so produces a straightforward progression on the level of V:

$$\frac{N_6\text{-}ii_{\substack{6\\5}}^{\emptyset}\text{-}V_2^4\text{-}I_6\text{-}V\text{-}I_6}{V_6}$$

followed immediately by the same progression on the level of IV_6.

Note particularly the dissonance at measure 3 where the three upper voices seem to outline an A C♯ E G chord. The G in the viola part definitely functions as a chord root, over which the A is a suspension and the C♯ a lower neighbor, the two dissonances being consonant with each other.

Fig. 10.11

Mozart, Quartet in C Major, K. 465, "Dissonant," first movement

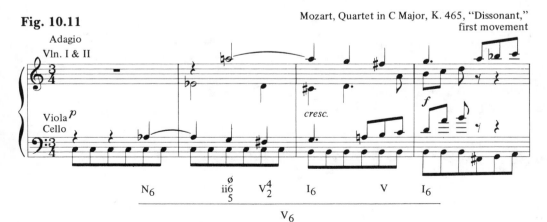

N6   ii⁰⁶₅ V⁴₂ I6   V   I6   iv6

IV6

♭III6   ii⁰⁶₆   i6   V⁷   I

Assignment 10.1. Harmonic Analysis. Each of these examples includes one or more features discussed in this chapter. Make harmonic analysis, including written commentary where necessary concerning multiple uses of analytical devices.

(1)

Schubert, Ländler in A♭ Minor, D. 790

(2) Andante con moto

Chopin, Ballade, No. 4, Op. 52

Bach, *Well-Tempered Clavier*, Vol. I,
Fugue No. 4

(3)

Brahms, *Romanzen aus Magelone*, Op. 33,
"Treue Liebe dauert lange"

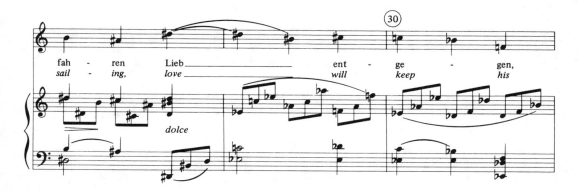

fah - ren   Lieb_____   ent - ge - gen,
sail - ing,   *love_____*   *will   keep   his*

treu - es_____ Blut.
loy - al_____ heart.

Und   wie   Ne - bel
Like   a   cloud   then

(5)

Graun, *Der Tod Jesu*, No. 2

(6) This next excerpt includes most of the development section of the sonata. It includes two principal analytical problems, measures 1-12 and 12 to the end. Consider measure 12 as a half cadence for the preceding measures, but at the same time, the tonic triad for the material beginning at this point.

Beginning at the third beat of measure 13, consider the tone C as a pedal tone against the diminished seventh chords until the end of measure 15. Use the same analysis in succeeding similar passages.

Compare the root movement of measures 24–28 with measures 28–32. Is this a variety of harmonic sequence, and if so, how would you describe it?

Beethoven, Sonata for Piano, Op. 53,
first movement

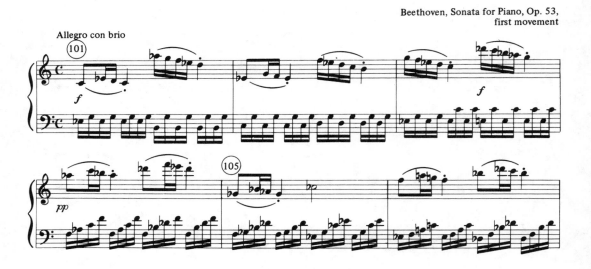

CHAPTER ELEVEN

The Close of the Nineteenth Century—
The Beginning of New Directions

Review of Traditional Harmony

The compositional techniques of the historical period c.1650–c.1900 have been the subject of our study in this text and its preceding volume, *Elementary Harmony: Theory and Practice.* We have seen that no matter how each composer of this period differed from another in his particular style of writing, all were governed by certain concepts and practices, the body of which has come to be known as the common practice of the period. In review, the most important of these concepts and practices are:

1. *Tonality.* In every composition there is one tone which assumes more importance than the others, and to which the others are related. This phenomenon is emphasized by the almost exclusive use of V-I progression (authentic cadence) at the close of a composition and its liberal use elsewhere.

2. *Scale systems.* Tonality in this period is expressed through two scale systems, major and minor, other scale systems of earlier times having fallen into disuse (review *Elementary Harmony,* pp. 303–307).

3. *Keys.* Each major and minor scale can be found on fifteen different pitch locations, called keys. These keys are systematized in two circles of fifths, one for major and one for minor.

4. *Chords.* Music of the common practice period is based upon the use of chords. A chord is defined as a simultaneous sounding of pitches spelled, usually, in major and minor thirds, the lowest note of these thirds being considered the root. Not all possible chord constructions in thirds were regularly used.

5. *Inversion.* A chord retains its identity whether or not the root is found as the lowest sounding voice.

6. *Chord succession.* The progression of one chord to another is based upon the movement of their roots, root movement by fifth being the most common. Certain progressions tended to become much more widely used than others, and not all possible root relationships within a key were regularly used. Chord suc-

cessions requiring the use of parallel fifths and/or octaves were carefully avoided.

7. *Nonharmonic tones.*   Tones not belonging to a chord may sound simultaneously with a chord structure. Such a dissonance must always be introduced and resolved in certain established ways.

8. *Melody.*   Melodic lines are so constructed that each tone will be part of a chord or an acceptable nonharmonic tone to that chord. A succession of melodic tones will usually imply an acceptable chord succession.

9. *Rhythm.*   Rhythmic patterns are usually organized into metric units of two, three, and four beats, the primary accent falling on the first beat of any metrical group. Any other accent in any melodic line is a syncopation against the primary accent.

10. *Harmonic rhythm.*   The rhythmic pattern created by the frequency of chord change conforms to the metric structures described in the preceding paragraph.

These, greatly generalized, are the basic concepts underlying the composition of music in the common practice period. Exceptions, though numerically quite frequent, actually represent only a very small percentage of the total output of the composers of the period. But this is not to imply that compositional techniques were stagnant and that no change in musical expression took place during this period of almost three hundred years. In any art form, in any science, in any institution, in life itself, change, for better or for worse, is the only constant known to human endeavor. The limitations listed above were subject to the attacks and inroads of change for the entire course of the historical period, so that by the end of the nineteenth century, no further change could take place within the style without destroying the style itself. True to predictable pressures of change, this is exactly what happened.

Of the basic concepts listed above, those concerning the sense of major and minor tonality bore the brunt of the early forces of change. The importance of the tonic was particularly subject to challenge. Composers, bound for centuries by the restrictions of a key and its closest relationships, now were breaking these bonds with a number of devices to postpone or to avoid achieving the harmonic goal and to lessen the influence of the tonic as the guiding tone of the composition. Although we have already encountered such devices in earlier composers, including the deceptive cadence, successive diminished seventh chords, direct modulations to remote keys, and less common root movements, the number and frequency of such evasive practices increase dramatically in the waning years of the nineteenth century. We will examine several such practices in this chapter.

Triads in Chromatic Third Relationship

Diatonic triads, roots a third apart, have two tones in common, for example, C E G-E G B. If one of the triads is altered to produce a different major or minor triad but with the same letter names or their enharmonic equivalents, in common, a chromatic third relationship results. Using C E G as an example, chord spellings in thirds are shown in Figure 11.1. These also include roots as spelled at the interval of the augmented second and diminished fourth, both of which are enharmonic with thirds.

Fig. 11.1

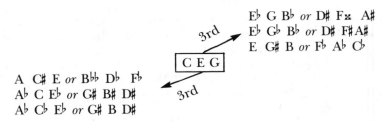

The use of this relationship is not original to the late nineteenth century. The music of Figure 11.2, a madrigal for five voices, is from the late sixteenth century, a short period of harmonic experimentation preceding the establishment of the conventional standards of the common practice period.

Fig. 11.2

Luzzasco Luzzaschi, *Quivi sospiri*

We have already seen this relationship in the use of the secondary dominant chord (Figure 1.1: I-A C♯ E to V⁷/vi-C♯E♯ G♯ B) and in a direct modulation (Figure 1.14: i in B♭ minor to i in F♯ minor). In Figure 11.3, the third relationship, A C♯ E-F A C initiates a passage on the secondary tonal level of F.

Fig. 11.3

Schubert, Sonata in A Major for Piano, D. 959, third movement, "Trio"

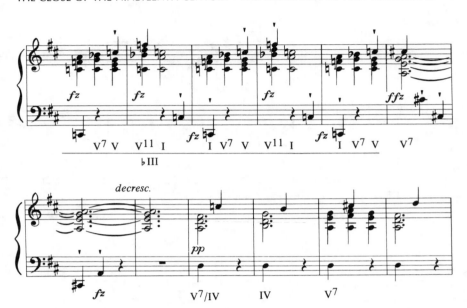

In the late nineteenth century, root movement by chromatic thirds is often used to create frequent changes of key, to cause delay in reaching the tonic, or to obscure the progress of the harmonic movement leading to the ultimate tonic cadence. This type of root movement is used in Figure 11.4 to mark off four separate short sections in as many keys: B♭, D, G♭, and B♭. The pitches of these successive tonics describe an augmented triad, though the tonic of D is preceded by the V of B♭, itself a root relationship by chromatic third, F A C to D F♯ A.

Fig. 11.4

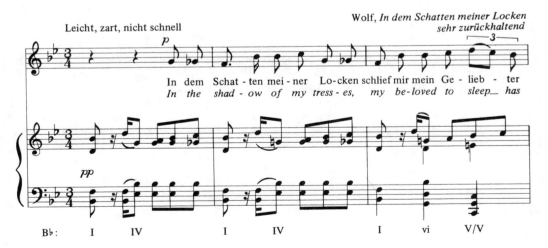

The opening measures of Figure 11.5 show the noncadential triad succession, E♭ G B♭-G♭ B♭ D♭-D F♯ A-G B D-E♭ G B♭, all but one by chromatic thirds. Note also in measure 17–20 the root progression E♭, D♭, C, moving towards a cadence in F major which never appears. The parallel movement of chords and the fifths in the inner voices suggest a similarity to examples of complete parallelism in the music of Debussy (presented in Chapter 12). Here, however, ties to traditional writing are maintained by the contrary motion in the outside voices.

Fig. 11.5

Wolf, *Mignon*

Root Movement by Tritone

Root movement by tritone has been seen in earlier music in such progressions as IV-vii°$_6$ and I-vii°$_6$/V, and, in a harmonic sequence, movement from root to root in the bass (review Figure 6.9 and following examples).

In other situations, root movement by tritone will often cause a sudden change in key orientation. Figure 11.6 opens with a harmonic sequence, down a tritone, up a fourth. The example contains one additional tritone movement, as well as a pair of seventh chords progressing by chromatic third (D F A♭ C-F A C E♭). The complete root movement, with tritones bracketed, is C-G♭-C♭-F-c-E♭-A-D° -F-B♭

Fig. 11.6

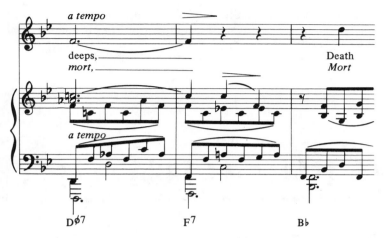

Reviewing Figure 10.2, the root movement by diminished fifth serves a different purpose. The antiphony between two different groups of instruments represents a coloristic and dramatic musical expression rather than two triads in a harmonic progression.

Evasion of Tonic

Music of the early common practice period is usually characterized by frequent reference to the tonic of the key, as in this Mozart example, where the tonic chord is sounded eight times in nine measures.

Fig. 11.7

Mozart, Sonata for Piano, K. 284

As time passed, composers continually sought freedom from the frequent return to the tonic. An example of one such attempt, the fifteen measures of Schumann's Sonata for Piano (Figure 11.8), shows no tonic chord between measures 2 and 15, and but one tonicized chord, IV, in measure 10.

Fig. 11.8

Music from the latter part of the century often is extended to even greater lengths, but usually by means of traditional devices, two examples of which follow.

Evasion of Tonic by Deceptive Cadence

Figure 11.9 shows evasion of tonic by deceptive cadence as a primary compositional device. Starting in E minor, the chord on the first strong beat seems to be ambiguous (E G B or C E G?) until the true intent, C E G, is shown in a later presentation of this theme at measure 29 (Figure 11.10). Each V or vii°⁷ of measures 1-10 progresses to the C E G sonority as a deceptive cadence, and no tonic appears until measure 36 where the B section of a ternary form begins.

Fig. 11.9

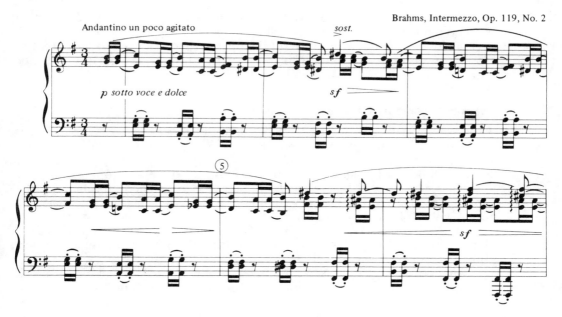

Fig. 11.10

Examination of the entire work is recommended to observe the contrasting B section in E major, which *does* contain tonic references, and the return to the A section continuing the procedures of the opening section, even to the extent of closing the entire composition with an imperfect rather than a perfect authentic cadence.

Evasion of Tonic by Chromatic Inflection

As in the preceding Brahms example, the music of Wagner in Figure 11.11 is made up of recognizable common harmonic progressions. In these passages, however, as few as two successive chords will imply a tonic (but without reaching a tonic), followed by similar short progressions on successive tonic levels. The movement of one such passage to the next is often accomplished by the modulatory process in which a pitch of one chord moves by chromatic half step to a member of the following chord. Measures 842–844 demonstrate the process. In the opening I-V of A♭ major, the G of E♭ G B♭ moves by chromatic alteration to G♭ of C♭ E♭ G♭, VI of E♭ minor, after which the music continues mostly in a similar manner throughout the excerpt.

Changes in implied keys, when not by chromatic pitch, are accomplished as *direct* change of key. No tonic chord is found after the opening I until measure

866, where a partial repetition of the opening of the passage is found. The result is a fluidity of tonic implications which precludes the establishment of any particular major or minor key.

In Figure 11.11, the arrows between Roman numerals indicate direct modulations, while the arrows below numerals indicate the two pitches of a half step chromatic alteration.

Fig. 11.11

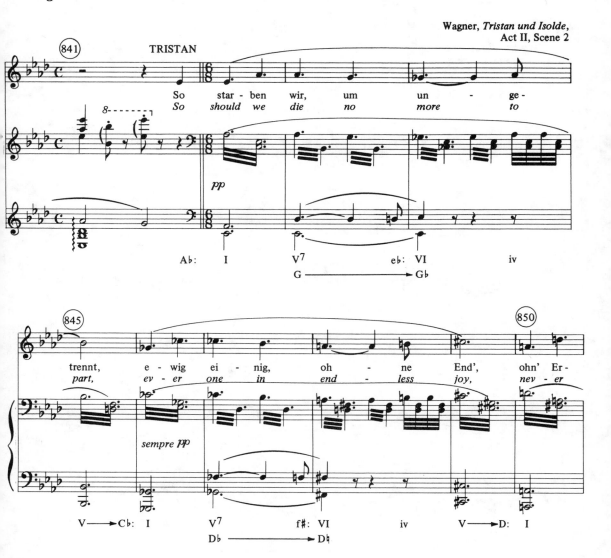

*The progression of the nonharmonic tone G to G♭ may be considered the chromatic half step modulatory link.

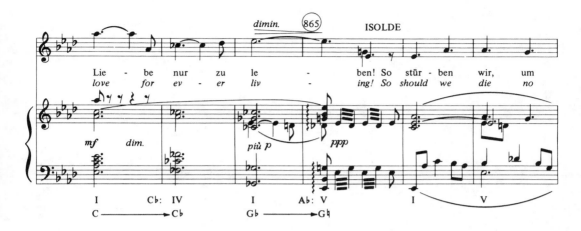

In addition to the processes of change of implied key, these procedures are also of interest:

1.

	Intervals of Root Movement	Intervals Between Actual or Implied Tonics
5th	6	2
3rd	7	7
2nd	10	1
Tritone	0	1

These figures show dramatically the departure from the use of the perfect fifth (fourth) as the principal interval between roots or tonics.

2. In root movements of a second, as in measures 845–846, parallel motion is avoided by placing the second of the two chords in second inversion, creating contrary motion between the outside voices.

It should be noted that *Tristan und Isolde,* finished in 1859, is not *late* nineteenth century music, but in spite of its early appearance, it is generally considered to represent the spirit and goals of the later progressive nineteenth century composers. Certainly it represents the ultimate accomplishment in avoiding tonic while at the same time operating within the tonal system of the common practice period.

Unconventional Root Movement

While chords built in thirds remained characteristic of the late nineteenth century, movements from chord to chord continually become freer, so that a composition might contain more exceptions than traditional progressions. In Figure 11.12, analysis by Roman numeral yields no meaningful results. A study of root movements reveals root movement by fifth to be only 7 of the total of 22, three of the remainder of which are by chromatic third, and three by tritone.

Fig. 11.12

Fauré, *La bonne chanson*, Op. 61,
"J'allais par des chemins perfides"

Indeterminate Tonic Implication

Figure 11.13, while appearing much simpler than several of the previous examples, is far more forward looking. While the examples of Brahms and Wagner demonstrate techniques which have reached their ultimate development, this short song by Mussorgsky includes features that anticipate styles of twentieth-century composition.

1.   The key signature of two sharps, with first and last bass notes on D, strongly implies D major. There is, however, only one implication of dominant harmony, the incomplete chord on A in measure 7 which resolves evasively.

2.   Much of the song includes progressions implying B♭ major. Again, there is only one dominant triad in this key, and it does not progress to its tonic.

3.   The modal inflection, E♮, in the implied key of B♭ occurs in measures 3–4 and 6.

4.   The series of first inversions, measures 9–10, between the E♭ and A♭ triads, ordinarily would produce these triads: E^b_6-d^o_6-c_6-B^b_6-A^b_6. With the use of the altered tones F♯ and B♮, the series becomes E^b_6-D_6-c_6-b_6-A^b_6.

5.   The work as a whole vacillates between the tonic centers of D and B♭, the two summed up in the final B♭ triad. The bass line of the last four measures implies a strong root progression in D, while the right-hand chord at the same time implies B♭. This is a rather remarkable instance of a single consonant triad implying two different tonal areas.

Fig. 11.13

Mussorgsky, *Sunless*,
"In the Crowd"

all.   I   first   felt   ex - alt - ed,   then   hum - bled,   So

high and   a - las, then so small.   It   all   hap - pened just   in   a   mo - ment,   but

told   me   the whole sor - ry   plot,   How   bliss - ful   it   was   while   it

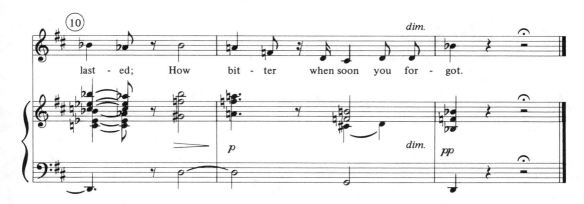

last - ed; How bit - ter when soon you for - got.

With the works of Wagner, Brahms, Wolf, and others of the late nineteenth century, the common practice period comes to an historical close. But contemporary with them were young composers such as Claude Debussy with new, fresh concepts of music composition, whose procedures will be covered beginning in the next chapter.

Even so, music based on the principles and techniques of the common practice period lived on in many composers, their musical styles often incorporating many of the newer ideas. Composers relying heavily on the old common practice principles are often known as "post romantic" composers. Among these are many famous names, including Mahler, de Falla, Rachmaninoff, Sibelius, and Richard Strauss. A group of songs by the latter for voice and orchestra, now usually titled *Four Last Songs,* written in 1948, is probably the final major composition strongly tied to the romantic tradition.

Assignment 11.1. Harmonic Analysis. Analyze the following excerpts, particularly for the devices described in this chapter. Use Roman numeral symbols where helpful; otherwise, describe in prose or verbally the principles governing the harmonic movement.

(1) The first excerpt is the piano reduction of the orchestral accompaniment to a very florid solo piano passage. At each asterisk, a two-measure repetition occurs in the original score.

Liszt, Concerto No. 2 for Piano

Franck, Prelude, Chorale, and Fugue
for Piano, "Chorale"

Wagner, *Tristan und Isolde,*
Act III, Scene 2

(4) In the following excerpt,

a) listen to measure one. Is the aural effect of the first three chords that of successive chromatic thirds? How is this effect actually achieved?

b) consider the triad after each diminished seventh chord as a tonic. How does the relationship of these tonics compare with that of Figure 11.4?

Wagner, *Die Walküre*, Act III, Scene 3,
"Magic Fire Music"

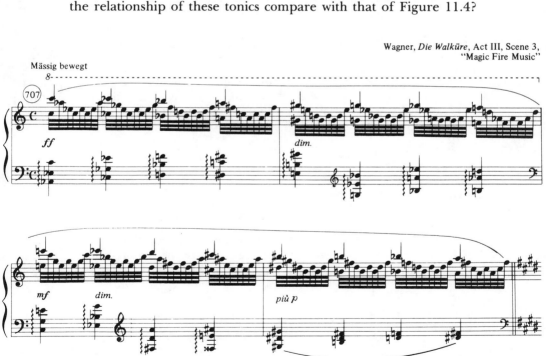

Assignment 11.2.   Spell chords in a chromatic third relationship to a given chord, using Figure 11.1 as an example. Spell chords from this list, or others as assigned.

D F♯ A,   B♭ D F,   D♭   F A♭,   F♯ A♯ C♯
F A♭ C,   E   G B,   G♯ B D♯,   B D F♯

Assignment 11.3.   Each bass note is the root of a major triad. Write in the three upper voices, continuing from those given. Use contrary motion between soprano and bass where possible.

Assignment 11.4.   Continue this sequence for about eight more chords. Roots move down an M3 and up an m3 (or enharmonically, down a d4 and up an A2, as needed). Use major or minor triads, as seem suitable.

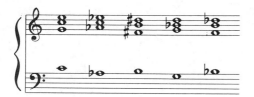

Assignment 11.5.   Continue this sequence, roots down a tritone, up a fourth. Conclude the sequence upon reaching the F♯ major triad.

Assignment 11.6.   *a)* The passage below is based on the progression I-V (or i-V) with the V progressing to the next triad by chromatic third, up or down. Continue this progression, bringing it to an authentic cadence several measures later.

b) Using this same passage, write a different conclusion by changing the direction of the root movement of the third at some point.

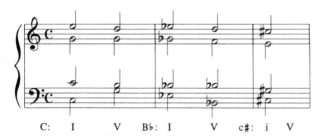

Assignment 11.7.   The passage below is that of Assignment 11.6 with nonharmonic tones added. Complete this example in a similar manner. Also, rewrite your solution(s) to Assignment 11.6*b* in this manner.

CHAPTER TWELVE

Debussy and Impressionism

Based on the date of his birth, study of the music of Debussy (1862–1918) could well have been incorporated in the previous chapter. However, the thirty-six years of his mature creative activity, beginning c. 1882, are divided exactly by the year 1900, and the nature of his creative accomplishments in breaking with nineteenth-century traditions demands that he be considered the first of the "modern" twentieth-century composers.

Impressionism

Debussy's compositional style is usually termed "Impressionism," a word borrowed from a school of French painters of that time, including Monet, Pissaro, Renoir, and others. The paintings of the impressionists avoid emphasis on the geometric or specific relationships of its subject matter; important is the expression of that illusive subjective feeling aroused in a mere momentary glimpse of the scene as portrayed on the canvas. Consequently, the artist may be primarily concerned with the interplay of light and reflection, of shadow and haze, and the many other elements one often disregards when viewing a scene objectively.

Though Debussy himself disclaimed that he was an "impressionist," his contemporaries felt that he achieved in music the characteristics of the impressionist paintings. In expressing a mood or conjuring up an atmosphere, Debussy follows the precept of Beethoven, who described his own *Pastoral Symphony* (the sixth) as, "More expression of feeling than tone-painting." Debussy's compositional style was accomplished in part through the introduction of an amazing number of new compositional practices, and in part through his rejection of many of the conventional devices of his early contemporaries, Brahms, Wagner, and others.

Tonality and Cadence Structure

There is no break with tonality in the music of Debussy. A key feeling is maintained though it is often vague, and at times missing for short periods by devices to be presented shortly (but never by the traditional series of diminished seventh chords). Frequent use of long pedal points on the tonic against more or less nonrelated progressions in the upper voices maintain tonal stability, as in Figures 12.2 and 12.3, much the same as in the Mussorgsky song in Figure 11.13.

Cadences are rarely simple V-I or IV-I progressions. These cadences, when employed, are usually camouflaged to diffuse the traditional positive cadential effect, as in this final cadence of Debussy's first known work, written at the age of fourteen.

Fig. 12.1

Observe the positive V-I of the cadential bass tones against which is sounded the progression V-iv-I+ preceding the final tonic.

A clearly stated V-I, when used, never includes a preceding tonic six-four, and its effect is weakened by some other closing progression. In the popular "Clair de lune" (from *Suite Bergamasque*), the "final" V-I is followed by seven measures using only the chords I, iii and ♭III, ending with ♭III₆-I (the third of ♭III is the dominant tone, so dominant-tonic appears in the bass).

The Whole Tone Scale

Debussy made extensive use of scales other than major and minor, both for use in melodic lines and as a basis for chord construction. One, the *whole tone scale,* equally divides the octave into six whole steps (Figure 12.2.).

Fig. 12.2

It is found in thirds in the upper clef of Figure 12.3, used contrapuntally against a single whole tone melodic line in the lower clef.

Fig. 12.3

Only two chords built in thirds can be derived from this scale, C E G♯ and D F♯ A♯. These are used in Figure 12.4 to accompany the melodic line first seen in Figure 12.3.

Fig. 12.4

One transposition only of this scale is available: C♭ D♭ E♭ F G A. In Figure 12.5, chords derived from this scale but not built in thirds are found as the double dotted eighth notes: D♭ E♭ A and C♭ D♭ G. The missing note, F, is prominently stated in the vocal line. The chords found as thirty-second notes preceding each whole tone chord are made up of notes "nonharmonic" to the whole tone scale.

Fig. 12.5

Debussy, *Trois Ballades de François Villon,*
"Ballade de Villon à s'ayme"

The Pentatonic Scale

The *pentatonic* (five-tone) scale is made up of the interval succession M2 - M2 - m3 - M2 - m 3, an easy example of which is the succession of black notes on the keyboard, Figure 12.6. Its use by Debussy is seen in Figure 12.7.

Fig. 12.6

(a)

Fig. 12.7

Debussy, *Préludes*, Book I, No. 2, "Voiles"

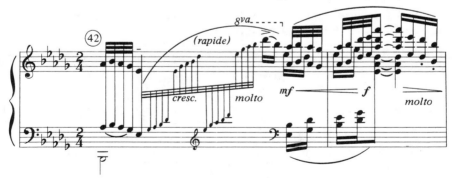

The Medieval Modes

Used infrequently since about 1650, modes other than major and minor became part of the Debussy style. Their use is not always obvious; complete compositions are not based on a given mode. Rather, one or several modes may be hinted at in short melodic fragments or in short chord successions during a composition. In Figure 12.8, the D♯ in a two-measure motive in A major provides the effect of the Lydian mode. Note also the harmonic progressions in chromatic thirds: F♯ A C♯-D F A in measure 1, and A C♯ E-C E♭ G in measures 2–3.

Fig. 12.8

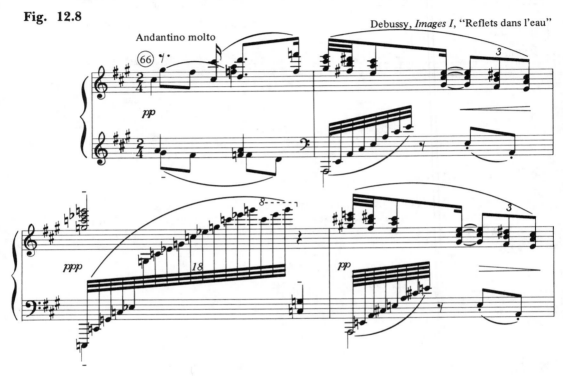

Debussy, *Images I*, "Reflets dans l'eau"

The Dorian scale, G♯ A♯ B C♯ D♯ E♯ F♯ G♯, is well defined in the progression leading to the final cadence of Figure 12.9.

Fig. 12.9

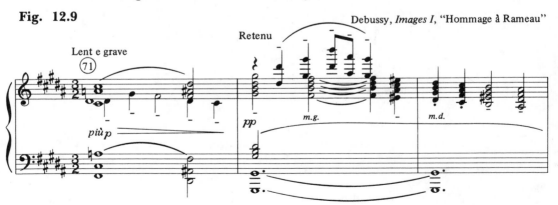

Debussy, *Images I*, "Hommage à Rameau"

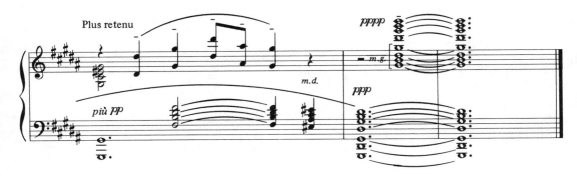

The complete Phrygian mode is the basis for the opening phrase of the
String Quartet.

Fig. 12.10

Debussy, Quartet for Strings, first movement

Animé et très décidé

Chords and Harmonic Progressions

Traditional chords built in thirds are commonly used, and these include all varieties from the triad through thirteenth chords. At the same time, a wide variety
of original sonorities, common in later music, first appear in the works of
Debussy. In either case, conventional root movement, as outlined in Table 12.1
of *Elementary Harmony* and Figure 4.1 of the present text, is almost nonexistent,
the few exceptions being passages of two to four chords. Chord types and methods of progression are so inextricably intertwined in most cases that they will be
discussed simultaneously.

Conventional Chords

Figure 12.11 shows a passage consisting of triads, and these with conventional
contrary motion between the outer parts. Yet the progression itself, I-iii-ii-I-
♭VII-IV-III-ii-I is most unconventional in common practice terms. Note also the
cadence treatment: the last two bass notes imply V-I during the arpeggiation of
the supertonic triad.

Fig. 12.11

Debussy, *Préludes*, Book II, No. 5,
"Bruyéres"

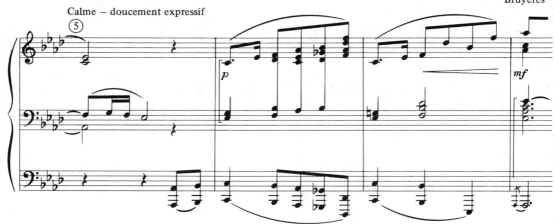

Still more unconventional is the use of the simple triads and seventh chords in extended parallelism, sometimes called "planing," as in Figures 12.12 and 12.13. In addition, note the use of progression by chromatic thirds—all of Figure 12.12 and the first measure of Figure 12.13. Also, review Figure 12.4 as an example of parallel augmented triads.

Fig. 12.12

Debussy, *Préludes*, Book I, No. 4, "Les sons et
les parfums tournent dans l'air du soir"

Fig. 12.13

Debussy, *Pour le Piano*, "Sarabande"

Parallelism is not limited to single types of chords in succession as Figure 12.14 shows. Further study of Debussy's music will show many different patterns of parallel motion, including uses of triads or larger chords in any inversion, or two sets of parallel chords in contrary motion to each other.

Fig. 12.14

Debussy, *Pelléas et Mélisande*,
Act III, Scene I

Quartal and Quintal Harmony; Added Tone Chords

In addition to tertian harmony (chords built in thirds), Debussy's music provides examples of quartal (fourth) and quintal (fifth) harmony. Figure 12.15 shows two chords in quartal harmony, B E A D, and D G C F, both with octave doubling in the upper voice.

Fig. 12.15

Debussy, *Pour le Piano*, "Sarabande"

Quintal harmony is shown on the bass staff of Figure 12.16*b* with the chords G D A and A E B. But there is another possible explanation of these sonorities. Chords in a similar passage in the first measure of the Prélude (Figure 12.16*a*) do not include the upper tones (A and B) of the quintal chords, leading to the conclusion that these may be *added tones* to the original progression. This use of fifths, however, is important as a precedent for its extensive use in the music of later composers.

Fig. 12.16

Debussy, *Préludes*, Book I, No. 10,
"La Cathedrale engloutie"

Triads with *added sixths* (example: C E G A) often appear, but it is usually difficult to determine whether the chord is really a first inversion of a seventh chord. There is no doubt about the chord A C# E F# in Figure 12.17, the final cadence chord[1] following the text, "The voice of our despair, the nightingale sings on."

Fig. 12.17

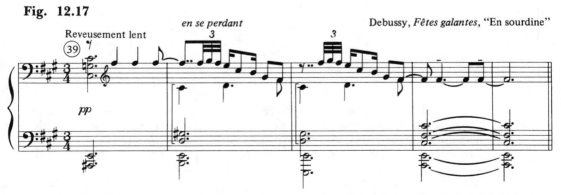

Debussy, *Fêtes galantes*, "En sourdine"

[1]An oft quoted example of an early use of this cadence is in the conclusion of Mahler's *Das Lied von der Erde (1908),* where it is held for seventeen measures to emphasize the effect of the vocal soloist's final word, "ewig" ("forever"). Debussy applied the same cadence eleven years earlier.

All the chords of Figure 12.18 are either added note chords or inversions of seventh chords in parallel motion. Since no seventh resolves as such, analysis as added note chords is plausible.

Fig. 12.18

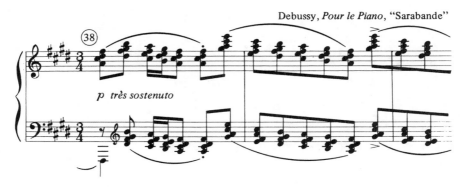

Debussy, *Pour le Piano*, "Sarabande"

The chords of Figure 12.5, described as derived from the whole tone scale, could also be considered chords with an added second, as D♭ E♭ A (implied D♭ F A with added E♭).

Tritones and Augmented Fifths

These intervals from earliest times have been considered unstable and their use has therefore been severely restricted.[2] The increased use of these intervals by Wagner is carried still further in the music of Debussy, where examination of almost any excerpt will demonstrate the greater frequency of their usage and the ultimate freedom in their movement, now without the requirement of a specific kind of resolution. Typical is the type of passage in Figure 12.19, where most of the chords contain tritones or augmented intervals.

Fig. 12.19

Debussy, *Pelléas et Mélisande*,*
Act IV, Scene 4

*The vocal line is omitted.

[2]Review the article, "The Devil in Music," in *Elementary Harmony*, pp. 275–278. A melodic example from Debussy's *Prelude to the Afternoon of a Faun* is included.

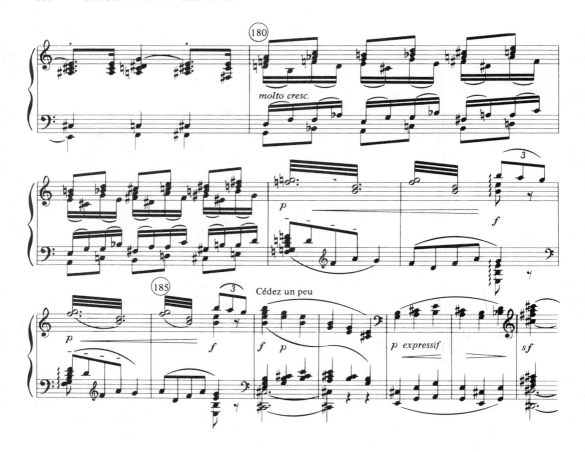

The short passage of Figure 12.20 is of interest because of its pivotal use of the tritone: C-F♯ of measure two becomes B♯-F♯ in measure three. Compare this with a similar progression by Rimsky-Korsakov in *Elementary Harmony,* page 278.

Fig. 12.20

Debussy, *Images I,* "Reflets dans l'eau"

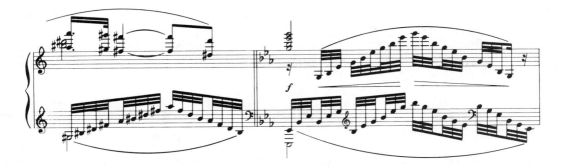

Conclusions

The preceding examples can only presume to be a small sampling of the multitude of devices used by Debussy in creating a startlingly new and refreshing style of writing. Debussy's impressionism cannot be defined as the use of any single device or any combination of these. Each composition is created through its own unique combination of chosen elements, the total effect of which must be heard as well as analyzed for complete comprehension.

Debussy's style, while revolutionary, did not set general patterns for twentieth-century composition, though his influence was most profound on certain other early twentieth-century composers; Ravel, Delius, and Scriabin, to name a few. Debussy's all-important contribution was his ability to break with the traditions of the previous three centuries, proving that a new direction in music, like that of the early seventeenth century,[3] was possible again in the early twentieth century.

Method for Analysis

Locate and describe both the traditional and the novel devices employed. These may include those illustrated in this chapter, or the device may require an original description on your part. Among the possibilities, look for these:

1. Whole tone scales and chords.
2. Pentatonic scales and chords.
3. Modal scales and chords.
4. Tritone chords (7ths, 9ths, 11ths, 13ths). Describe the resolution or the nonresolution of the dissonance and the movement of its root.
5. Added tone chords.
6. Root movement by chromatic thirds.
7. Parallelism (planing).

[3]Review the article, "The Theory of Inversion" in *Elementary Harmony*, pp. 205–210.

8. Other traditional or nontraditional chord progressions. For the latter, describe the nature of the harmonic movement.

9. Quartal and quintal chords, and any other chords built other than in thirds.

10. Describe nonharmonic tones, in relation to either traditional or nontraditional chord types.

An analysis of Figure 12.17 would include:

Measure 1:   The chord is a diminished seventh, A♯ C♯ E G, with the melody line F♯ suspended over it.

Measure 2:   V^{13} in A major, or, the C♯ may be considered an appoggiatura (without note of approach) to the 7th, D. The progression in measures 1–2 is ♯vi^{o7}-V$^4_3$ (functional spelling: F× A♯ C♯ E to E G♯ B D; review page 46).

The melody line emphasizes the nonharmonic tones F♯ (the first and last notes of the measure) and C♯ (accented by its length relative to surrounding tones).

Measure 3:   Same as measure 2 with root in bass.

Measure 4:   I of the V-I cadence with added sixth in soprano, and doubled an octave lower.

Assignment 12.1.   Make a complete analysis of any of the examples of this chapter, especially Figure 12.19.

Assignment 12.2.   Continue analysis with the following examples.

Debussy, *Chansons de Bilitis*,
"Le tombeau des Naïades"

dis ri - aient les na - ia - des.

Il pren-ait de grands mor-ceaux froids,   et les sou-le-vant vers le ciel

pále,   il re - gar-dait au tra - vers.

Debussy, *Préludes*, Book I, No. 6,
"Des pas sur la neige"

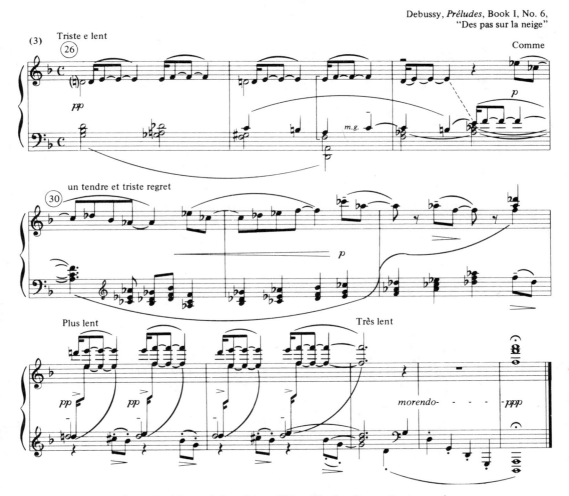

Debussy, Quartet in G Minor,
first movement

(5) The next example is from the works of Ravel, the younger of the two most important impressionist composers. The work, *Le Tombeau de Couperin*, is a tribute to the Baroque composer, François Couperin (1668–1733). Figure 6.13 (page 158) is an excerpt from another such tribute by Grieg for Ludvig Holberg (1658–1754), a Norwegian author and contemporary of Couperin. Both works use a device common to Baroque music. Compare Figure 6.13 with measures 20–29 below to discover this device, and describe the difference in its use.

Ravel, *Le Tombeau de Couperin*,
"Rigaudon"

CHAPTER THIRTEEN

After Debussy: An Introduction to Twentieth-Century Music

The success of the musical practices of Debussy effectively marked the end of the common practice period. No longer constrained by former limitations, composers searched for new modes of musical expression, resulting in a wide diversity of musical styles and the technical means to achieve their creative efforts. These processes, both evolutionary and revolutionary, continue to the present day, and, grouped as a whole, are not explainable by any single theoretical principle. Thus, without the controls experienced in common practice styles, such as common root movements, standard use of nonharmonic tones, and so forth, music of the twentieth century can only be considered on the basis of each individual composer's practice.

Analyzing twentieth-century music, then, is similar to the manner in which we investigated the music of Debussy. We look both for features that differ from those used in the common practice period, as well as any that are the same, or modified, from that period. For example, a composer's use of pitch combinations may be highly original, but at the same time expressed in traditional rhythmic patterns and metrical units. Looking back at the example by Fauré, Figure 11.12, we see a highly unconventional harmonic progression combined with a rhythmic and metrical pattern that could have occurred any time in the common practice period.

Analysis of twentieth-century music can be simplified to some extent by recognizing four major groups of compositional practices.

1. *New approaches to traditional materials.* This category includes music produced through evolutionary processes: extensions and modifications of earlier practices, such as chords built with intervals other than thirds, scale patterns other than the major and minor modes, new varieties of rhythmic groupings, and many others included in later discussions.

2. *Original systems.* Music based on new systems of melodic, harmonic, or rhythmic organization, such as the "dodecaphonic" ("twelve-tone") method, and its derivations.
3. *New sound sources.* Music based on the sources for production of sound never before available, such as the synthesizer and the computer.
4. *New performance practices.* Music based on improvisation and aleatoric devices, transferring from the composer to the performer much of the responsibility in the compositional process.

Discussions of theoretical developments and processes within each of these groupings will imply neither that a particular composer's style is based solely on those described nor that they are used only by that composer. A composer's musical style still, as in previous eras, depends upon the choice of theoretical materials and the relative frequency of their usage. There are many examples of music which include features from two or more of these categories, the choice itself being a component part of that composer's unique writing style.

Many examples of twentieth-century music are fully comprehensible only when heard as written by the composer. In contrast, we can reduce the score of a Mozart symphony to a score for piano, or for most any combination of instruments, and still recognize its harmonic, melodic, and rhythmic elements and the interplay among these features. Looking ahead to Figure 14.19, measure 1, we find three instruments, each playing its own triad, B♭ D♭ F, C E G, and E G♯ B simultaneously and in the same general range. Performance on the piano produces a muddy mixture of dissonances, whereas hearing these triads, each played by an instrument with its own unique timbre as indicated in the score, allows each to be set off clearly from the others, with a considerable lessening of the dissonant effect. All examples written for combinations of orchestral instruments should be heard as originally conceived; if heard at the piano, enough imagination should be exercised to reproduce mentally the composer's intentions.

Lastly, it should be understood that adequate coverage of a subject as vast as that of twentieth-century music can be accomplished only by a volume or volumes dedicated to that subject alone. The diversity and quantity of compositional experimentation allows us only to cover some of the more important highlights in the limited space available in a text such as this. For further information, see some of the currently available books on twentieth-century music:

Austin, William W., *Music in the 20th Century.* New York: W. W. Norton & Co., 1966

Cope, David H., *New Directions in Music—1950–1970.* Dubuque, Iowa: Wm. C. Brown Co., 1971

Dallin, Leon, *Techniques of Twentieth Century Composition,* 2nd ed. Dubuque, Iowa: William C. Brown Co., 1964

DeLone, Richard, et al., *Aspects of Twentieth-Century Music.* Englewood Cliffs, N.J.: Prentice-Hall, Inc., 1975

Hansen, Peter, *An Introduction to Twentieth Century Music,* 2nd ed. Boston: Allyn and Bacon, Inc., 1967

Machlis, Joseph, *Introduction to Twentieth Century Music*. New York: W. W. Norton & Co., 1964

Marquis, G. Welton, *Twentieth Century Music Idioms*. Englewood Cliffs, N.J.: Prentice-Hall, Inc., 1964

Martin, William and Drossin, Julius, *Music of the Twentieth Century*. Englewood Cliffs, N.J.: Prentice-Hall, Inc., 1980

Persichetti, Vincent, *Twentieth Century Harmony*. New York: W. W. Norton & Co., 1961

Perle, George, *Serial Composition and Atonality*, 5th ed. Berkeley, California: University of California Press, 1981

Read, Gardner, *Modern Rhythmic Notation*. Bloomington, Indiana: University of Indiana Press, 1978

Reti, Rudolph, *Tonality-Atonality-Pantonality*. Westport, Conn.: Greenwood Press, 1958

Salzman, Eric, *Twentieth-Century Music: An Introduction* 2nd ed. Englewood Cliffs, N.J.: Prentice-Hall, Inc., 1974

Slonimsky, Nicolas, *Music Since 1900*. New York: C. Scribner's Sons, 1971

Stone, Kurt, *Music Notation in the Twentieth Century*. New York: W. W. Norton & Co., 1980

Stuckenschmidt, H. H., *Twentieth Century Music*. New York: McGraw-Hill Book Company, 1969

Ulehla, Ludmila, *Contemporary Harmony*. New York: The Macmillan Co., 1966

CHAPTER FOURTEEN

Twentieth-Century Music: Melody, Rhythm, and Harmony

This chapter will be concerned with compositional practices from the first of the four groups described on page 336. The music ranges from styles only slightly removed from the common practice period to those remote enough to make any relationship difficult to ascertain. Yet all do show compositional procedures derived, however tenuously, from practices of the past, in contrast to the material of the next chapter in which composers strive for new and unique basic concepts in music composition.

Melody

One obvious and simple reaction to the three-century usage of the major and minor modes was an adoption of scale patterns suggestive of the medieval modes. In the work of which Figure 15.1 is an excerpt, the theme is a hymn in the Phrygian mode by Thomas Tallis (1505–1585).[1] Development of this theme shows fragmentary influence of the Phrygian and other modes. Measures 78–81

Fig. 14.1

Vaughan Williams, *Fantasia on a Theme by Thomas Tallis*

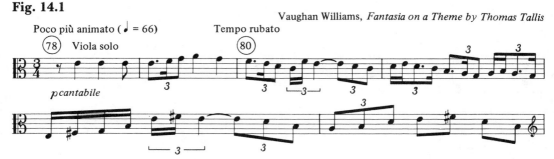

[1]The complete hymn in four voices can be seen in *Music for Sight Singing*, number 543.

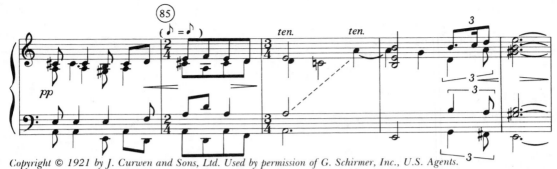

of the solo viola are clearly Phrygian on E. Changing F to F♯ in measure 82 creates a Dorian mode on E. The final C♯ of the solo becomes the third of A major, progressing in that key to the ¾ signature, where the mode is Aeolian on E.

The scale of Figure 14.2 seems to have two implications. The vocal line with its tonic implication of G displays the Dorian scale G A B♭ C D E F G, while the accompaniment, with its tonic implication of B♭, uses the same scale tones for the Lydian mode, B♭ C D E F G A B♭. Observe the use of "relative modes." Just as B♭ major and G minor are relative keys, so B♭ Lydian and G Dorian are related.

Fig. 14.2

Britten, *Seven Sonnets of Michelangelo*, Op. 22, "Sonetto LV"

Simultaneous use of two modes is shown in Figure 14.3, the melody based on the Lydian mode on F against the major mode accompaniment in D♭. This procedure is known as bimodality.

Fig. 14.3

Milhaud, *Trois Poemes de Jean Cocteau*,
"Fête de Bordeaux"

Melodic lines in the twentieth century are more likely *not* to be restricted completely by scale or key implications. The melody of Figure 14.4 implies no particular continuous scale form, and only a vague relationship to a key or keys. The first twelve notes include all twelve notes of the chromatic scale,[2] and included therein are melodic outlines of the G minor and E♭ minor triads. The notes within each of the next three brackets may suggest the indicated but questionable key, perhaps because of conditioned traditional hearing. For example, under C (?), the note B followed by C may imply leading tone to tonic in C, while the C itself implies the same to the following note D♭. The pentatonic passage interrupts any feeling for key until the strong repeated D♭'s accompanied by a descending G♭ major scale, all ending with a cadence chord incorporating all the notes of the pentatonic scale (C D E G A).

Fig. 14.4

Hindemith, Symphonie, "Mathis der Maler,"
third movement

[2]This twelve-tone series is not used as a "tone-row" or in the "twelve-tone technique," discussed in Chapter 15.

Many melodic lines cannot be analyzed through description of specific devices used. The melody of Figure 14.5 looks superficially similar to melodic lines from earlier in the century, and in fact, begins with three measures clearly in A major. From this point on, key implications change rapidly until the return to the original starting note via an Aeolian scale on E.

Fig. 14.5

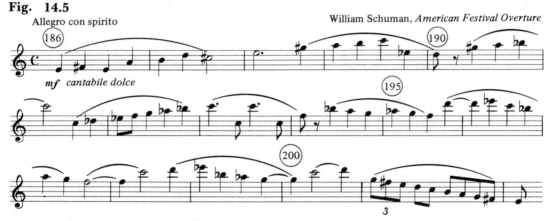

Melodic doubling was common in earlier centuries, but limited to octave sonority doubling (review page 121) and doubling in thirds and sixths, the varying sizes of these intervals, major and minor, determined by the key of the passage. Twentieth century practice allows doubling at any interval. Figure 14.6 shows doubling at the constant interval of the major sixth. Since the lower line does not have to conform to the "key" of the upper line, several cross relations result, such as F♯-F♮, first and third notes.

Fig. 14.6

Included in this same movement are these additional passages displaying melodies doubled at various intervals:

1. Minor thirds at rehearsal number 33
2. Minor sevenths at rehearsal number 45

3. Perfect fifths at rehearsal number 60
4. Major seconds at rehearsal number 90

Meter and Rhythm

Meter and rhythm as used in earlier centuries still play an important role in twentieth-century music. The regularly recurring accents and measure lengths so typical of the common practice period are still found in much of the music written since 1900, as shown in some of the previous examples such as Figures 14.2, 14.3, and 14.6. Of the three principal elements of music—melody, harmony, and rhythm—characteristics of nineteenth-century rhythm have been retained in the twentieth century to a much greater extent than those of melody or harmony.

A marked increase in the use of syncopation often gives the impression of a radical change in rhythmic practices. But if we define syncopation as the accenting of beats or parts of beats other than those of the regularly recurring accent, these being heard against a regular metric pattern, either sounded or implied, then at least in principle there is no change in style brought about by syncopation, except in degree. Increase in frequency was accompanied by more irregularity in the placement of syncopated notes in order to create rhythmic patterns not typical of the nineteenth century. The well-known example from Stravinsky, Figure 14.7, demonstrates an early and still exciting instance. The accents, however, being heard against an implied regular duple simple meter, still constitute syncopation in the accepted nineteenth-century meaning of the term.

Fig. 14.7

Stravinsky, *Le Sacre du Printemps*

More significantly, twentieth-century composers have often returned to principles of rhythmic and metric structure commonly found in sixteenth-century musical composition.[3] The rhythm of the music of that era, particularly vocal music, often seems extremely free and even unregulated by standards of the common practice period. Figure 14.8a is the first part of a song by John Dowland, quoted in full in *Music for Sight Singing*, number 544.[4] For our present figure, we have omitted bar lines, just as it was written in the sixteenth century. To ascertain the location of the accents, it becomes necessary to locate the accents in the poem. Then, by adding bar lines and time signatures as needed, we find we have a composition of changing meters. The four notes after the first quarter rest, for example, prove to be in $\frac{6}{8}$ meter in modern notation rather than syncopation in $\frac{3}{4}$ meter (Figure 14.8b).

Fig. 14.8

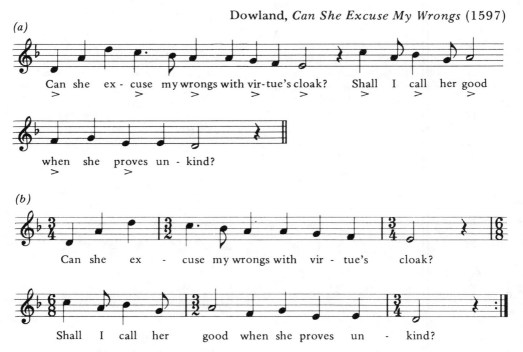

Dowland, *Can She Excuse My Wrongs* (1597)

Twentieth-century music makes extensive use of this irregular metric structure and is notated usually in one of two ways. In the first way, a single time signature precedes regularly recurring bar lines, with the actual metrical accents to be determined by the performer. Scansion of the text of Figure 14.9a determines the metrical interpretation to be shown in Figure 14.9b.

[3]Review article, "Another Metrical Concept" in *Elementary Harmony*, page 139.

[4]In *Music for Sight Singing*, see also numbers 538, 540, and 543. In *More Music for Sight Singing*, see numbers 935, 938, 944 and others between numbers 932 and 954.

Fig. 14.9

Britten, *Five Flower Songs*, Op. 47, "To Daffodils"

Secondly, the meter changes are shown as successive changes in time signatures, as seen in Figure 14.10, particularly important in instrumental music where no text is available to guide the interpretation. (For an example in instrumental music comparable to Figure 14.9, see the excerpt from Bartók's Quartet No. 4 in *Elementary Harmony*, page 142.)

Fig. 14.10

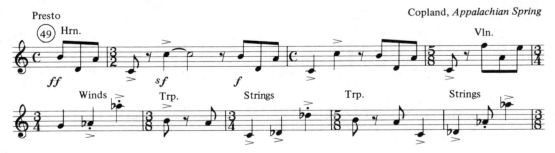

Copland, *Appalachian Spring*

Meter signatures rarely or never used in earlier periods abound in twentieth-century music. Besides the numerators 5 and 7 used earlier to some degree, we now find numerators from 1 through 21, used over a variety of denominators.[5]

Alternating meters, written as $\frac{3}{4}\frac{2}{4}$ or $\frac{3}{4}+\frac{2}{4}$ can occasionally be found in the nineteenth century.[6] These, along with meters indicating irregular groupings within the measure, such as

$$\frac{3+2+3}{8}$$

are again common in the twentieth century, while fractional meters such as $\frac{4\,1/2}{4}$ or $\frac{3\,2/3}{8}$ are sometimes seen. The reference in footnote 5 lists a repertoire of these and other current metric devices.

The use of two or more meters simultaneously (*polymeter*) is seen only rarely in traditional music. An exceptional example is found in Act I of Mozart's *Don Giovanni* where three orchestras play in the meters of $\frac{3}{8}$, $\frac{2}{4}$, and $\frac{3}{4}$ simultaneously, together with the horns playing triplets in $\frac{3}{4}$, producing the effect of $\frac{9}{8}$.

From Brahms, we see in Figure 14.11, that the phrasing in measures 112–113 of the piano part produces a meter of $\frac{3}{4}$ against the $\frac{6}{8}$ of the singer's line. In measure 114, the left hand joins the voice in $\frac{6}{8}$, finishing in measure 115 with all voices in $\frac{6}{8}$.

Fig. 14.11

Brahms, *Von ewiger Liebe*, Op. 43, No. 1

[5]See Gardner Read, *Music Notation,* 2nd ed., Boston: 1969, pages 159–163 for a listing of fifty-three different time signatures (other than the common ones) and compositions in which they are used.

[6]Brahms, Trio, Op. 101: example of $\frac{3}{4}\frac{2}{4}$ in *More Music for Sight Singing,* melody number 786; and Mussorgsky, *Boris Gudonov;* example of $\frac{3}{4}\frac{5}{4}$ in *Music for Sight Singing,* melody number 556.

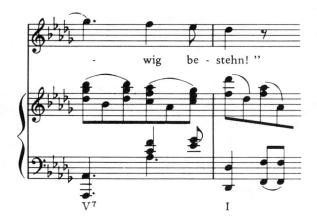

The excerpt from Stravinsky, Figure 14.12, shows six metrical patterns sounding simultaneously.

Fig. 14.12

Stravinsky, *The Rite of Spring*[7]

*This is not the complete score. Instruments duplicating these meters have been omitted.

[7]This is not the complete score. Instruments duplicating these meters have been omitted.

In the piccolo parts, the prominence of the alternating octave leaps creates the effect of a downbeat at those points, the composite of the two voices creating a $\frac{3}{8}$ meter.

Fig. 14.13

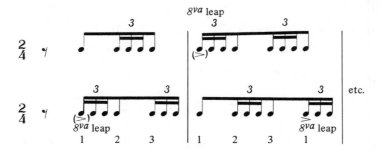

The oboe part in $\frac{2}{4}$ is accented on each 2nd beat, the English horn, also in $\frac{2}{4}$, plays steady eighth notes, while the viola sounds as $\frac{6}{8}$, created by two triplets per measure. The melodic configuration of the cello and bass parts contributes to a composite $\frac{3}{4}$ meter. The same $\frac{3}{4}$ effect can be created by starting on any eighth note.

Fig. 14.14

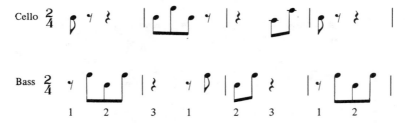

The success of jazz in popular music has had its impact on a number of composers other than jazz specialists. While one all-important aspect of jazz, that of improvisation, cannot be utilized in a composition where definite pitch and duration values for all notes are given, another characteristic, its rhythm, can be easily transferred to concert music as in the well-known works of George Gershwin—*Rhapsody in Blue* and *An American in Paris*. In Figure 14.15, measure 10, note the groups of three notes in a measure where metrical groups of four are implied, and in measures 11–14, accents alternating between off beat eighth notes and metrical strong beats. In Figure 14.16, polyrhythm is created by the $\frac{3}{8}$ meter of the treble staff against the meter of the bass staff, which could be that of the time signature, but more likely a $\frac{3}{4}$ meter with the downbeat on any chosen note.

Fig. 14.15

Fig. 14.16

Milhaud, *La Création du Monde* (1923)

Harmony

The twentieth-century use of tones in vertical combinations are so varied and numerous as to defy any system of classification. In the reaction against the consistent use of chords built in thirds by earlier composers, multitudes of new chordal combinations, some already seen in the music of Debussy, have been conceived during the present century. The triad and other chords built in thirds have not been discarded entirely, however, as seen in Figures 14.17–14.20.

Modal melodies are often harmonized with chords of traditional construction, the chord type on any scale step dependent upon the mode being used. In the Mixolydian melody of Figure 14.18, the lowered seventh scale degree requires the use of v (minor) and $\flat$VII. The composer also uses $\flat$III, probably to avoid the diminished triad, iii° (G B$\flat$ D$\flat$) required by the mode.

Fig. 14.17

Vaughan Williams, *The Water Mill*

Measures 1–4 of Figure 14.18 are triadic when considering the pitch D as an internal pedal. The next four measures, though slightly more dissonant, also show implications of traditional writing. The D-C♯ dissonance of measure 5 (two lowest voices) is created when the two melodic lines move in contrary motion. The C♯ is held over as though it were to be a suspension, but never to resolve, becoming part of a chord structure at the end of measure 6. An expected cadence at measure 8 is foiled, again as a result of the contrary soprano and bass lines. The actual cadence occurs in measure 9, the D major tonic chord also acting as the first chord of the next section.

Fig. 14.18

Shostakovich, Prelude No. 5,
Twenty-four Preludes and Fugues, Op. 87

Allegretto (♩ = 120)

p dolce

sempre arpeggiato

*Prelude No. 5 Dmitri Shostakovich From TWENTY FOUR PRELUDES AND FUGUES, Op. 87
By DMITRI SHOSTAKOVICH
Edited by JULIEN MUSAFIA*

Superimposed triadic lines as in Figure 14.19 can create a highly dissonant effect. It is this example we cited on page 337 in advising that passages such as these should not be judged as they sound at the piano, but as originally scored.

Fig. 14.19

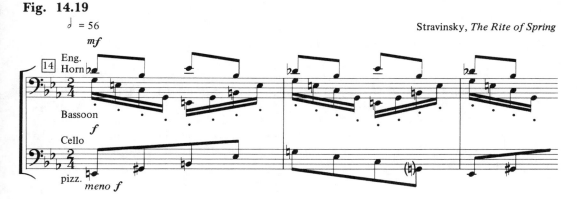

♩ = 56

Stravinsky, *The Rite of Spring*

mf

[14] Eng.
Horn

Bassoon
f

Cello

pizz.
meno f

In Figure 14.20, simple triads are seen in contrary motion. An added complexity is the use of two sets of ascending parallel six-four chords, the upper set the same as the lower set, but one beat later. At measure 118, the two contrasting lines change directions and swap the characteristics of measures 2–3.

Fig. 14.20

Milhaud, *L'Orestie d'Eschyle*, III,
"Les Euménides"

Both seventh chords and chords built in sevenths occur in Figure 14.21. Disregarding the pedal B♭, the first chord is a seventh chord, D F (A) C, and the second a chord built with sevenths, from the lowest note up, G F E♭. Both types appear in parallel motion, the seventh chords either in root position or in first inversion. Note in measures 21–23 a series of four parallel traditional seventh chords followed by four chords built with superimposed sevenths.

This excerpt is also an example of *pandiatonicism,* music based on traditional diatonic scales, and making use of both traditional chords (though not in functional progression) and original types of chords. Measures 17–23 use only members of the B♭ major scale, changing to the use of the G major scale at measure 24. This technique was a reaction against what many composers thought to be the excess of chromaticism, especially that of the "12-tone" composers discussed in the next chapter.

Fig. 14.21

Copland, *Twelve Poems of Emily Dickinson,* "Why do They Shut Me Out of Heaven?"

The music from which Figure 14.22 is an excerpt is remarkable for the variety of its chord types, all used in parallelism, and for the fact that it was written so early, in 1906. At measure one, we find superimposed augmented triads, D F♯ B♭ and E G♯ C, the six pitches comprising a whole tone scale. A series of five such triads in parallel motion leads to chords built in fourths at measure 3, the first one, B♭ D♯ G♯ C♯ F♯ B; at measure 6 are chords built on alternate intervals of the tritone and the perfect fifth, G♭ C G C♯ G♯ D A. Each of these types is sounded in parallel motion until the next type is stated.

Fig. 14.22

Ives, *Central Park in the Dark*

During the course of this background played by the strings, various tunes sound over it, as sounds heard from a distance in the night air. The most remarkable superimposition is that of a ragtime piano marked allegro, Figure 14.23, against the *molto adagio* of the strings, the latter informed to stop anywhere in its chordal sequence when the rest of the instruments come to their final chord!

Fig. 14.23

Ives, *Central Park in the Dark*

Methods for juxtaposing notes to create vertical sonorities vary widely and are limited only by the imagination of the composer. In Figure 14.24, the chord at each * is a combination of seconds and thirds. The completed chord in measure one uses the same five pitches in both the treble clef and in the bass clef, though the spacing between notes is different. The same is true of each of the remaining two similar sonorities. These chords, spelled beginning with C, are:

measure 91:   C D♯ E G G♯

measure 95:   C E F G♯ B

measure 96:   C E♭ G A♭ B

Fig. 14.24   Carter, Sonata for Flute, Oboe,
                                        Cello, and Harpsichord

Beats 1 and 2 of each measure of Figure 14.25 are alternately consonant and dissonant. As the bass line falls by fourths, each bass note is repeated. At the first repetition the upper voices move to triads dissonant with the bass, and at the next to a triad of which the bass is the root, after which the pattern is repeated as a type of harmonic sequence.

Fig. 14.25

The bass line of Figure 14.26 is reminiscent of the harmonic sequence of the common practice period. Rather than serving as a foundation for a series, roots down a third, up a fourth, the harmony above the sequential bass is controlled by an ascending chromatic line, beginning on D♯ in measure 8, and, while disappearing into the harmonic texture in measure 9, is still traceable to the B♭ at the end of measure 10.

Fig. 14.26

An additional harmonic sonority, called a *cluster*, consists of three or more consecutive tones sounding simultaneously. Figure 14.27 shows alternating three-note clusters. A B C♯ and B♭ C D, used as a harmonic device.

Fig. 14.27   Bartók, Quartet No. 4, fourth movement

Copyright 1929 by Universal Edition. Renewed 1956. Copyright and Renewal assigned to Boosey & Hawkes, Inc. for the U.S.A.

From these examples it can be seen that the construction of dissonant vertical sonorities need not be haphazard. Careful examination and study of even a seemingly forbidding score will usually reveal the thought processes of the composer and the logic behind his choice of sonorities.

Analysis

The procedures we have used in analyzing the examples of this chapter should be applied to the assignments in analysis. Consider the elements of melody, rhythm, and harmony, looking for

1. features resembling or related to traditional aspects of these elements.
2. features not characteristic of earlier centuries.
3. combinations of traditional and novel elements.
4. systematic approaches, particualrly repetition and sequence, whether identical or varied.
5. devices used consistently, if not systematically, in establishing the style of the music.

Study of formal structures should be included when the excerpt is sufficiently complete for this purpose. See the author's *More Music for Sight Singing*,

Part 5 (melodies 968–1021) for complete or extended sections of twentieth-century melodies. In addition, several anthologies offer a good variety of music for analysis including

Brandt, William et al., *The Comprehensive Study of Music*, vol. 4, "Anthology of Music from Debussy Through Stockhausen." New York: Harper's College Press, 1976

Burkhart, Charles, *Anthology for Musical Analysis*, 3rd ed. New York: Holt, Rinehart and Winston, 1978

Wennerstrom, Mary, *Anthology of Twentieth-Century Music*. Englewood Cliffs, N.J.: Prentice-Hall, Inc., 1969

Wennerstrom, Mary, *Anthology of Musical Structure and Style*. Englewood Cliffs, N.J.: Prentice-Hall, Inc., 1983

Assignment 14.1. Analysis

Milhaud, *Saudades do Brasil*, VIII, "Tijuca"

Bartók, *Mikrokosmos*, Vol. 6, No. 141

Hindemith, *Ludus Tonalis*, "Interludium"
preceding "Fuga quinta in E"

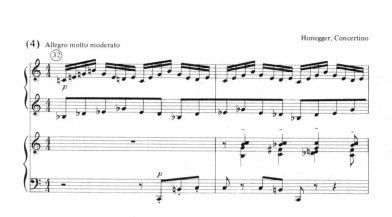

(4) Allegro molto moderato

Honegger, Concertino

Messiaen, *Vingt Regards sur l'Enfant Jésus*,
"Regard de l'Esprit de joie"

Très modéré, Tempo rubato (♪ = 104)

(Dans un grand transport de joie)

Barber, *Hermit Songs*, Op. 29,
"The Praises of God"

(6) Un poco allegro (♩. = 66)

How fool - ish the
man   Who does   not raise ____ His voice ____ and   praise ____ With joy - ful words, ____

Suggested Writing Activities

Study of the literature of music is always enhanced through the experience of writing original music, as we have done throughout the course. This continues to be true for twentieth-century music, but our approach must be somewhat different. The current century is one of experimentation and has produced a diversity of styles that cannot yet be linked to a common basic principle. Therefore part-writing, or harmonizing melodies and realizing bass lines, will not suffice as a basis for writing projects.

Instead, your own experimentation is the best way to participate in the writing experience. Following is a list of suggestions, based on the music examples of Chapters 12 and 14. Different ideas but of a similar nature should occur to you as you study these examples and other repertoire of the twentieth-century literature.

1. *a*) Choose one of the medieval modes. Write a melody of 8–16 measures based on this mode, experimenting both with smooth traditional lines, and with nontraditional procedures such as wide leaps, use of tritones, and so forth. *b*) Harmonize the melodies with triads based on the chosen mode. An occasional altered triad may be used, as in Figure 14.18

2. Write a melody of 8–16 measures, using modal inflections, but derived from more than one mode. Use Figure 14.1 and accompanying discussion as a guide.

3. Experiment with bitonality by setting your melodies to accompaniments in either major or minor keys. Refer to Figure 14.3.

4. Using a poem from Assignment 5.6 (page 149), or one of your choice, write a melody using a conventional time signature and regular measure lengths, but with an irregular metrical pattern as in Figures 14.8 and 14.9. Note: Poetic lines that appear to be in a single meter with regularly recurring accents can actually be accommodated with several meters. Review Figure 5.30, page 147.

5. Write melodies without texts, but with alternating meters or with changing meter signatures. Review Figure 14.10.

6. Write several series of parallel triads using different root movements in each. (Compare the root movements of Figure 12.8, page 320, and Assignment 12.2 (1), page 328.) b) Write a melodic line against one of these chord successions, as in Assignment 12.2 (3), measures 4–6, page 331.

7. Repeat number 6, using parallel seventh chords or parallel added tone chords. Find examples in Chapter 12.

8. Experiment with triads and/or larger chords in contrary motion, as in Figure 14.20.

9. Devise a system of chord construction and a system for their progression, as in Figures 14.21, 14.22, 14.24, and 14.25.

CHAPTER FIFTEEN

Serial Composition and Later Twentieth-Century Practices

Extended use of chromaticism in the late nineteenth century, especially in music such as *Tristan und Isolde,* imposed severe restrictions on further developments within the major-minor tonal system. Hence, we have seen in the preceding chapters (12–14) examples of the many attempts to generate new and effective styles of music composition. Not included in the previous chapter was the work of Arnold Schoenberg (1874–1951), who among others, ultimately developed a new systematic approach to music composition, one which exerted significant influence on music of the twentieth century.

Schoenberg's early compositions, written in Vienna in the period shortly after Wagner's death, often clearly show the latter's influence, as in this excerpt, Figure 15.1, dating from 1900–01.

Fig. 15.1

Schoenberg, *Gurre-Lieder,* Part III
(piano transcription by Alban Berg)

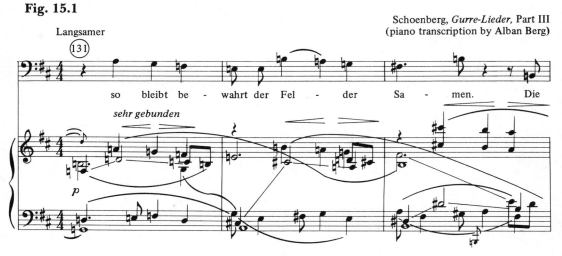

Used by permission of Belmont Music Publishers, Los Angeles, California 90049.

This type of music, like that of Wagner, practically eliminated the feeling of being in any one key, while at the same time expressing functional relationships which were infrequently achieved and which changed in rapid succession. For Schoenberg, realizing the futility of continuing in this style, the next goal was the release of music from its dependence and allegiance to a given tonic tone and, consequently, from the necessity of changing tonics in rapid succession.

Early progress toward this goal is shown in Figure 15.2. The chords played by the right hand are mixed tertian and quartal, while the melody in the left hand, which is a melodic sequence and could, by itself, be harmonized traditionally, actually has little harmonic relationship to the harmonic progression in the upper staff. The startling V-I progression closing the first phrase demonstrates the continuing strong influence of traditional writing, as does the added sixth chord at the final cadence (Figure 15.2*b*).

Fig. 15.2

a) opening measures

Schoenberg, *In diesen Wintertagen,*
Op. 14, No. 2

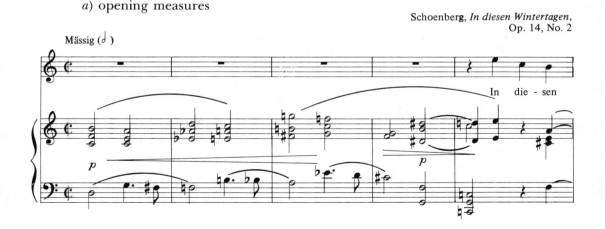

Win - ter-ta - gen,   nun sich das   Licht __   ver - hüllt,

b) closing measures

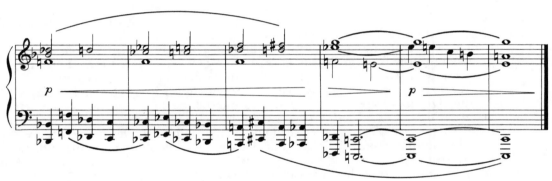

Atonality

Beginning in 1908, Schoenberg achieved the goal of complete or near-complete divorcement from a tonic note, resulting in music which is usually referred to as *atonal* (lacking in tonality in the traditional sense). In Figure 15.3*a*, the contrived scale in the cello line includes eleven of the twelve possible chromatic tones, the missing G being prominent as the first note (concert pitch) in the clarinet part. Calculating vertical structures of the instrumental parts on each beat shows only four intervallic combinations reminiscent of traditional chords: (1) measure 1, beat 3, B F♯ A, (2) measure 3, beat 2, G D, (3) measure 4, beat 3 B♭ C E, and (4) beat 4, G D. The final cadence, Figure 15.3*b*, is completely lacking in traditional harmonic concept, the final "chord" consisting of the notes, as spaced, E A C, F D♯, and G, or spelled consecutively, C D♯ E F G A.

Fig. 15.3

a) opening measures

b) closing measures

Used by permission of Belmont Music Publishers, Los Angeles, California 90049.

The vocal line demonstrates a notation devised by Schoenberg to express a unique singing style. The stem of the note includes an "x" ♪, indicating the approximate pitch of a *spoken* word. The text is a recitation, its method of performance known as *Sprechstimme*.

Twelve-Tone Systems

Having achieved an atonal style, Schoenberg worked for nine years (1914–1923) to develop a system for atonal composition, much as traditional music had a system for tonal writing. The result is described in Schoenberg's own words as a "method of composing with twelve tones which are related only one with another," but is more popularly known as the "twelve-tone system," the "twelve-tone technique," "serialism," or "dodecaphonic writing." First demonstrated in 1923 in his *Five Piano Pieces,* Op. 23, and the *Serenade,* Op. 24 (for seven instruments and voice), his theoretical basis for atonal composition was a predetermined "row" (or "series" or "set") consisting of the twelve notes of the chromatic scale. By using all twelve tones before repeating any note of the row, it is impossible that any pitch can assume the role of tonic. The row itself constitutes the basic organizing principle of a composition, rather than as in the past, a harmonic progression leading to a tonic.

The concept of the row can be demonstrated by illustrating its first complete use in the fifth movement of Op. 23.[1] Observe from Figure 15.4 that the first twelve notes in the treble clef include each of the twelve notes of the chromatic scale, these constituting the row as shown in Figure 15.4b. (Octave displacement of some of the notes is explained in item 3, page 373.)

Fig. 15.4

(a)

Schoenberg, *Fünf Klavierstücke*, Op. 23, No. 5, "Walzer"

© 1923; Edition Wilhelm Hansen, Copenhagen, Denmark.

[1]The previous movements display row technique, but not with all twelve tones.

(b) row for Op. 23, No. 5

Order numbers, as shown in Figure 15.4b, indicate simply the location of a given pitch in a row.

Also useful in twelve-tone analysis are *pitch class (pc)* numbers. These are derived by writing a chromatic scale starting on order number 0 of the row, and numbering each note in successive numerical order. For Figure 15.4*b,* the pc numbers are:

C♯	D	D♯	E	F	F♯	G	G♯	A	A♯	B	C
0	1	2	3	4	5	6	7	8	9	10	11

A pc number refers to *any* enharmonic spelling of that pitch. In this row, for example, pc number 9 refers equally to A♯, B♭, and C♭♭. In a composition any spelling of pc 9 is acceptable since sharps and flats do not indicate tendencies of resolution. Choice is usually based on the spelling easiest in its context. The row, Figure 15.4*b,* expressed as pc numbers, is:

C♯	A	B	G	A♭	F♯	A♯	D	E	E♭	C	F
0	8	10	6	7	5	9	1	3	2	11	4

Thus each pc number refers to the number of half steps between it and the first number, 0, of the row. In this row, pc 4 is four half steps above C♯, and can be spelled E♯, F, or G♭♭.

Following are the basic considerations in the use of the row:

1. The choice of a row is predetermined, and used as the basis for the composition, just as mode and key were chosen in traditional writing. The concept of the row and its musical implications may occur simultaneously, similar to simultaneous concepts of theme, mode, and key in traditional music.

2. The notes of the row are numbered. Originally the numbering was 1–12, but recent developments in the use of the row have made the numbering system 0–11 more practical.

3. Any note of the row may appear in any octave. Note that we have written Schoenberg's row using the closest possible intervals for ease in use. The first two notes in the row are 0 and 1, a major third, but used as a minor sixth in the composition. The theory of inversion still holds for this type of music.

4. Any pitch may be spelled enharmonically. The F♯ of measure 2 and the G♭ of measure 5 in Figure 15.4, for example, are both number 5 in the row and also by coincidence pc number 5. This procedure will often result in a changed appearance of an interval, F♯-B♭ instead of F♯-A♯, for example. This is no matter, since there is no intervallic function as in traditional music.

5. No note of the row may be repeated (except for immediate repetition with no intervening notes) until all other tones of the row are sounded. Occasional other exceptions include repetition of a short melodic figure, or an ostinato, often in fifths. But, as the system developed over the years, composers relaxed these severe restrictions, allowing further exceptions for musical reasons. This, of course, is no different from what we have learned in working with traditional music: regular procedures predominate, but are relaxed when an exception is a better choice.

6. A row may utilize any rhythmic pattern or patterns during the course of the composition.

7. A row does not necessarily coincide with a theme or a motive. Either may end during the course of a row, the next theme or motive starting with one of the remaining notes of the row.

8. The row need not necessarily follow one melodic line or be confined to a single clef. In addition to the row designated in Figure 15.4, we find the complete row both in measures 1–2, and in 2–4, as shown in Figure 15.5.

Fig. 15.5

9. The row may be used harmonically, as well as melodically. The row of Figure 15.6 also supplies an underlying harmonic structure in these measures.

Fig. 15.6

Schoenberg, Quartet No. 4,
first movement

(a) the row (Violin 1)

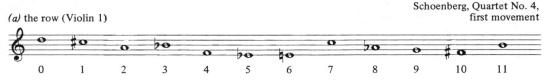

(b)

Vln.1	0		1		2		3	4	5
Vln.2	3	8	10			6		11	1
Vla.	5	6	9			7		10	2
Cello	4	7	11			8		9	0

In this example, the chords are derived by dividing the row into four units: 0 1 2, 3 4 5, 6 7 8, and 9 10 11. The units are so chosen that they combine with the row in the Violin 1 part to produce four consecutive complete rows.

10. The row may be varied on one of three ways:

a) *Inversion.*   Each note of the row proceeds by the same interval, but in the opposite direction. The first three notes of the row in Figure 15.6, D down to C♯ down to A, are found as D up to E♭ up to G in inversion. The complete row in inversion is shown in Figure 15.7*a*.

b) *Retrograde.*   The row is presented backwards, starting with the last note and ending with the first note. The row of Figure 15.6 begins on D and ends on B. In retrograde, the row begins on B and ends on D. See Figure 15.7*b*.

c) *Retrograde Inversion.*   The retrograde is in inversion, the relationship being the same as the prime row and its inversion. The example in Figure 15.7*c* is also transposed, as will be explained in the next section.

Fig. 15.7

(a) Inversion   Schoenberg, Quartet No. 4

(b) Retrograde

(c) Retrograde Inversion

0 1 2 3   8 9 10 11
        4 5 6 7

11. *Transposition.*   Each form of the row may be transposed to each of the twelve chromatic tones, resulting in 48 rows. These may be shown in a *grid* or *matrix*. The matrix for the row from the Fourth Quartet is shown as Figure 15.8.

P = Prime Series and is read from left to right. The row of the Fourth Quartet is P^0. Other superscript numbers refer to the number of half steps in the transposition. A prime series starting on E♭ (instead of D) is P^1 because E♭ is a half step higher than D; P^4 is the prime row starting on F♯, four half steps above D.

I = Inversion and is read from top to bottom. The I^0 column is the same as Figure 15.7*a*.

R = Retrograde and is read from right to left. R^0 is the same as Figure 15.7*b*.

RI = Retrograde Inversion and is read from bottom up. Figure 15.7*c* starts on F♯ and is RI^1, since RI^0 starts on F.

Fig. 15.8

Matrix for Schoenberg's Fourth Quartet, first movement

	I^0	I^{11}	I^7	I^8	I^3	I^1	I^2	I^{10}	I^6	I^5	I^4	I^9	
P^0	D	C♯	A	B♭	F	E♭	E	C	A♭	G	F♯	B	R^0
P^1	E♭	D	B♭	B	F♯	E	F	D♭	A	A♭	G	C	R^1
P^5	G	F♯	D	E♭	B♭	A♭	A	F	D♭	C	B	E	R^5
P^4	F♯	F	D♭	D	A	G	G♯	E	C	B	B♭	E♭	R^4
P^9	B	B♭	G♭	G	D	C	C♯	A	F	E	E♭	A♭	R^9
P^{11}	C♯	C	A♭	A	E	D	D♯	B	G	F♯	F	B♭	R^{11}
P^{10}	C	B	G	A♭	E♭	D♭	D	B♭	G♭	F	E	A	R^{10}
P^2	E	E♭	B	C	G	F	F♯	D	B♭	A	A♭	D♭	R^2
P^6	G♯	G	E♭	E	B	A	B♭	G♭	D	D♭	C	F	R^6
P^7	A	A♭	E	F	C	B♭	B	G	E♭	D	C♯	F♯	R^7
P^8	B♭	A	F	F♯	C♯	B	C	A♭	E	E♭	D	G	R^8
P^3	F	E	C	C♯	G♯	F♯	G	E♭	B	B♭	A	D	R^3
	RI^0	RI^{11}	RI^7	RI^8	RI^3	RI^1	RI^2	RI^{10}	RI^6	RI^5	RI^4	RI^9	

Here is another example from the Fourth Quartet. First determine the form of the row. The row is in inversion. It starts on C♯, eleven half steps above the first note of I^0, so the row therefore is I^{11}.

Fig. 15.9

Schoenberg, Quartet No. 4

I^{11} ㉑

Assignment 15.1. Complete the row analysis of Figure 15.4. The row begun with the notes 0–4, lower staff of measures 3–4, is continued in measure 5. This segment of the row (0–4) has a dual role, both as part of a complete row in measures 3–4, and as the first five notes of a row of its own. The next complete row starts in measure 6, lower staff.

Assignment 15.2. Analyze this excerpt, the final measures for which Figure 15.4 is the beginning. Follow these suggestions:

(1) All rows are P^0 except one, which is either I^0, R^0, or RI^0.

(2) In measure 106, the notes C♯ and A in the bass are simultaneously the last two notes in one row and the first two notes in the following row. Look for a similar overlap later in the excerpt.

(3) In the last four chords, the rows are incomplete.

Schoenberg, *Fünf Klavierstücke*,
Op. 23, No. 5, "Walzer"

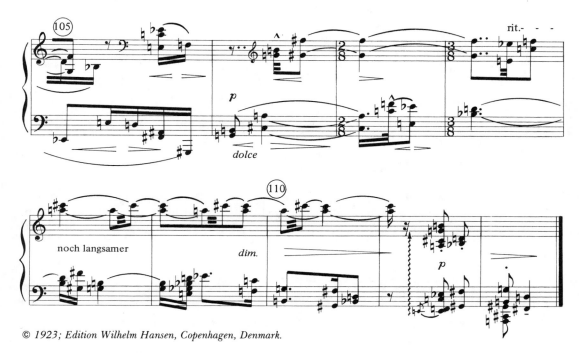

Assignment 15.3.   Using the matrix, Figure 15.8, identify these rows from Schoenberg's Fourth Quartet, first movement.

1. Measures 95–98, cello

2. Measures 120–121, violin 1 and viola

3. Measures 34–37, viola and cello

4. Measures 155–156

Assignment 15.4.   Analyze this excerpt from Schoenberg's Fourth Quartet. It contains six complete rows, including all forms, some in transposition. Identify each from the matrix, Figure 15.8. In the first measure, the violin 1 and violin 2 parts together comprise the row.

Row Variants

Almost limitless are the numbers of ways a row can be devised, each to serve some musical purpose. Of these, we select three of sufficient variety to indicate the scope of these possibilities.

Three-Note Cells

The *Concerto for Nine Instruments* by Anton Webern (1883–1945), a student of Schoenberg, is based on a row divisible into four three-note sections, or cells.

Fig. 15.10

Each cell includes a minor second and a major third, each in a different configuration.

Fig. 15.11

cell 1	half step down, major third up	B B♭ D
cell 2	major third up, half step down	E♭ G F♯
cell 3	major third down, half step up	G♯ E F
cell 4	half step up, major third down	C C♯ A

By identifying any cell as the P form of a three-note row, each remaining cell is in an I, R, or RI relationship to it. If the first cell is called P, then the subsequent cells in order are R^6, RI^7, and I^1.

These three-note cells are used consistently throughout the work, both melodically and harmonically. Figure 15.12 illustrates the melodic use of the cells in the row, beginning with the P^0 row, measures 1–3, and the I^1 row, measures 4–5. Webern's melodic writing, characterized by wide melodic leaps, is often called "pointillism," a term first used to describe a technique in painting in which the picture is made up of a large number of tiny dots and strokes, and first used by Georges Seurat (1859–1890).

Figure 15.13 demonstrates the harmonic use of Webern's row. It begins with three three-note chords followed by a three-note motive, all derived from P^7 of the row in Figure 15.10: F♯ F A, B♭ D C♯, E♭ B C, G G♯ E.

Fig. 15.12

Webern, *Concerto for Nine Instruments,*
Op. 24, first movement

Fig. 15.13

Webern, *Concerto for Nine Instruments,*
Op. 24, third movement

Assignment 15.5. Construct a matrix for Webern's *Concerto for Nine Instruments*. A matrix may easily be constructed as follows.

1. Write out the row as a horizontal line of numbers.

2. Write the I^0 form of the row reading down from the first note (0) of the row. In Figure 15.8, 0-1 of the row is a half step down, therefore, the second note of the vertical row is a half step up (row is D-C♯, inversion is D-E♭). Continue to complete a twelve-note vertical row.

3. Calculate the interval from 0 to 1 in the P^0 row (in Figure 15.8, a half step down). Consider each note of the I^0 row as the first note of this interval and write the second note in the second vertical column, continuing until the second vertical row is complete. Notes 1–2 of the row in Figure 15.8 are a descending major third; write a descending major third after each note of the second column. Continue until all vertical columns are complete, and the matrix will be complete. *Remember,* only pitch classes are important—B♭ down to G♭ and B♭ down to F♯ are the same for this purpose.

4. Number each row based on the pitch class number of the row. Example: the P^0 row of Figure 15.8 starts on a D, therefore, P^1 starts on E♭, P^2 on E, P^3 on F, and so forth. I^0 also starts on D, therefore I^1 starts on E♭, I^2 on E, and so forth. Note that P and R rows share the same number (R^5 is the retrograde of P^5), while I and RI rows share the same number (RI^7 is the retrograde of R^7).

Assignment 15.6. Analyze the remaining portions of Figures 15.12 and 15.13. Look for three-note groupings outlining one of the patterns of Figure 15.11 and identify each row by its P, I, R or RI number. (*Note:* For all instruments, the notation sounds as written.)

Combinatoriality

Initially devised by Schoenberg, this concept was later augmented and given its name by Milton Babbitt (1916–   ). In Schoenberg's words,[2]

the inversion a fifth below of the first six tones, the antecedent, should not produce one of those six tones, but should bring forth the hitherto unused six tones of the chromatic scale. Thus the consequent of the basic set, the tones 7 to 12, comprises the tones of this inversion, but, of course, in a different order.

This can be illustrated from Schoenberg's *Klavierstück*, Op. 33b. The first six notes (*hexachord*) of P^0 and the first hexachord of its I^5 version together furnish a twelve-tone row, and can therefore be used together as a row. The notes of the second hexachord in P^0 and I^5, of course, also contain the twelve notes of the row, but these two hexachords do not have the intervallic relationships as do the first hexachords of the two rows.

Fig. 15.14

Schoenberg, *Klavierstück*, Op. 33b

Row: P⁰

PC numbers   0   2   6   4   10   9

[2]Schoenberg, *Style and Idea*, N.Y.: Philosophical Library, 1950

Row: I⁵

PC numbers   5   4   11   1   7   8

In this work, the rows R⁰ and RI⁵ are in a similar relationship, with all pc numbers accounted for.

Assignment 15.7. *a*) Write out the rows for R⁰ and RI⁵. *b*) In the opening measures of Op. 33b following, rows R⁰ and RI⁵ are used combinatorially. Identify the opening row, P⁰, and the pairing in succeeding measures. Be sure to eliminate from your calculations the frequent repeated notes.

Mässig langsam (♩ = 64)

Schoenberg, *Klavierstück*, Op. 33b

Assignment 15.8. In this excerpt from Op. 33b, the first two measures display the four forms of the row, P⁰, R⁰, I⁵, and RI⁵ separately, followed by a pair used combinatorially.

Schoenberg, *Klavierstück*, Op. 33b

© *1932 by Arnold Schönberg. Renewed 1959 by Gertrud Schönberg.*

Assignment 15.9. Analysis of this excerpt will divulge the other pair used combinatorially.

Schoenberg, *Klavierstück*, Op. 33b

© *1932 by Arnold Schönberg. Renewed 1959 by Gertrud Schönberg.*

A row may be devised to act combinatorially with more than two pairs. In Op. 33a, for example, the combinatorial rows are: R^0 and R^5, P^2 and I^7, P^7 and I^0, and R^7 and RI^6. In the row from Webern's Cantata, Op. 29, (Figure 15.15) not only are P^0 and I^7 combinatorial, but the second hexachord of P^0 is the I^7 form of the first hexachord. Therefore, R^7 is identical to P^0. Try it!

Fig. 15.15

Conservative Use of the Row

Alban Berg (1885–1935) often used the row to produce music with links to the tonal past. In his Violin Concerto, numbers 0–8 of the row consist of intervals of thirds, any consecutive three of which produce a triad, while numbers 8–11 form a four-note whole tone scale.

Fig. 15.16

As used in the introductory measures of the concerto, the use of the row in producing triadic movement is quite obvious.

Fig. 15.17

Other Uses of Serialism

Use of serialism for pitches has led some composers to try serializing other factors, such as rhythmic patterns, dynamics, tempi, and so forth. In Figure 15.18, durations are serialized. Beginning with the first note in the upper staff, a thirty-second note, the value of each successive note is increased by one thirty-second: 1/32, 2/32, 3/32 . . . ending with 23/32. The lower staff is a retrograde, starting with 23/32, 22/32, 21/32 . . . ending with 1/32, the two rows sounding simultaneously.

Fig. 15.18

Assignment 15.10. As its title indicates, this short but complete work is concerned only with melodic lines, using straightforward examples of the P^0 row and transpositions of each of the P, R, I, and RI rows. Members of the rows sometimes move from one staff to another, providing several crossings of the three melodic lines. Only one row, starting on beat 4 of measure 9, is incomplete, with a gap of two tones.

Look for these contrapuntal features:

1. stretto: the theme against itself, the second starting shortly after the first
2. themes in simultaneous contrary motion
3. stretto in contrary motion

Dallapiccola, *Quaderno Musicale Di Annalibera*,
No. 3, "Contrapunctus Primus"

Music Since 1950

The term most appropriate to describe in general the nature of composition in the last few decades is "eclecticism." Compositional practices and related techniques described in Chapter 14 continue to be an important part of the new music, and the use of serialism, though it reached its zenith in the decade 1955–1965, continues to be a significant element in the music of many composers.

But new practices and concepts began to emerge shortly after the close of World War II, concepts which now appear to be a natural reaction to the complexities and restrictions inherent in serialism, much of this music being far more complex than we have shown in our examples, and often appealing almost exclusively to the intellect at the expense of emotional impact. Upon reaching that state where analysis is of more interest than hearing or performing the score, a reaction was surely inevitable. But in its favor, serialism, along with the exploratory devices of Debussy, must be credited not only with the creation of much significant music, but equally with the opening of new pathways at a time when nineteenth-century practices could no longer provide a stimulus for fresh ideas in music composition.

The new types of music which most obviously expressed this reaction are known by several names: *indeterminancy, chance music, random music,* and *aleatory music* (or *aleatoric*).[3] All refer to music in which there is a lessening of the restrictions of precise pitch, specific melodic patterns, exact rhythms or meters, or of any other element of notation in music composition. Although each of the four terms supposedly has its own meaning, all are used rather loosely, with different composers using different terms to express the same concepts.

In any case, indeterminancy can apply to all or any part of a work, or to one or more of its elements (pitch, rhythm, and so forth), in any combination.

Probably the earliest form of chance music is the "jamming" by a jazz combo, free improvisation by several instruments simultaneously, based on a given tune and chord progression, though even earlier, the Baroque practice of realizing a figured bass produced results that were not totally predetermined. Chance music, however, gives the performer, and sometimes the conductor, the choice of what to play, when, and for how long, from a group of composed or

[3]The term was devised by Pierre Boulez from the French *aléa* (chance).

implied possibilities, or improvisation on any of these possibilities, or any combination of scored music and improvisation. Conventional instruments, electronic instruments, prerecorded tapes, and human voices may join in the chance or improvisatory ensemble. Works in conventional style (to be played as written) often include sections in aleatoric style.

Since aleatoric music will vary from performance to performance, analysis is not possible in the traditional sense; we can look at a score and try to predict what might occur, but with few exceptions, the actual music will never be committed to paper.[4]

The most violent reactions to the extremes of traditional notation were compositions based either on no notation whatsoever, or notation without specific meaning. Playing a piece of music without notation implies improvisation, which, of course, is the direct opposite of completely controlled notation, while nonspecific notation implies the necessity of symbols newly created for the purpose.

Figure 15.19 is "a composition" written "for ensemble," and is from a large collection of similar events.[5]

Fig. 15.19

Stockhausen, *From the Seven Days*

MEETING POINT

everyone plays the same tone

lead the tone wherever your thoughts
lead you
do not leave it, stay with it
always return
to the same place

English version © 1968 by Universal Edition A.G., Wien. All rights reserved. Used by permission of European American Music Distributors Corporation, sole U.S. agent for Universal Edition.

In another non-notated event by John Cage, *Variations III (For One or Any Number of People Performing Any Actions)*,[6] the player is furnished with 42 plastic discs to be dropped on a flat surface. Those not touching another are removed

[4]We have already seen a form of indeterminancy in Figures 14.22 and 14.23, Ives' *Central Park in the Dark* (1906), the indeterminancy of the strings playing against the piano's ragtime. Ives can also be credited with first use of a row, *Tone Roads No. 3* (1915), though a row is simply repeated throughout the composition against a background not using the row.

[5]The term "event" in avant garde music is commonly used to indicate the duration of a complete unit of activity. This example is a single event; larger works may consist of several events.

[6]New York, Henmar Press, 1963

after which the performer, noting the number touching and their relationships, performs "suitably" before going on to another group.

Notated aleatoric music often makes use of *graphic notation,* symbols of any kind, usually unique to a particular music composition. This notation, therefore, is found in many guises, three of which are seen in Figure 15.20, 15.21, and 15.25. When graphic notation does not express a specific pitch or metric value, it serves, in a way, the same purpose as eighth century neumes (Review *Elementary Harmony,* page 39).

Fig. 15.20

Feldman, *In Search of an Orchestration*

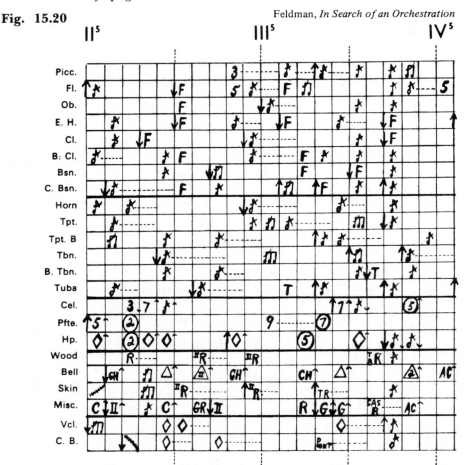

In Figure 15.20, each square is equivalent to MM 88, a specific metrical concept. Symbols in the squares indicate the activities for each of these periods of time. As with most such scores, it is necessary that a list of symbols and their meanings be included.[7] In this work, for example, a number indicates how

[7]See Smith Brindle, *The New Music,* for an 11-page list, beginning on page 188, of "some new notation symbols." The list is probably far from complete.

many sounds to make, or, if in a circle, how many to make at once (no particular sounds). The symbols ♪ and ♩ indicate "short" and "long" grace notes; ♩ . . . . indicates a sustained note. Arrows indicate whether to play high or low notes. A total of 37 symbols are listed by the composer.

Walaciúski's notation in Figure 15.21 refers to performance at the keyboard, including use of the palm of the hand on the strings, percussive sounds on wood or metal inside the piano, percussive sounds other than on the piano, and so forth,

Fig. 15.21   Walaciúski, *Allaloa*

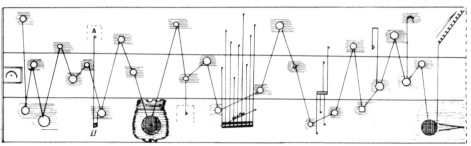

The current trend is away from such extremes. Aleatoric ideas are expressed in more conservative ways, usually combined with conventional staff notation as in Figure 15.22, measured but with only approximations of pitch, and in Figure 15.23, without measured time, but with specific pitch.

Fig. 15.22   Penderecki, *Ecloga VIII* (for six male voices)

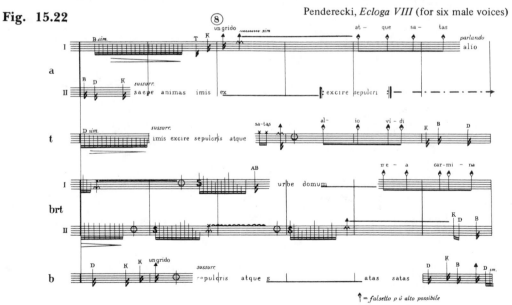

Fig. 15.23

Crumb, *Madigrals*, Book I, iii,
"Los muertos llevan alas de musgo"

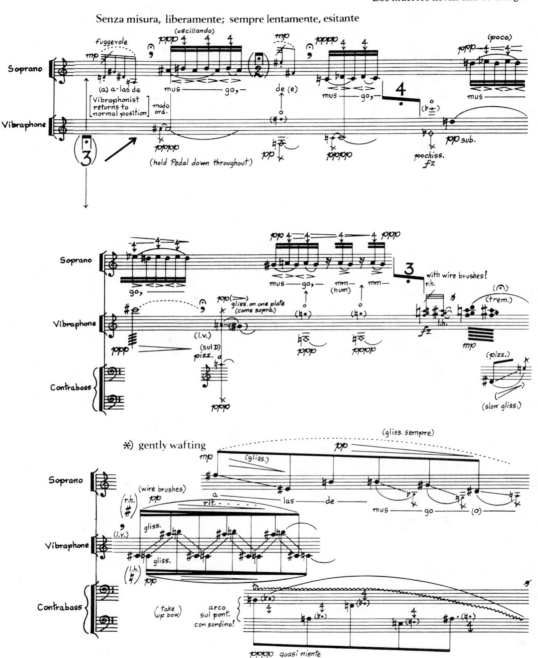

It can be said that regardless of their musical accomplishments, the aleatoric composers have contributed much to music composition by freeing it from its rigid adherence to rhythmic and pitch values, just as serialism freed music from its dependency on the major-minor tonal systems.

New Sound Sources

In all the preceding examples, we have studied those factors which differentiated twentieth-century writing from that of earlier eras. Yet, no matter to what degree they have differed, there is still a remaining constant characteristic in common. In any era the sources of musical sound have been the same: the vibrating string, the vibrating air column, and the vibrating membrane. Therefore, the kind of sound for which composers write has been basically the same (though of course with constant refinements and improvements) from the time when man first blew on a reed, plucked a taut string or struck a stretched skin.

The twentieth century has provided, for the first time in music history, new resources in sound itself. There are two varieties of such sounds: (1) electronic manipulation of natural sound and (2) electronic production of new sounds.

The first development in this area, known as *musique concrète*, combines old sound sources, including various forms of noise, with manipulation of these sounds by various techniques through the use of the tape recorder. A conventional sound or group of sounds is recorded on tape. The taped sound can be manipulated in many ways, for example, by changing the speed of the machine or by reversing the tape. Tapes can be cut up and spliced together to achieve desired effects, and sounds from other sources can be superimposed upon existing taped sounds. These procedures, among others, provide a composer with almost unlimited possibilities for imaginative musical creation. There is no score for such a composition; the final tape is the score itself. No notation is required since the composition will be heard only when the tape is played on a machine. The effect of this kind of music is enhanced by stereo reproduction of the sounds on the tape using two and often more than two speakers.

Electronic music takes advantage of the fact that a vacuum tube or a transistor is capable of producing audible sound. These sounds can be organized and controlled, as in the electric organ, to the point where they can duplicate fairly realistically existing natural sounds such as those produced by orchestra and band instruments. But they can also produce a wide range of sounds never before heard by the ears of man. These sounds are produced on a machine known as a synthesizer, which, to the uninitiated, recalls the complexities of a telephone switchboard or the dashboard of a Boeing 747. The synthesizer not only produces tones but can modify them in an almost unlimited number of ways. In addition to a wide variety of timbres, it is able to produce microtonal pitches, resulting in the possibility of creating scale formations with almost any number of desired equal tones to the octave. These sounds, along with *white noise,* a mixture of many simultaneous frequencies, are combined and juxtaposed in countless combinations on magnetic tape. Other sounds from nature, as in *musique concrète,* are often included as part of the texture of the completed composition.

Electronic music is performed in several ways: (1) by a playing of the completed tape alone, (2) by playing the tape along with an instrument or voice, or with an ensemble, with a conventional score for the conventional performers, and (3) by using the synthesizer as one of the instruments of the ensemble, played by a soloist with or without simultaneous performance of prerecorded tapes.

Electronic music is usually subject only to aural analysis, as the tape for the improvisation *is* the score. Stockhausen has provided a graphic score for an early electronic work, Figure 15.24, (in his words, "the first Electronic Music to be published"). On the upper part, the horizontal lines represent pitches ranging from Hz 100 to 17,200. The vertical lines indicate the outer limits of pitches, and overlapping areas represent simultaneous sets of pitches. Duration of sound is indicated in terms of tape speed, 76.2cm per second, while in the lower section, intensity is shown in terms of decibels. All these factors are explained in detail in the published score.

Fig. 15.24   Stockhausen, *Nr. 3 Elektronische Studien,*
"studien II"

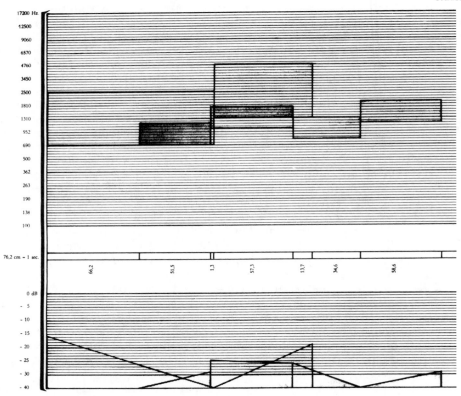

Figure 15.25 is an excerpt from a work for symphony orchestra, using a conventional orchestral score.

Fig. 15.25

Ellis, *Kaleidoscope*

One section of the work, however, is aleatoric, making use of both conventional instruments and electronic sounds. Our figure shows the score for the electronic sounds in this aleatory section; additional pages in this section provide aleatory passages for each of the string, woodwind, brass, and percussion sections of the orchestra. From these pages, the conductor during the performance chooses, and indicates by hand signals (two of which are shown), which "events" will be played by the respective sections of the orchestra. He is free to select in any order any passage or any combination of passages, and to continue the aleatory part of the piece for as short or as long a time as he pleases. Successive performances of this work, then, will usually differ greatly from each other.

The circle at the top of the page represents a prerecorded endless tape loop containing several "events" as pictured around the circle. At the given hand signal, the tape is played, beginning at random at any point on the circle, or, a live performer at the keyboard of a synthesizer may choose any point on the circle and improvise according to the diagram at that point. Among the many notational devices shown, we will describe a few: (1) the horn-like symbol at the left represents crescendo of a tone, rise in pitch, addition of pitches to be sounded simultaneously, and a modulating timbre, indicated, reading left to right, as a change from a "sine" wave to a "square" wave; (2) white noise sounds at the upper right are indicated in only approximate pitch locations; (3) conventional notation at the bottom of the circle is combined with electronic instructions. A different hand signal will cue in one of the prerecorded ostinato patterns at the bottom of the score.

Computer music takes electronic music a step further. Here, the machine is the composer. The human element is the programmer who prepares for the computer a codification of the "styles" or "rules" within which the computer will do its work. The machine then produces random sounds within the programmed framework and these sounds are recorded on tape. According to the information fed to the computer, it can compose "original" music varying in style from simple "pop" tunes to the most complex display of electronic sound combinations.

Multi-media is an art form combining several varieties of aural and visual stimulation simultaneously. Its basis is usually electronic music, using a tape, performance at a synthesizer, or both, combined with almost any other presentation of events, including projections—motion pictures, pictorial slides, random colors, laser configurations, and so forth—as well as dancers, instrumental or vocal soloists, staged effects, or whatever the composer's imagination can produce. The practice can be said to date from Scriabin's *Prometheus: Poem of Fire* (1910) for orchestra and a "color organ" of the composer's invention.

Summary

Music of the last half of the twentieth century finds composers heading in many directions, using exclusively or in any combination the tone row, serialism, systematic or nonsystematic principles of harmonic and contrapuntal development, electronics, and indeterminacy. As the century proceeds, expansion of experimentation seems to be the order of the day rather than consolidation of the achievements of earlier decades. Consequently, the present volatile state of the art may continue for some time before the true accomplishments of the century are known and a rational and comprehensive theory of the music can be developed. For the student and listener, this means that an understanding of new developments as they occur depends in great part upon the ability to analyze new sounds and techniques and to compare them with known practices both of the recent past and of previous eras.

The Essentials of Part-Writing

These essentials represent the basic procedures of part-writing. In no sense are they intended to include the countless variations in part-writing techniques that can and do exist. The need for and usefulness of this information is stated in the article "Rules? Why Rules?" found on page 97 of *Elementary Harmony*.

The Single Chord

Approximate Range of the Four Voices

Soprano: $d^1 - g^2$ Alto: $a - c^2$
Tenor: $f - f^1$ Bass: $F - c^1$

Triad Position

In *open position,* the distance between the soprano and tenor is an octave or more. In *close position,* the distance between the soprano and tenor is less than an octave. The distance between adjacent voices normally does not exceed an octave, although more than an octave may appear between bass and tenor.

Usual Doubling

The tonic, subdominant, and dominant tones in a key can ordinarily be doubled freely. To go beyond this generalization, some common doubling procedures are listed here:

Diatonic Major and Minor Triads
1. Root in bass: Double the root.
2. First inversion: Double the soprano note.

3. Second inversion: Double the bass note.

4. Exception: Minor triads, root or third in bass. The third of a minor triad is often doubled, particularly when this third is the tonic, subdominant or dominant note of the key.

Diminished Triad (usually found in first inversion only).   Double the third: when the fifth is in the soprano, the fifth is usually doubled.

Augmented Triad.   Double the bass note.

Seventh Chord.   Usually, all four voices are present. In the major-minor seventh chord, the root is often doubled and the fifth omitted.

Altered Triad.   Same doubling as nonaltered triads: avoid doubling the altered note unless that note is the root of a chord.

Chord Connection

The following are commonly used procedures, expressed as rules, for connecting any pair of chords. Page numbers refer to *Elementary Harmony*.

Triad Roots

When two successive triads have their roots in the bass, check the interval between these two roots, and then use one of the appropriate procedures listed below.

Rule 1 (p. 79).   When roots in the bass are repeated, both triads may be written in the same position, or each may be in a different position. Triad position should be changed

a) when necessary to keep voices in correct pitch range;

b) when necessary to keep correct voice distribution (two roots, one third, and one fifth);

c) to avoid large leaps in an inner voice.

Rule 2.   When roots in the bass are a fifth (fourth) apart;

2A (p. 82) retain the common tone: move the other voices stepwise;

2B (p. 83) move the three upper voices in similar motion to the nearest tones of the next triad;

2C (p. 84) move the third of the first triad up or down the interval of a fourth to the third of the second triad; hold the common tone and move the other voice by step;

2D (p. 85) at the cadence, the root of the final tonic triad may be tripled, omitting the fifth.

Rule 3 (p. 167).   When roots in the bass are a second apart, the three upper voices move contrary to the bass.

Rule 4.   When roots in the bass are a third apart,

4A (p. 325) hold the two common tones: the other voice moves stepwise.

4B (p. 325) When the soprano moves by leap, the second triad may be in either close or open position, depending on vocal range and whether octaves and fifths have been avoided.

Rule 5 (p. 326).   Exception to Rules 1–4: When it is impossible or undesirable to follow Rules 1–4, double the third in the *second* of the two triads; however, if this third is the leading tone or any altered tone, double the third in the *first* of the two triads.

Triads in Inversion

Rule 6.   When in two successive triads one or both triads are in inversion, use the following procedures:

6A (*p. 195*) When one of the two triads is in inversion, first write to or from the doubled note of the triad in inversion, using oblique or contrary motion if possible, and then fill in the remaining voice.

6B (*p. 196*) When both triads are in inversion, each triad must have a different doubling to avoid parallel octaves, or the same doubling may appear in different pairs of voices. Avoid doubling the leading tone or any altered tone. Approach and leave each doubled tone using Rule 6A.

Position Changes

Rule 7 (p. 199).   Triad position may be changed

a) at a repeated triad.
b) using Rule 2C.
c) at a triad in inversion or a triad with unusual doubling, following Rule 6A.

Nonharmonic Tones

Rule 8 (p. 283).   A nonharmonic tone temporarily replaces a harmonic tone. Write the triad with normal doubling if possible and substitute the nonharmonic tone for one of the chord tones. Approach and leave the nonharmonic tone according to the definition of the nonharmonic tone being used.

Seventh Chords

Rule 9 (p. 395).   The seventh of a seventh chord, its note of approach and its note of resolution comprise a three-note figure similar to certain nonharmonic tone figures: passing tone, suspension, appoggiatura, and upper neighbor. The seventh usually resolves down by step.

Altered Chords

Rule 10 (p. 427).   Use of altered chords does not change part-writing procedure. Do not double altered note unless it is the root of the chord. Follow Rule 6A if unusual doubling occurs.

General Rule

Rule 11.   In any part-writing situation observe the following:

a) Move each voice the shortest distance possible.

b) Move the soprano and bass in contrary or oblique motion if possible.

c) Avoid doubling the leading tone, any altered note, any nonharmonic tone, or the seventh of a seventh chord.

d) Avoid parallel fifths, parallel octaves, and the melodic interval of the augmented second.

Instrumentation: Ranges, Clefs, Transposition

Range

The range given for each instrument is approximately that ordinarily used by the average player. Neither the lowest nor the highest note playable by the instrument is necessarily included. These ranges will be found satisfactory for purposes of this text.

Clef

Each instrument regularly uses the clef or clefs found in the musical illustrations under "Range." Exceptions or modifying statements are found under the heading "Clef."

Transposition

Unless otherwise indicated under this heading, pitches given under "Range" sound concert pitch when played. (Concert pitch: $a^1 = 440$ vibrations per second; the note a^1 on the piano keyboard is concert A). All transposing instruments sound their name when written C is played; for example, a Clarinet in B♭ sounds B♭ when it plays a written C.

String Instruments

Violin

Viola

Clef. Alto clef is used almost exclusively. Treble clef is used occasionally for sustained high passages.

Violoncello ('Cello)

Clef. Bass clef is ordinarily used. Tenor clef is used for extended passages above small a. Treble clef is used for extreme upper range (not shown).

Double Bass (Bass Viol, Contrabass)

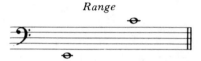

Transposition. Notes sound an octave lower than written.

Woodwind Instruments

Flute

Oboe

Clarinet: B♭ and A

Transposition *a*) Clarinet in B♭. Notes sound a major second lower than written. Use signature for the key a major second *above* concert pitch.

b) Clarinet in A. Notes sound a minor third lower than written. Use signature for the key a minor third *above* concert pitch.

Bassoon

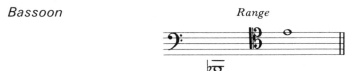

Clef. Bass clef is ordinarily used. Tenor clef is used for upper range.

English Horn (*Cor Anglais*)

Transposition. Notes sound a perfect fifth lower than written. Use signature for the key a perfect fifth *above* concert pitch.

Horn (*French Horn*)

Clef. Treble clef is commonly used.

Transposition. Notes sound a perfect fifth lower than written. Key signatures are not ordinarily used. Write in all accidentals. In many published horn parts, notes written in the bass clef sound a perfect fourth higher than written. Consult with player of instrument before writing horn part in bass clef.

Horn parts are occasionally written in D, E♭, and E.

Saxophones: E♭ Alto, B♭ Tenor, and E♭ Baritone

Transposition *a*) E♭ Alto Saxophone. Notes sound a major sixth lower than written. Use signature for the key a major sixth *above* concert pitch.

b) B♭ Tenor Saxophone. Notes sound a major ninth (an octave plus a major second) lower than written. Use signature for the key a major second *above* concert pitch.

c) E♭ Baritone Saxophone. Notes sound an octave plus a major sixth lower than written. Use signature for the key a major sixth *above* concert pitch.

Brass Instruments

Trumpet or Cornet, B♭ and C

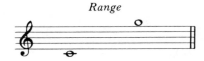

Range

Transposition   *a*) Trumpet or Cornet in B♭.   Notes sound a major second lower than written. Use signature for the key a major second *above* concert pitch.
   b) Trumpet or Cornet in C.   Nontransposing—sounds as written.

Trombone

Range

Clef.   Both tenor and bass clefs are commonly used.

Tuba

Range

Index

Added sixth chords, 324
Aeolian mode, 340
Aleatory (aleatoric music), 388
Altered chords, less common, 273
Applied dominant, 1
Arpeggiated harmony, 123
Atonality, 368
Augmented fifths (in Debussy), 325
Augmented minor seventh chord, 238
Augmented second, melodic, 46
Augmented sixth chords, 217
  less common uses, 224–27
Augmented sixth interval, 218
Augmented triad, 197

Babbitt, Milton, 382
Bach, C. P. E., Sonata in G Major for Flute and Figured Bass, 212
Bach, J. S.:
—Chorales, 7, 13, 19, 32, 33, 37, 38, 48, 109, 111, 112, 127, 158, 167, 180, 181, 200, 219
Christmas Oratorio, 162
English Suite, 34
Mass in B Minor, 17
Orgelbüchlein, 187
Prelude in D Major (organ), 159
Sonata No. 1 for Flute and Figured Bass, 170
—Well-Tempered Clavier, volume 1: Prelude 2, 124; Prelude 3, 280; Fugue 4, 283; Fugue 17, 161
Bach, W. F., Sonata for Piano, 227
Barber, Samuel, Hermit Songs, 363
Bartók, Béla:
  Concerto for Orchestra, 342
  Mikrokosmos, Volume 6, 359
  Quartet No. 4, 357
Beethoven, Ludwig Van:
  Concerto for Piano, Op. 37, 202
  Fidelio, 81
—Quartets: Op. 18, No. 3, 46; Op. 18, No. 5, 80, 89; Op. No. 2, 203; Op. 59, No. 3, 47; Op. 95, 62; Op. 127, 232
  Sonata for Cello, Op. 5, No. 2, 231, 258
  Sonata for Cello, Op. 102, No. 1, 239
—Sonatas for Piano: Op. 10, No. 3, 15; Op. 13, 16, 117, 125; Op. 27, 59; Op. 28, 57; Op. 31, No. 1, 128; Op 53, 286, Op.

101, 222; Op. 106, 45; Op. 109, 204; Op, 110, 184
—Sonatas for Violin and Piano: Op 12, No. 1, 230; Op. 23, 227, Op. 47, 15, 227
—Symphonies: No. 3, Op. 55, 55, 183, 257; No. 5, Op. 67, 49; No. 7, Op, 63
Berg, Alban, Violin Concerto, 385
Berlioz, Hector:
  La Damnation de Faust, 105
  Les Nuits d'Été, 237
  Symphonie Fantastique, 274
Bimodality, 341
Binary form, 77
  rounded binary, 84
Bizet, Georges:
  Carmen, 198
  Les Pécheurs des Perles, 44
Borrowed chords, 177
Boulez, Pierre, 388
Brahms, Johannes:
  An die Nachtigall, Op. 46, No. 4, 105
  Ballade, Op. 118, No. 3, 160
  Dein blaues Auge, Op. No. 8, 56
  Dein Herzen mild, Op. 62, No. 4, 49
  Ein deutsches Requiem, 190
—Intermezzi: Op. 76, No. 7, 41; Op. 117, No. 1, 120; Op. 117, No. 2, 164; Op. 118, No. 2, 20, 103, 205
  Liebeslieder Walzer, Op. 52, 78, 179
  Neue Liebeslieder Walzer, Op. 65, 92
  Quartet, Op. 51, No. 2, 195
  Romanze, Op. 118, No. 5, 122, 123, 267
  Romanzen aus Magelone, Op. 33, 284
  Sankt Raphael, 113
  Sextet, Op. 18, 14
  Sonata for Cello, Op. 38, 224
  Symphony No. 2. Op. 73, 182, 263
  Symphony No. 3, Op. 90, 193
  Trio for Violin, Horn and Piano, Op. 40, 278
  Trio in B Major for Violin, Cello and Piano, 57
  Von ewiger Liebe, Op. 43, No. 1, 346
Britten, Benjamin:
  Five Flower Songs, 345
  Seven Sonnets of Michelangelo, 340

Carter, Elliott, Sonata for Flute, Oboe, Cello, and Harpsichord, 355
Cells, 379
Chance music, 388
Change of mode, 183, 276
Chopin, Frédéric, 283
  Ballade, No. 4, Op. 52, 283
—Mazurkas: Op. 56, No. 1, 10, 104, 236; Op. 56, No. 3, 266; Op., No. 3, 126
—Nocturnes: Op. 15, No. 3, 102, 201; Op. 27, No. 2, 128; Op. 37, No. 1, 39; Op. 48, No. 2, 51; Op. 62, No. 1, 265; Op. 72, No. 1, 260
  Polonaise, Op. 40, No. 1, 180
—Preludes: Op. 28, No. 4, 100; Op. 28, No. 26, 194; Op. 45, 184
Chromatic melodic line, 99
Chromatic thirds, 291
Clérambault, Louis, Suite du premier ton, 259
Closely related keys, 6
Cluster, 357
Combinatoriality, 382
Common chord (modulation), 6
Commonly used progressions (review), 97
Composing an original melody and accompaniment, 145
Compositional style, 127
Computer music, 396
Continuo, 129
Copland, Aaron:
  Appalachian Spring, 345
  Twelve Poems of Emily Dickinson, 353
Corelli, Arcangelo, Concerto IX, 169
Couperin, François, Gavotte, 86
Crossed voices, 108
Cross relation, 64, 342
Crüger, Johann, Jesus, meine Zuversicht, 154
Crumb, George, Madrigals, Book I, 392

Da capo aria, 80
Dallapiccola, Luigi, Quaderno Musicale Di Annalibera, 387
Debussy, Claude:
  Chansons de Bilitis, 329
  Fêtes galantes, 324
  Images I:
    Hommage à Rameau, 320
    Reflets dans l'eau, 320, 326
  Nuit Étoiles, 317

Pélleas et Mélisande, 323, 325
Pour le Piano, 322, 323, 325, 328
—Préludes, Book I: *No. 2*, 318, 319; *No. 4*, 322; *No. 5*, 322; *No. 6*, 331; *No. 10*, 324
Quartet, 321, 332
Trois Ballades de François Villon, 319

Deutsch, Otto, 4
Diatonic seventh chords, 152
in harmonic sequence, 155
Diminished minor seventh chord, 34
Diminished seventh chord, 34
cross relation, 64
leading tone chord, 37
modulation, 52
nondominant, 46
resolution, premature, 36, 38, 42, 75
resolution, regular, 36
secondary leading tone chord, 39
spelling variant, 45
terminology variant, 36
Diminished third, 191
Diminished triads, 31
Direct change of key, 11
Distance between voices, abnormal, 108
Dorian mode, 340
Double pedal, 124
Doubling:
melodic, 126, 342
sonority, 121
unusual, 108
Doubly augmented six-four-three, 223
Dowland, John, *Can She Excuse My Wrongs*, 344
Duparc, Henri:
Extase, 216
Soupir, 264
Dvořák, Antonin:
Biblical Songs, Op. 99, 102
Concerto for Violin, 199
Quartet, *Op. 105*, 261
Symphony *No. 9, Op. 95*, 226

Electicism, 388
Electronic music, 393
Eleventh chord, 262
Elgar, Sir Edward, *Enigma Variations*, 91
Elision, 97
Ellis, Merrill, *Kaleidoscope*, 395
Event, 389
Extended harmony, 120
Extended part-writing procedures, 107

Fauré, Gabriel:
Au bord de l'eau, 226
La bonne chanson, Op. 61, 304
Les roses d'Ispahan, 155
Lydia, 178
Poéme d'un jour, 94
Requiem, 276
Feldman, Morton, *In Search of an Orchestration*, 390
Figured bass realization, 129, 388
Foreign key, 6
Form, 77
binary, 77
incipient ternary, 84
rounded binary, 84
ternary, 79
three-part, three-part song, 77
three-part period, 83
two-part, two-part song, 77
Franck, César:
—Chorales: *No. 1*, 227; *No. 2*, 229; *No. 3*, 233
Prelude, Chorale, and Fugue, 309
Symphonic Variations, 161, 262
Symphony in D Minor, 232
Franz, Robert, *Am leuchtenden Sommermorgen*, 146
Free voicing, 121
French sixth chord, 219

German sixth chord, 219
alternate spelling, 222
Gershwin, George, 348
Gluck, Christoph:
Alceste, 217
Orfeo, 80
Gounod, Charles, *Faust*, 233
Graphic notation, 390
Grieg, Edvard:
Holberg Suite: 79, 158
In der Heimat, 259
Letzer Frühling, 200

Half diminished seventh chord, 34
Handel, George Frederic:
Messiah, 98, 110, 153, 154
Sonata in B Minor for Flute and Figured Bass, 175
Sonata for Violin and Figured Bass:
Op. 1, No. 10, 130
Op. 1, No. 13, 131
Harmonic progression, complex, 275
Harmonic sequence:
change of mode, with, 276

diatonic seventh chords, 155
diminished seventh chords, 40
enharmonicism, with, 276
interlocking, 279
modulatory, 9
Neapolitan sixth chord, 195
ninth chords, 262
secondary dominant chords, 3
third relationships, 314
twentieth century usage, 356
Harmonizing a folk song, 139
Harmony, twentieth century, 350
Haydn, Franz Joseph:
The Creation, 273
Mass in C, 113
—Quartets: *Op. 71, No. 1*, 48; *Op. 74, No. 1*, 60; *Op. 77, No. 1*, 43
—Sonatas: D Major for Piano, 85, 87; E♭ Major for Piano, 3; G Major for Piano, 128
Symphony *No. 92*, "Oxford," 221
Symphony *No. 101*, 53
Hexachord, 382
Hindemith, Paul:
Ludus Tonalis, 356, 360
Mathis der Maler, 341

Impressionism, 316
Improvisation, 388
Incipient ternary form, 84
Indeterminancy, 388
Indy, Vincent d', *La Rêve de Cynyras*, 239
Instrumental style, 116
Instrumentation, 401
Interlocking harmonic sequence, 279
Internal pedal, 351
Interrupted pedal, 124
Inversion:
diatonic seventh chords, 158
diminished seventh chords, 25
Neapolitan sixth chord, 191
ninth chord, 260
row (twelve-tone), 374
use of (review), 97
Inverted pedal, 124
Italian sixth chord, 219
Ives, Charles,
Central Park in the Dark, 354
Tone Roads, No. 3, 389

Janacek, Leoš, *M'sa Glagloskaja*, 356

Kuhlau, Friedrich, Sonatina, *Op. 55, No. 2*, 84

Leading tone seventh chord, 37
Liszt, Franz, Concerto for Piano, *No. 2*, 307
Lully, Jean Baptiste, *Cadmus et Hermione*, 132
Luzzaschi, Luzzasco, *Quivi sospiri*, 292
Lydian mode, 340

MacDowell, Edward, *My Jean*, 103
Major seventh chord, 152
Marcello, Benedetto, Sonata for Flute or Violin, 137
Massenet, Jules, *Manon*, 189
Matrix (twelve-tone row), 375, 382
Melismatic text setting, 198
Melodic doubling, 126, 342
Mendelssohn, Felix
Elijah, 112
Piano Trio, Op. 49, 238
—*Songs Without Words: Op. 38, No. 1*, 239; *Op. 53, No. 2*, 263; *Op. 85, No. 2*, 126
Messiaen, Olivier:
Cantéyodjoyâ, 385
Vingt regards sur l'Enfant Jésus, 362
Meter:
poetic, 145
twentieth century, 343
Milhaud, Darius:
La Création du Monde, 350
L'Orestie d'Eschyle, 352
Saudades do Brasil, 358
Trois poémes de Jean Cocteau, 341
Modes:
medieval, 319, 339
harmonization, 350
Modulation: 5
augmented sixth chord, 234
change of mode, 183
closely related keys, 6
common chord, 6
diminished seventh chord, 52
direct,
formal sequence, 10
melodic chromatic alteration, 11
phrase, 11
pivot tone, 12
Neapolitan sixth chord, 196
pivot chord, 6
remote keys, 6
transient, 3
Mozart, Wolfgang Amadeus:
—Concerto: A Major for Piano, K. 488, 1; C Major for Piano,

K. 503, 277; F Major for Piano, K. 459, 159
Don Giovanni, K. 527, 186
The Magic Flute, K. 620, 108, 192
Quartet, K. 465, 281
Quintet, K. 593, 89
Quintet for Clarinet and Strings, K. 581, 42, 194
Requiem, 113
Serenade, "Haffner," K. 250, 47
—Sonatas for Piano: K. 279, 38; K. 280, 47; K. 281, 121; K. 284, 297; K. 330, 118, 128; K. 331, 126; K. 533, 156; K. 545, 7
—Sonatas for Violin and Piano: K. 377, 122, 124; K. 380, 267; K. 454, 241
—Symphonies: *No. 35*, K. 385, 104; *No. 38*, K. 504, 222; *No. 39*, K. 543, 196; *No. 40*, K. 550, 99, 232; *No. 41*, K. 551, 10
Trio for Violin, Cello, and Piano, K. 542, 18
Multi-media, 396
Musique concréte, 393
Mussorgsky, Modeste:
Boris Gudonov, 240
Pictures at an Exhibition, 206
Sunless, 305

Neapolitan sixth chord, 191
pivot chord, 196
secondary dominant of, 193
Ninth chords, 255
incomplete, 26, 277
inversion, 260
irregular resolution, 261
sequence, 262
Nondominant diminished seventh chords, 46
Notation,
graphic, 390
non-specific, 389
vocal, 148

Offenbach, Jacques, *La Créole*, 48
Order numbers, 372

Pandiatonicism, 353
Parallelism, 322
Part-writing, essentials of, 397
Pedal point, 123
Penderecki, Krzystof, *Ecloga VIII*, 391
Pentatonic scale, 319
Phrygian mode, 321, 339
Pitch class numbers, 372
Pivot chord, 6
Pivot tone, 12

Planing, 322
Poetic meter, 145
Pointillism, 379
Polymeter, 346
Post romantic composers, 307
Premature resolution:
diminished seventh chord, 36, 38, 42, 75
ninth chord, 256
Prime series (twelve-tone row), 375
Progressive cadence, 3
Purcell, Henry:
Amphitryon, 106
Dido and Aeneas, 155
I Envy Not a Monarch's Fate, 136
The Virtuous Wife, 161

Quartal harmony, 323
Quintal harmony, 324

Rachmaninoff, Sergei:
Concerto No. 2 for Piano, 52
Symphony No. 2, 106
Random music, 388
Range, instrumental, 127
Reger, Max, *Valet will ich dir geben*, 104
Remote keys, 6
Retrograde, 374
Retrograde inversion, 374
Retrogression, 97
Rhythm, twentieth century, 343
Root movement, unconventional, 303
Rossini, Gioacchino:
Anodine I I I I, 17
Comic Duet for Two Cats, 201
Messe Solenelle, 185, 266
Rounded binary form, 84
Row (tone row), 371

Schoenberg, Arnold:
Gurre-Lieder, 366
In diesen Wintertagen, Op. 14, No. 2, 367
Klavierstücke, Op. 23, 371, 376
Klavierstücke, Op. 33b, 382–84
Pierrot Lunaire, Op. 21, 369
Quartet No. 4, Op. 37, 373–78
Schubert, Franz:
Adagio and Rondo, D. 506, 85
Die Forelle, D. 550, 78
Die schöne Mullerin, "Wohin," D. 795, 83
Impromptu, D. 946, 4
Jägers Liebeslied, D. 909, 187
Ländler, D. 790, 282
Litanei, D. 343, 185

Moments musicals, 11
Nur wer die Sehnsucht kennt,
    147
Quartet, "Death and the
    Maiden," *D. 810,* 268
Quintet in C Major, *D. 956,*
    61, 192
Rosamunde, D. 768, 124
—Sonatas for Piano: *D. 664,*
    187; *D. 845,* 39, 236; *D. 850,*
    59, 237; *D. 959,* 292; *D. 960,*
    54
Wanderers Nachtlied, 123
—*Winterreise, D. 911:*
    "Frühlingstraum,"
    147; 148; "Das Wirtshaus,"
    178; "Die Post," 148
Schuman, William, *An American
    Festival Overture,* 342
Schumann, Robert:
    *Album for the Young, Op. 68,
        No. 10,* 125
    *Album for the Young, Op. 68,
        No. 43,* 33
    Auf einer Berg, 154
    Concerto in A Minor for
        Piano, *Op. 54,* 40,
        201, 231
    Dichterliebe, Op. 48, 231
        "Am leuchtenden
            sommermorgen,"
            146, 223
        "Das ist ein Flöten und
            Geigen," 163
        "Ich grolle nicht," 265
        "Im wunderschönen
            Monat Mai," 119
    Liederkreis, Op. 39,
        Waldesgespräch,"
        275
    Myrten, Op. 25,
        "Hochländers
            Abschied," 5
    Novelletten, Op. 21, No. 6,
        50
    *Nur wer die Sehnsucht
        kennt,* 147
    Quartet, *Op. 41, No. 3,*
        193
    Sonata for Piano, *Op. 11,*
        298
Secondary dominant chords, 1
    cadence, use in, 3
    embellishing, 2
Secondary leading tone seventh
    chords, 39
Secondary leading tone triads,
    31
Secondary tonal levels, 13, 281

Sequence, *See* Harmonic
    Sequence or Melodic
    Sequence
Serialism:
    pitches, 371
    uses of, 385
Series (twelve-tone), 371
Set (twelve-tone), 371
Seurat, Georges, 379
Seventh chords:
    diatonic, 152
    diminished, 34
    diminished-minor, 34
    half-diminished, 34
    major, 152
Shostakovich, Dimitri, Prelude
    No. 5, 351
Smetana, Bedřich, *The Moldau,*
    12
Sonority doubling, 121, 342
Spacing between voices, 127
Sprechstimme, 370
Stockhausen, Karlheinz:
    Elektronische Studien, 394
    From the Seven Days, 389
    Variations III, 389
Stravinsky, Igor, *Le Sacre du
    Printemps,* 343, 347, 351
Strophic songs, 148
Style, 116
Syllabic text setting, 198
Syncopation, 343
Synthesizer, 393

Tallis, Thomas, 339
Telemann, George Phillip:
    Partita 5, 132, 157
    Sonata für Blockflöte und
        Basso Continuo, 133
    Sonata in F Minor for Flute
        and Figure Bass, 211
Ternary form, 79
    incipient ternary, 84
Text setting, melismatic, syllabic,
    198
Thirteenth chord, 262
Thorough bass, 129
Three-part form; three-part
    song form, 77
Three-part period, 83
Through-composed songs, 148
Tonic:
    evasion by chromatic
        inflection, 300
    evasion by deceptive
        cadence, 299
    indeterminate, 305
Tonicization, 1

Transient cadence, 3
Transient modulation, 3
Transposition, twelve-tone row,
    375
Tritone:
    in Debussy, 325
    in root movement, 296
Tschaikowski, Peter:
    Eugene Onegin, 225
    Nur wer die Sehnsucht kennt,
        147
    The Nutcracker, 259
    Romeo and Juliet, 262
Twelve-tone systems, 371
Two-part form, two-part song
    form, 77

Vaughan Williams, Ralph:
    *Fantasia on a Theme by
        Thomas Tallis,* 339
    The Water Mill, 350
Verdi, Giuseppe, *Il Trovatore,*
    221
Vivaldi, Antonio:
    Concerto Grosso, *Op. 3, No.
        6,* 192
    Concerto Grosso, *Op. 3, No.
        10,* 202
    Concerto in Fa, 134
Vocal notation, 149

Wagner, Richard:
    Goetterdaemerung, 261, 263
    Lohengrin, 43, 257
    Siegfried, 58
    Tristan and Isolde, 12, 301,
        310
    Die Walküre, 224, 266, 313
Walacinski, Adam, *Allaloa,* 391
Walton, William, Concerto for
    Viola, 165
Weber, Carl Maria von, *Der
    Freischütz,* 99, 191
Webern, Anton, Concerto for
    Nine Instruments,
    380–81
White noise, 393
Whole tone scale, 278, 317
Wilder, Alec, Woodwind
    Quintet, *No. 3,* 349
Wolf, Hugo:
    Auf einer Wanderung, 198
    In den Schatten meiner Locken,
        293
    Mignon, 295
    *Und willst du deinen Liebsten
        Sterben sehen,* 228
    Zur ruh, zur Ruh!, 225